W9-AGI-300

Bloom's Modern Critical Views

Bloom's Modern Critical Views

HISPANIC-AMERICAN WRITERS
New Edition

Edited and with an introduction by
Harold Bloom
Sterling Professor of the Humanities
Yale University

BLOOM'S
LITERARY CRITICISM
An imprint of Infobase Publishing

Library of Congress Cataloging-in-Publication Data

Hispanic American writers / edited and with an introduction by Harold Bloom. —New ed.
p. cm. — (Bloom's modern critical views)
Includes bibliographical references and index.
ISBN 978-0-7910-9623-9 (acid-free paper) 1. American literature—Hispanic American authors—History and criticism. 2. Hispanic Americans in literature. 3. Hispanic Americans—Intellectual life. I. Bloom, Harold.

PS153.H56H56 2008
810.9'868—dc22

                              2008031221

Contents

Editor's Note

My Introduction, composed more than a decade ago, remains relevant, and speaks for me only.

Juan Bruce-Novoa studies Chicano theater's reorienting of myths of origin, after which Jeffrey Cass meditates upon so-called "Orientalism" in Rudolfo Anaya's *A Chicano in China*.

The influence of Spanish-American literature upon U. S. Latino writing is traced by Juliana de Zavalia, while Silvia Spitta surveys aspects of *mestizo* ideology.

Anne Connor employs the symbols of disfigured countenances in analogizing identity problems in *Latino* literature, after which Miriam DeCosta-Willis states the importance of Martha K. Cobb in developing Afro-Hispanic criticism.

Oscar Hijuelos is seen by Richard F. Patteson as being worthy of serious comparison to Marcel Proust, the strongest novelist of the twentieth century, while Pat Mora's *House of Houses* is also related to themes of temporal flow by B. Marie Christian.

Identity again is a concern, this time for Fiona Mills in relation to Afro-Latino writing, while Jason Frydman explores masculinity and violence, after which this volume concludes with Nicolás Kanellos on reviving the Hispanic-American immigrant literature of the early twentieth century.

HAROLD BLOOM

Introduction

HISPANIC-AMERICAN WRITERS

Unfortunately, in the current cultural climate of the United States, Hispanic-American writers are subject to many of the same hazards that afflict the better African-American and other "multicultural" literary endeavors. Overpraise, generally allied to ideological enterprises, emanates endlessly from our resentful academics and journalists alike. Perhaps two generations will have to pass before Hispanic-American literature will be judged by authentic cognitive and aesthetic standards. Myself, Bloom Brontosaurus, the academic dinosaur, I am well aware that I can no more intrude traditional canonical considerations than I can intervene helpfully in any of our current multicultural contexts. This Introduction therefore in no way contests or quarrels with the critical judgments reprinted in this volume. Rather, I wish only to raise the problem of influence and its anxieties in regard to the Mexican and Chicano *corrida*, the border ballad. As my primary text I will take Américo Paredes' *With His Pistol in His Hand: A Border Ballad and Its Hero* (1958, 1971). Paredes tells us that:

> Corrida, the Mexicans call their narrative folk songs, especially those of epic themes, taking the name from correr, which means "to run" or "to flow" for the corrida tells a story simply and swiftly without embellishments.

Paredes and his work, both as scholar and as poet, have been praised by José E. Limón, in his *Mexican Ballads, Chicano Poems: History and Influence in Mexican-American Social Poetry* (1992). Limón's critical heroes in this book—besides Paredes himself—are the Marxists Raymond Williams and Fredric

Jameson. The critical villain is the aesthete Harold Bloom, whose books on poetic influence are severely chastised by Limón for their palpable ignorance of "the sociopolitical realm." Having acknowledged that I am Limón's devil to Paredes' angel, I shall not venture to defend myself, but instead shall question both Paredes and Limón as to their shared argument, which is that the influence of the *corrida* produced a strong poetry in English in the work of Paredes himself and in that of political Chicano poetry of the 1960's and 70's composed by José Montoya, Rudolfo Gonzales, and Juan Gómez-Quiñones.

Paredes, in his study of the Mexican border ballad, emphasizes the continuous strength of an oral tradition that goes back to the border conflicts of the 1860's. Limón, after comparing Paredes' own poetry to the *corrida* argues that *With His Pistol in His Hand,* Paredes' study of the *corrida,* is actually a "strong sociological poem," rewriting the ballads in a true Return of the Dead. By the same logic, Limón's *Mexican Ballads, Chicano Poems* is a strong misreading of Paredes, a process that could continue indefinitely. In such a continuity, poetry perpetually dims and politics grows more and more intense. The Chicano movement, admirable from the perspective of any striving for social justice, is no more an inevitable source of poetic strength than is any other protest against injustice. The English-language ballads that Limón quotes are very sincere but, as Oscar Wilde observed, all bad poetry is sincere. I refrain from quoting any excerpts or texts praised by Limón, because they cannot bear quotation. The heroic *corrida* of the oral tradition frequently had a rough vigor; its imitations are strident, and poetically self-defeating. If Chicano poetry is to survive its own Mexican heritage, then the poets will have to go beyond the constraints and repetitions of politics. Ideology at best can produce period-pieces, not poems.

JUAN BRUCE-NOVOA

Chicano Theater:
Editing the Origin Myth

Every mythical account of the origin of anything presupposes and continues the cosmogony.

Mircea Eliade, *Myth and Reality,* 21.

Introduction

The construction of origin myths is a vital task of ideology. The act of foundation, far from being a simple historical event casually related to the present, is a hierophanous charting of causal relationships traversing space and time, a typology in all its informing authority, an energizing source for recharging tradition because, as Mircea Eliade points out, it reaffirms a group's concept of cosmic order. Yet, it is always a retrospective action, a recreation of the creation of the tradition which, in turn, empowers the present group to evoke their myth. Although typology is defined as "a form of prophecy which sets two successive events into reciprocal relations of anticipation and fulfillment" (Brumm, 27), a definition which naively establishes a past-to-present flow of causality, it more accurately names a strategy of projecting into the past an ideological conceptualization of a model to justify a vision of the present as one steeped in tradition and history. Moreover, since the function of the text or ritual in the present is to establish paradigmatic authority in the past, it is incumbent on the

GESTOS, Teoria y Practica del Teator Hispanico, Volume 7, Number 14 (November 1992): pp. 105–116. Copyright © 1992 GESTOS.

author/practitioner to model the evocation text on the evoked foundation act, thus exemplifying the validity of the typological practice in its continued utilization as essential model. The two acts form a closed circuit transcending time and space, claiming authority through the fusion of the present author with the original author—a circle in which all temporal and spatial, mediating practitioners are implicitly included to form the unbroken line of authenticating tradition. As mystical as this may sound, I find it at the heart of much interpretive discourse, not only on traditionally oriented subjects like folklore or ethnic studies, but the practice of critical analysis in general. It lies behind the pro forma references to founding critics and their texts that are invoked to authorize the utilization of a method by followers. In recent essays I have treated the typological manipulations in U.S. colonial literature, the novel of the Mexican Revolution, Chicano narrative, and mid-century Latin American writing. Here, in keeping with the focus on historiography of this collection of essays, I turn, not to theater per se, but to a key critical text on Chicano theater and its origin myth—a text which in its own right has become a foundation myth.

One tires of reminding readers that myth is not synonymous with lie or untruth, but a symbolic representation of what is held to be true by the group generating the narrative. "Myth narrates a sacred history ... how, through the deeds of Supernatural Beings, a reality came into existence, be it the whole of reality, the Cosmos, or only a fragment of reality ... it relates how something was produced, began to be" (Eliade, 5–6). Of course, in our hyperbaroque age nothing remains innocent or straightforwardly transparent, least of all texts which purport to be innocent transparency—the evocation of mythic authority is a style, a self-conscious positioning, but not for all that less sincere in its intent of convincing readers. The specific textualization of an origin myth I will be discussing should not be taken as a falsification, but rather a well intentioned act of emic anthropological description, of the thick sort championed by Clifford Geertz.

Historical Context

In 1965, a group of Filipino agricultural workers in the area of Delano, California, went out on strike against the grape field owners. They sought support from the National Farm Workers Association, for whom the now famous César Chávez had worked for years trying to organize the California fields. Chávez persuaded his associates to back the strike. This is as good a point as any to pick up the trajectory of events that led Chávez that same year to establish the United Farm Workers Union under his leadership, organize national boycotts against agribusiness corporations, and the eventual, although ephemeral and ambiguous, triumph of official recognition for his union as a legitimate representative of agricultural workers in

California. In a decade of social unrest and multiple projects for reform and even revolution, Chávez assumed the image of a leader in the eyes of many Mexican Americans, or Chicanos as the young activists of the period called ourselves in the late 60s.

For many, Chávez appeared to be "El Jefe" [The Leader], although others like Rodolfo Corky Gonzales of the Colorado based Crusade For Justice and Reies López Tijerina of New Mexico competed for the title. But Chávez had more national appeal, perhaps because he also had more national media exposure and a less radical political program. For many reasons not pertinent here, Chávez seemed to many the most likely to unite the disparate Chicano communities.

It was an illusion, admittedly, another of the bittersweet 60s dreams, because Chávez never unified the Mexican-origin communities which have proved to be as ideologically and historically diverse as they are geographically dispersed. In Chávez' defense, he never aspired to the leadership of an ethnically based social movement, much less a third political party. His project, more modestly and pragmatically oriented, tightly focused on specific economic goals attainable through unionizing. Nevertheless, he attracted, in some ways monopolized, the attention of the national and international press, which covered him through the grid they had developed for another ethnic leader about whom they knew much more, Martin Luther King. But it must be confessed that Chávez appealed to many Chicanos as well, incarnating a desired identity, personifying a valued tie to the earth—it even could be said that he and his union represented a sentimental nostalgia for the lost rural past, a direct tie to the earth, and even Mexican Revolutionary ideals of land for the workers of it, all mythologized in popular tradition. In Chávez one could contact the noble worker of the earth, the oppressed human base of the economy, which also, through no fault of its own, still had not been alienated from the traditional labor customs of the ancestors, for some only a generation back in time. This romantic vision must be filtered, however, through the sieve of statistics: "the 1930 census reported that 50.8 percent of all Mexican-heritage families [in the United States] lived in urban regions" (Griswold, 95); and by the 60s it had risen to eighty percent. But the urban population had and has retained a vision of its group identity as rural—proving once again that identity is not merely the function of the real material base, but of a much more complex mixture of memory, desire, tradition, and, yes, illusion and blindness. We should not discount, either, the fact that, contrary to the popular belief that most Chicanos can trace their immigration roots to the Mexican Revolution exodus, in the twenty years following W.W.II, more Mexicans immigrated to the United States than in the previous one hundred years combined (Griswold, 113). To this statistic we must add that the ruling political party of modern Mexico serving as the feeder nation of this mass immigration had been carrying out an intensive populist propaganda campaign that, for reasons best known to the party's social theorists, utilized and manipulated a demagogic rhetoric, exalting rural life at the same time that government policies were aimed at modernization, producing a popular self-image similar to that held by Chicanos in the U.S. At the risk of over schematizing this contextualization, I must move on to the main subject, summarizing that in the public imagination César Chávez' campaign to win recognition for his union was centered as the most authentic struggle for Mexican American civil rights—sometimes also called the Chicano Movement.

Shortly after Chávez had established the United Farm Workers Union, Luis Valdez came to him at his headquarters in Delano, California, and offered to organize dramatic presentations for the strikers. The performances would be designed to both entertain and instruct. Valdez had personal, professional, and ideological credentials to support his offer. A Chicano native of Delano, Valdez had worked as a laborer in the very fields Chávez aimed to organize. But he also had a long association with drama, beginning in high school, activities which won him a university scholarship and an eventual degree in drama from San Jose State, where he had written and staged two of his own plays: *The Theft* and *The Shrunken Head of Pancho Villa*. Furthermore, he had worked for a year with one of the country's most innovative and politically leftist street theaters, The San Francisco Mime Troupe, where he learned to adapt the traditional *commedia dell'arte* techniques to contemporary popular theater (Jiménez, 124, 130). Chávez agreed to an experiment with the strikers, setting the scene for Valdez' first performance as Luis Valdez of El Teatro Campesino.

Constructing Origins

With the Teatro Campesino's rise to unchallenged leadership among Chicanos, as well as to international fame and admiration that have endured to the present, that first meeting has assumed more and more significance, becoming the origin myth of Chicano theater per se.[1] Jorge Huerta, the leading critic in the field, placed the event at the opening of Chapter 1 of his *Chicano Theater*. The following quotation is long but revealing and necessary for my exposition:

> "[Valdez] and a small group of striking farmworkers are meeting in a little pink house . . . Valdez talks for a while, but he knows that he will have to get the people themselves to demonstrate their situation. Speaking to the *campesinos* in a mixture of Spanish and English, Valdez urges members of his audience to step up in front of the others and show what happened in the strike that day. He has brought signs to hang around these "actors" necks,

identifying the characters, and asks for two volunteers to portray *huelguistas,* or strikers, and a third volunteer to play an *esquirol,* or scab. Everyone is reluctant to play the part of the despised strikebreaker, but finally a brave young farmworker says he'll do it.

'Now show us what happened today on the picket line,' Valdez tells these three farmworkers, and immediately the two "strikers' begin yelling at the "esquirol," who good-naturedly shouts back at them. The other people in the room join in the fun and laugh and shout as they witness this rudimentary recreation of their own experiences. Another person volunteers to take part; suddenly the room is filling up with people from nobody knows where, all laughing and having a good time . . . [Everyone present wants to participate.]

Valdez now triumphantly pulls out another theatrical device, a pig-like mask which is immediately identified by the jeering crowd as *El Patroncito,* the "boss" or grower. There, for all to see, is a face that could belong to no one else, and the people respond with glee at the prospect of seeing a portrayal of a despised figure—the wealthy grower who refuses to negotiate with the union. "Who wants to play *El Patroncito?"* asks the director, and the volunteers rush forward, eager to make their individual comments about the villain in their lives. . . .

With each improvisation of their daily struggles, these *campesinos* demonstrate to Valdez that there is a message to be dramatized and that the talent to dramatize it is in this room. . . . Valdez' vision of the theater that will speak of the Chicano and Mexican struggles in the fields is more than just a possibility—it has come alive this evening.

At the close of the first improvised session, the Teatro Campesino has been born . . . those that choose to get involved will become the collective authors of the Teatro's first *actos:* improvised scenes that present the realities of the struggle. The improvisations this evening are the seeds of what will follow; under Valdez' guidance, his group will explore the characters and situations that must be exposed in order to educate the farmworkers about the need for a union. . . .

Long after the people have gone, Valdez is still thinking about his new venture" (11–13).[2]

Let's start with the obvious. The somewhat ingenuous tone of admira-tion aside—a tone many of us adopted in the early, euphoric days of creating a body of positive and supportive criticism—the passage conveys the key feature of the early Teatro Campesino *aficionados* have come to expect: use of signs to title characters, masks, satiric and burlesque comedy, laughter, political intent, focus on specific social issues directly related to current events.[3] Beyond these surface characteristics, Huerta reveals a desire—his and perhaps the community's as well—to couch Chicano cultural production in collective terms: the impression is created that the Teatro Campesino was a virtually spontaneous creation of an anonymous group of common people. Second, this desire manifests itself also as an assumption of a natural authenticity located in the common people. Third, supreme value is placed in representing "the real," of "what happened." Combining these points, we comprehend that this vision of Chicano Theater privileges mimesis, the expression of the supposedly unmediated voice of the people, the direct communication between performers as common people and the public. Even more, there is a tacit prejudice against trained, professional actors and an esteem for the untrained amateur. There is an unstated, but clear, postulation that any farm worker can assume, not only the role of a character, but the "role of an actor." In all of this there is yet another tacit prejudice against textualization; that is to say, this theater supposedly directs the oral tradition of the community straight through the voices of its own members to itself in a closed circle of speech, evoking the presence of the word incarnate and constituting a return to the preliterate, preindustrial, pre-alienated world of the organic community of primary orality. We should understand that, during the 60s and 70s, these points were never questioned in an open forum, rather accepted as intrinsic to Chicano theater, probably because they coincided in great part with the populist ideology of the political movements of the period. All of the above can be read as supporting evidence for Huerta's statement in the Introduction that "Chicano theater was born of and remains a people's theater" (3).

Huerta, however, and in spite of himself, reveals contradictions. He lets us see, for instance, that the Teatro Campesino was not actually a spontaneous, group creation by farm workers, rather the product of one individual's planned effort; the idea, the motivation and the direction arose from a trained artist, who, although having his roots in farm working, was by then distanced from them by education, experience and his horizon of realistic expectations. For Valdez, no longer a migrant farm worker, but a university graduate and professional actor with one of the country's elite troupes—an urban one at that—the creation of the Teatro Campesino represented a homecoming to his ethnic and class roots. Nevertheless, it also represented his chance to function in a setting where no one or nothing would limit his actions or question his decision. He could direct, mold, and manipulate a group of technically unsophisticated participants, naive and malleable.

We must note, as well, that the expression of a free, direct, and unmediated voice, one capable of conveying the community's most heartfelt preoccupations, does not coincide with the indicators of control and direction which emerge in Huerta's narrative. Valdez did not begin the meeting by inquiring what was on the farm workers' minds or what kind of entertainment they wanted. Instead, Valdez directed them to "show us what happened today on the picket line." From the start, Valdez spoke in the imperative mode—a tone naive critics have attributed to his recent period, sometimes reading it as a sign of a major change and a betrayal of his own initial principles. In other words, from the start Valdez is depicted employing the mode of director/producer in total control of a production he initiated, shaped, guided, and—a very significant point—watched and judged from a vantage point of an outside observer. Valdez determined the choice of characters, the limited range of which imposed a binary structure of opposition, one we might read as that of cultural conflict, although this would be a pedantic mask for the basic, radical binary of good and evil.[4]

When the farm workers did not radicalize the conflict between workers confronting each other on a horizontal level of equals—the scab worker responded "good-naturedly" when taunted by strikers—Valdez heightens their emotions by evoking hatred through the introduction into the equation of a vertical hierarchy of inequality with the mask of the field owner. As simplistic as this representation's interpretation of the socioeconomic situation was, let us grant it a basic validity for the purpose of its producers. After all, neither Valdez nor Chávez wanted their organizing efforts to bog down in the subtleties of close analysis.

We should not overlook, however, Valdez's role as director, and even author of the performance through the premeditated use of props. He infused a mediating element to provoke the farm workers, not to express themselves directly, but exactly the opposite: they hid behind masks, correctly identified by Huerta as a "theatrical device," adding them to the signs they already were wearing to distance them from themselves in order to speak. Hardly straightforward expression, nor the spontaneous choice of topic from an open field of possibilities. Huerta, consciously or not, revealed that this theater, far from a naive, direct exposition of reality, was, rather, a demonstration of theater's power to harness the imagination to transform and transcend reality when guided by a trained, talented and empathetic expert granted full control of the cast and production.

Huerta tells us that Valdez intended to form a consciousness raising group. However, neither Valdez nor Huerta wanted to create a high consciousness of the directorial presence. Huerta tries to ameliorate the impact of Valdez the individual, underplaying his status as a professional dramatist, information he introduces only later in the chapter, after the origin scene has been played out. And since in an earlier version of the same event, Huerta had told the story differently, we can only conclude that he judged it counter-productive to the goals, not necessarily of the first meeting of the Campesino, but of the narrative commemorating it.[5] Both Valdez and Huerta dissimulate the function of the director behind the facade of the amateur. "These are not actors portraying characters from a playwright's pen; they are people express-ing their own experiences by donning signs or masks" (13). The difference drawn here is yet another binary of opposition, that of restricted written text versus supposed free-moving improvisation, a binary of exclusion easily in-validated by information from the same narrative. Huerta and Valdez both hope the public will accept the momentary displacement of the author of the representation—he is metaphorically moved off center stage, to the periphery of our vision, a position Valdez would often assume in Teatro Campesino performances over the years. This tactic is necessary; in the final analysis, the ultimate proof of success of an author who seeks to create a representation of the people's natural and direct voice lies in his or her ability to convince the public and the actors that they are experiencing, not a re-presentation, but the presence itself of reality.

And yet, Huerta could not erase entirely the signs of contradiction. First, the "signs and masks" dangle, not just from the actors, but in the middle of his sentence tracing a line back to the supplier of the props, whose semiotic control functioned like a writer's pen to guide the action. Later he wrote, "All the people who have crowded into the house this evening return to their respective homes with spirits lighter than usual, for they have enacted the triumph of their cause and released some of their frustrations through the laughter aroused" (13). This new theater was neither realistic nor mimetic, but idealistic and therapeutic. Represented by strikers to strikers, it informed no one of what they didn't already know. To be didactic the group would have had to go outside the closed context and address their performance to people not convinced already of the rightness of the cause. Finally, to achieve his goal, Valdez had to transform some of the campesinos into actors—that is, in order to represent the farm workers as Valdez wanted them to see themselves, they could not remain as they were, but had to be transformed into Others, to literally become another, first in appearance through props, and secondly, by becoming actors—a transformation which prefigured the eventual change of those workers chosen by Valdez to join his troupe into professional actors playing at still being farm workers for audiences far from the fields.

There arises a distance between the populist version of theater and the reality of the process, a distance reflected in the manner in which Huerta closed the narrative of the scene. After the now happy workers return to their homes, Huerta's narrative narrows back down to Valdez, alone, contemplating what has occurred and wondering about the possibilities of channeling the results. Significantly, Huerta specifically centers our attention and Valdez's simultaneously on a retrospective view of what has just been narrated, and calls it "his [Valdez's] new venture" (13).

The next three paragraphs bridge from the first gathering of a collectivity of amateurs to the recreation of Valdez's professional history. Only then do readers receive the vital facts about his education and work in professional theater that have prepared him for the encounter with the farm workers, facts that I introduced beforehand to create an ironic distance which in Huerta's text—at least this version of it—arises only *a posteriori*. The effect of Huerta's structuring is to position collective ritual as the source of the personal through spatial and logical precedence. He even inserts Valdez's birth and ethnic personal history within the creation narrative for greater effect, yet, as mentioned above, leaving the professional data for later, outside of the myth of origins. It is as if the collective were necessary for the emergence of the individual, an ideological position binding the personal to the communal often assumed by 60s cultural activists and required of ethnic literature by critics.[6] Nevertheless, readers find themselves focused finally on the individual artist, slipping flashback fashion into his history, all as a bridge to the creation of a future that appears in the text's next subheading, the opening sentence of which depicts Valdez naming the plays "he and his group were collectively creating," the importance of which "he understood."[7] In short, Valdez's singular grammatical subjectivity rules, and what flows from this point on in the subsection is essentially a repetition and extrapolation of the initial origin scene.

Cosmogony of Origin Myth

Origin myths are created, not in the supposed founding action itself, rather in and through the act of recalling—inventing—the scene of the first act of the creation of the group which now narrates its foundation as a reenactment. Such a narrative functions typologically, its features constitute a cosmic order being promoted, not simply as memory, but as a viable model for the present, accepted and promoted by the practitioners evoking the myth. The narrative of the myth both imitates and reveals the underlying cosmogony, albeit at times palimpsestically, conveying the essential cosmogonic message through an apparently profane, unsubstantial surface.

This case simulates a birthing myth: "the Teatro Campesino has been born" (Huerta, 12). Origin myths need not begin from nothing: "the 'World' was already there, even though its structure was different, though it was not yet *our* world. Every origin myth narrates and justifies a 'new situation'" (Eliade, 21), an interruption of one historical flow to commence another. Huerta used two devices to evoke mythical space. First, unlike the earlier version of the same event (see note 3), for his book Huerta composed the narrative of the scene of the meeting entirely in the present tense, grammatically placing it in that limbo of time outside of specific time, outside of history, the space where action reverts to the atemporal moment of beginnings that always are the same and therefore non-sequential. Second, he employs the perspective of omniscient narrator, floating freely into Valdez's mind, repeating verbatim spoken dialogues without recourse to citations of sources, making interpretive assessments of feelings and emotions; in short, despite the appearance of an unmediated event, the writer is in total control, a position not limited even by the customary restrictions of academic protocol—and this positioning mirrors that of Valdez within the scene.

That a new situation has come into existence during the evening is reflected in the change in the participants: the people go home enlivened and renewed, "with spirits lighter" (13), as if having attended a religious revival. They disperse back into the world from a small enclosure, a womb-like "little pink house" (11) into which Valdez, and the text, has gathered them for what can be read as a transformation ritual.[8] Inside the womb, the people have been remade, molded, emerging with an altered perspective of their place in the world and with enhanced possibilities of action. Moreover, they have been infused with a sense of control over their situation, one based on a new faith—or perhaps a renewed confidence in the old faith.

At a different level, however, the particular cosmogony of this scene involves the presence of a guiding figure who directs creation, predetermines the spectrum of choices, even imposes identity, and, in return for satisfactory performance within those parameters, delivers that sense of well-being described at the close of the meeting. Valdez's solitary pondering at the meeting's end resembles that of the Biblical Supreme Being resting after creating the earth in Genesis, Chapter 2, just before completing the remaining project of developing his original creation.

The cosmogony evoked is a patriarchal one in which females are not even given a specific and substantive role.[9] That the patriarchal face—whether wearing the mask of Valdez the director, Huerta the omniscient narrator, or the farm workers as actors playing themselves—represents itself as the collective community should not surprise us. It is part and parcel of demagogic ideologies and conveys the impression of deriving its power and plan of action from the free will of the common people. This impression was maintained by Valdez for over a decade. Only after 1975, when Valdez began to develop *Zoot Suit* as a personal "property," did observers begin to criticize his new individualism, also accusing him of patriarchal chauvinism.

Yet, if we reread this origin myth, editing out both our present nostalgia and the original desires and naivete, we can learn to see it no longer as merely the fortuitous coincidence of spontaneous expressions of our communal reality. The campesinos were involved, of course, but the naive belief in the collective, ingenuous, innocent generation of an art form from nothing is no longer necessary to maintain. We should accept that Chicano theater, as practiced by the Teatro Campesino, was, on one level, the product of the talent, vision, and direction of Luis Valdez, the man who, in every sense of the word, deserves the title of father of contemporary Chicano Theater; and that on another level entirely, our image of the origin is largely the result of a carefully crafted narrative molded to reflect the intent of the critic, Jorge Huerta.

NOTES

1. Certainly the Chicano theater movement came under the guiding influence of Valdez and his style of performance, but that the creation of the Teatro Campesino has been studied as if nothing else existed, to the exclusion of other forms, for instance Rodolfo Corky Gonzales' plays from the same period, is a subject Chicano theater critics have yet to address. Gonzales may have had no lasting influence in theater, but his performance activities in the 60s raise questions that problematize the view we have had, and still maintain, of early Chicano theater. The fact that his plays were both more traditionally structured into acts and realistic in their style reflects a different light on the current opinion sometimes expressed by critics that the new generation of Chicano dramatists, who write in this same vein, are no longer really Chicano. Perhaps the obsessive focus on only one typology of Chicano theater in the 60s was possible only through the marginalization and silencing of other competing forms. The studies of the history of U.S. Latino theater by such critics as Nicolás Kanellos leads one to a similar conclusion.

As this article was in final stages of preparation, the Crusade For Justice announced the imminent publication of Gonzales' plays.

2. Huerta himself had given a slightly different account of the same event: "When Valdez met with a group of huelguistas for the first time, he brought some signs and masks with him, hoping that he could get the campesinos to portray their own realities. The crowd was curious to see who this fervent young man was, and how he might help them. 'You can't talk about theater,' he thought to himself, 'you have to *do* it.' So he asked the group what it was they were going through and which were the experiences they wished to share with others. Immediately, a campesina began relating an experience she had undergone with another campesino who was an esquirol, and Luis interrupted her and asked if she could demonstrate what occurred. 'Here's a sign that says "campesina,"' he told the group, 'and here's another which says "esquirol." Who saw what happened to the señora and wants to play the esquirol?' 'Yo lo vi,' said a modest looking campesino, and he jumped up to put on the sign which would label him a scab. Knowing the importance of masks, Valdez then gave the gentleman a comic mask and asked him to put it on. Everyone laughed at the man's transformation, and behind that cover of production this humble campesino who had never been on a stage in his life became, for the moment, an actor." "From the Temple to the Arena: Teatro Chicano Today," *The Identification and Analysis of Chicano Literature*, ed. Francisco Jiménez, Ypsilanti: Bilingual Press, 1979, 91.

3. For a list of characteristics of the early Chicano theater works, see Jorge Huerta, "Difference Between Teatro Chicano and Traditional Theatre," in *Pláticas del Sexto Festival Nacional de los teatros chicanos*, San Antonio, Texas, 1975, 7–8.

4. Had Huerta stayed with the earlier version of this founding meeting, quoted in note 3 above, Valdez's directorial mode would have been less powerfully

emphasized. Note that in the first version Valdez does consult the workers and leaves the choice of topic to them. Furthermore, the specific scene is more than suggested, it is initiated by a woman. And the worker who volunteers to play the esquirol enters into the performance in a different manner. Valdez himself has remembered the event yet differently again: "The first huelguista to portray an esquirol in the teatro did it to settle a score with a particularly stubborn scab he had talked with in the fields that day" "The Actos," in *Actos, El teatro campesino*, Fresno: Cucaracha Press, 1971, 5.

Obviously, we are not reading mere "facts," but a rhetorical reconstruction of an event highly susceptible to coloring, shading, toning—in other words, Huerta's narrative is, like all historical narration, more an artifact constructed for effect than an "accurately reported objective fact" whatever that might be.

5. In "From Temple to the Arena," ibid, Huerta introduces the biographical data in the second paragraph of the essay, a page before the narrative of the first meeting with the workers.

6. See the early readings of Tomás Rivera's . . . *y no se lo tragó la tierra* or the critical attacks on José Antonio Villarreal's *Pocho*.

7. "Before Valdez gave the designation of *acto* to the improvisations he and his group were collectively creating, he understood the importance of the form." Huerta, 14.

8. Carlos Morton also used a birth image to characterize the founding of the Campesino: "born out of the labor pains of the 1965 *Huelga of grapepickers*," "*La Serpiente Sheds Its Skin, The Teatro Campesino*," *The Drama Review*, 18, 4 (Dec. 1974), 71. Valdez himself, however, referred to the meeting place in much less "rosy" terms: "We started in a broken-down shack in Delano," "El Teatro Campesino," *Aztlán, An Anthology of Mexican American Literature*, Luis Valdez and Stan Steiner, eds, New York: Knopf, 1972, 360.

9. In contrast to the version cited in note 3, in the book version Huerta has eliminated the detail of female campesina being, not only the first volunteer to answer Valdez's call for participants, but the source of the first scene ever acted out. Thus, the two different versions of the same event once again create significantly different readings of the origin myths. For another example of the patriarchal cosmogony behind the mask of collectivity in a key literary text from the Chicano Movement phase of contemporary literature, see Rodolfo Corky Gonzales' *I Am Joaquín / Yo soy Joaquín*, New York: Bantam Books, 1972.

WORKS CITED

Brumm, Ursula. *American Thought and Religious Typology*. New Brunswick: Rutgers University Press, 1970.

Eliade, Mircea. *Myth and Reality*. New York: Harper and Row, 1963.

Geertz, Clifford. *The Interpretation of Cultures*. New York: Basic Books, 1973.

Griswold del Castillo, Richard. *La Familia, Chicano Families in the Urban Southwest 1848 to the Present*. Notre Dame: Notre Dame University Press, 1984.

Huerta, Jorge A. *Chicano Theater, Themes and Forms*. Ypsilanti: Bilingual Press, 1982.

———. "Difference Between Teatro Chicano and Traditional Theatre," in *Pláticas del Sexto Festival Nacional de los teatros chicanos*. San Antonio, Texas, 1975, 7–8.

————. "From the Temple to the Arena: Teatro Chicano Today," *The Identification and Analysis of Chicano Literature,* ed. Francisco Jiménez. Ypsilanti: Bilingual Press, 1979, 90–116.

Jiménez, Francisco. "Dramatic Principles of the Teatro Campesino," *The Identification and Analysis of Chicano Literature.* Ypsilanti: Bilingual Press, 1979, 117–132.

Valdez, Luis. *Actos, El teatro campesino.* Fresno: Cucaracha Press, 1971.

JEFFREY CASS

A White Man's Fantasies: Orientalism in Rudolfo Anaya's A Chicano in China

She walked with measured steps, draped in striped and fringed cloths, treading the earth proudly, with a slight jingle and flash of barbarous ornaments. She carried her head high; her hair was done in the shape of a helmet; she had brass leggings to the knee, brass wire gauntlets to the elbow, a crimson spot on her tawny cheek, innumerable necklaces of glass beads on her neck; bizarre things, charms, gifts of witch-men, that hung about her, glittered and trembled at every step. She must have had the value of several elephant tusks upon her. She was savage and superb, wild-eyed and magnificent; there was something ominous and stately in her deliberate progress. And in the hush that had fallen suddenly upon the whole sorrowful land, the immense wilderness, the colossal body of the fecund and mysterious life seemed to look at her, pensive, as though it had been looking at the image of its own tenebrous and passionate soul. (76)

Joseph Conrad, *Heart of Darkness*

China is a jealous woman. She has not let me go since I arrived. She holds me and makes love to me over and over again until I am exhausted. She has become my mistress: I, her slave. I understand now why, throughout history, foreigners have been drawn to China. (79)

Rudolfo Anaya, *A Chicano in China*

Critica: A Journal of Critical Essays (Spring 1998): pp. 43–51. Copyright © 1998 Jeffrey Cass.

Although the first passage reflects Conrad's ambiguous experiences in the Belgian Congo of the 1880s and the second passage recalls Anaya's naïvely enthusiastic romp through Deng Xiao Ping's China of the 1980s, both construct gendered narratives that essentialize and reify an alien "Other." Conrad's harshest critic, Chinua Achebe argues that while Conrad may criticize the European colonization of Africa, his ersatz "liberalism" mirrors the colonialism from which he seeks to detach himself. Conrad's description of Kurtz's African woman-warrior only confirms what Achebe has labeled as Conrad's "thoroughgoing racism" (11). She is "superb," "barbaric," "magnificent." Embodying the tragedy and triumph, the beauty and the danger of African fecundity, Conrad's imagined figure of an African woman-warrior recapitulates the very imperialism that he allegedly detests. In his essay "An Image of Africa: Racism in Conrad's *Heart of Darkness*," Achebe writes, "Conrad saw and condemned the evil of imperial exploitation but was strangely unaware of the racism on which it sharpened its tooth" (19). Edward Said reiterates Achebe's argument in *Culture and Imperialism:* "Conrad's tragic limitation is that even though he could see clearly that on one level imperialism was essentially pure dominance and land-grabbing, he could not then conclude that imperialism had to end so that 'natives' could lead lives free from European domination" (30).[1]

Achebe's critique manifests an acute awareness of his own subject positions relative to the Anglo literary culture that has attempted to circumscribe and colonize him. Achebe discerns how Conrad has subsumed his skin color into the tangle of African cannibals who menace from the shores, even as his British education and training bind him to a "white English subject position." By contrast, Anaya is blithely unaware of how thoroughly he has embraced his colonialist and Orientalist fantasies: For Anaya, China is his athletic sex pot, exhausting his sexual energies and, by extension, his imaginative ones. Lacking Achebe's self-reflexivity, Anaya not only fails to discern the specificities that undergird Chinese culture, he never sees them in the first place, precisely the imaginative condition Said describes in *Orientalism*. Although at times gushing in his praise of and exuberance for Chinese culture, Anaya unwittingly becomes the white man. For it is the intensity of Orientalist fantasies that ironically reinforce the inequalities that have persistently governed the discourse between the colonizer and the colonized.

What is profoundly disturbing about Anaya's Orientalism are his claims to a colonized subject position and his insistence that Chicanos simply do not have the necessary imaginative space in Anglo-American culture to do their work. Of course, Chicano scholars and activists have long taken this critical line. Bruce-Novoa argues in the opening sentence of "Charting the Space of Chicano Literature" that "Chicano literature is an ordering response to the chaos which threatens to devastate the descendants of Mexicans who now reside in the U.S.A." (114). Gloria Anzaldúa's description of this chaos is even more riveting: "The U.S-Mexican border is *una herida abierta* where the Third World grates against the first and bleeds" (3). Implicit in both Bruce-Novoa's and Anzaldúa's claims is the agonizing assertion of cultural difference, the "open wound" of a cultural war that can never heal because the dominant culture seeks to extirpate or colonize the subdominant strains within it. In Anzaldúa's view, the colonizing grip of Anglo-American culture strangles competing subcultures even as they emerge because these cultural competitors are either eliminated or, even more likely, co-opted. To survive, as Bruce-Novoa suggests, Chicano literature must chart an imaginative course that permits its Mexican-American readers to negotiate between the cultural space they physically inhabit and the imaginative spaces that they need and desire.

The political and aesthetic ideologies that erupt from the search by Chicanos for their own imaginative spheres, however, do not necessarily immunize them from becoming the very colonizers they abhor. In an essay published three years after *A Chicano in China,* Anaya appears to continue his push for the space in which Chicanos may negotiate their identities, yet he ironically outlines a "totalizing" form of that identity, one undergirded by both the Spanish "aggressive, conquest-oriented part" of itself and the Native American side of its nature that remains "harmonious" and "earth-oriented" (21). Chicano identity as "New World Man" remains conventionally yet irrevocably "oriented" between Spanish aggression and Native American passivity, between the colonizer and the colonized. Anaya's "orientation" even genders the creation of a "New World Man." The Spanish father, the paternal seed that provides language and writing, copulates with the Indian mothers of Mexico and the Southwest, the maternal "substratum" of Anaya's work (21). It is the mother who "reveals the symbols and mythology of the New World" (21). By his own admission, Anaya has grounded his writing in a state of perpetual colonization; the Spanish father aggressively copulates with the Native-American mother. For Anaya, this is how his writing is rendered as intelligible and symbolically meaningful.

In *Bless Me, Ultima,* Anaya foreshadows the colonialist duality of *A Chicano in China* by reifying the familial differences between the Lunas and the Márez. In effect, they become the imaginative incarnations of Antonio's consciousness, a boy's consciousness that seeks to explore and explain itself and its origins through myth (the Golden Carp) and white magic (Ultima's owl/familiar). Already torn by the colonizing restlessness of his father's blood, Antonio's soul can only be brought into balance by Ultima's healing ministrations. It is her *curanderismo* that appears as the deconstructive supplement of Christian spirituality, overturning the vacuity of Christian ritual with the rich weavings and castings of her *brujería*. She represents, as Anaya continually insists, the power of the forgotten mother. But even as the 'mother' (in the character of Ultima) resurfaces, haunting the New Mexican *llano* and reminding us of her restorative force, she still sacrifices herself in the face of the 'father's' violence. The long *velorio* for Ultima at the end of the novel attests to the inevitable spread of the father's colonizing religion and, with Ultima dead, the continued marginalization and displacement of the mother's indigenous religious beliefs.

In writings subsequent to *Bless Me, Ultima*, Anaya manifests his previously submerged colonialist ambitions. Far from committing himself to an ideology that struggles against the historical accidents of colonization, Anaya later demythologizes Chicano identity, a recuperative process that he initially describes in *Bless Me, Ultima* as being singularly mythological. Because the father's language ultimately cannot be understood without the mother's symbolic logics, Anaya has unwittingly become complicit in a colonialist paradigm, guaranteeing the perpetual rape of the Native-American mother. In this context, Antonio's realization that "there is also the dark, mystical past . . . the past of the people who lived here and left their traces in the magic that crops out today" (220) becomes a poignant reminder that the historical "traces" of colonization do not lie safely in the dark, unrecoverable past; rather, they continue to emerge from the subterranean blackness of personal and national history, spreading out and infecting everyday life.

Unlike *Bless Me, Ultima*, *A Chicano in China* openly recapitulates Anaya's incipient colonialism. Anaya's appropriations of Chinese culture merely confirm his ambitions.

> I had a friend in the Taos Pueblo, the commune of the Taos Indians. Cruz, an old man who taught me to hunt. Cruz, old man of the Pueblo, governor, cadre, hunter, farmer, communal man, man of power . . . He was a dragon man . . . *Those thousands of years separated from the Orient, separated from Asia, thousands of years since the migration from Asia and he still carried the supreme sense of the dragon in his soul . . . So now I have Cruz and my grandfather to guide me through China. I have the dragon coiled in my body.* I feel I am a new man. *A Chicano Chinaman.* (emphasis mine, 47)

In this passage, Anaya unintentionally supplants Aztlán, the mythical birthplace of the Aztecs and emblem of both Chicano origins and identity, with the aboriginal Orient. Crossing the Bering Strait twenty thousand years ago, Anaya's aboriginal Chicanos actually provide the genetic material for the "New World Man," permitting the "New World Man" to be decoded, reconfigured, and redeployed when he eventually returns to China, his 'actual' (and not mythical) birthplace. Anaya's outrageous conflation of the Chinese Tao with Cruz ("dragon man") and the Taos Indians reduces the complexity of Chicanismo's social, cultural, and political character to dormant Asian genes. Therefore, while the "Chicano Chinaman" may appear, from Anaya's perspective, to be merely another iteration of the Mexican-American's cultural hybridity, it actually transforms Chicano history into a rhetoric of eugenics. *La raza* has literally become a "race"—a race in diaspora. Anaya writes that "China sent part of her memory to the Americas and memory may sleep for thousands of years, but it will awaken" (152). Once Chicanos "awaken" from their diaspora, they will reclaim their 'Oriental' heritage and recolonize their lost homelands, armed with knowledge that has lain biologically submerged for generations.

But if Anaya looks to the aboriginal past for the seeds of "dragon power," he looks to a utopian future for its fullest expression. For Anaya, "Chicanitos" of the future "will dream of Chinese umbrellas and Chinese chocolates. Dragons will flutter in the blue sky of New Mexico. Mao jackets will appear. [Anaya's] paisanos "will dream in Chinese characters" (15). That future Chicanitos cannot read these Chinese characters does not unduly disturb Anaya because they will viscerally comprehend the meanings even if they cannot articulate the literal signification. Anaya concedes that "language is a code" and that he has "not been able to enter the Chinese reality" since he does not speak Chinese (138). Still, he feels that because he has incessantly heard the Chinese language, "the sound of China is sucking [him] into its soul, into its language" (138). Armed with the symbolic logics of the Southwestern mother, Anaya believes he can interpret a language he does not consciously know. At one point in the narrative, Anaya, reading the *China Daily*, drinks a beer and discovers the linguistic coincidence between *Tsingtao*, the name of the beer, and *Chingao*, the Spanish oath. He muses that a Southwestern beer named *Tsingtao* "would become more popular than Coors. Instead of going up to the bar and saying, '*Dáme un* Bud,' one would say, '*Dáme un Chingaso!*'" (141). Anaya concludes happily: "Tsingtao beer: *Chingao!* I feel connected" (141).

Nevertheless Anaya's "connectedness" depends upon orientalizing the Chinese dragon and appropriating its physical properties in order to assert an imagined scene for a revitalized and repoliticized Chicanismo. Having settled its body "along [his] spine and heart and liver and stomach" (45), Anaya parasitically feeds off his newly-acquired "dragon power." He proclaims:

> We will send our Chicano dharma bums to the mountains of Tibet to study with the Buddhist priests even as we send them to unravel the secrets of the Aztecs and the Mayans. We will grow with dragon power. We will grow in the spirit of the Buddha. In the holsters at our hips, we carry Mao and Pancho Villa, in our hearts we carry Buddha and Quetzalcóatl. (49)

As Achebe and Said might have predicted, Anaya's pseudo-Kerouackian call to "dharma bum" arms erases the very cultural differences that attract Anaya to Chinese culture in the first place. Anaya all too easily incorporates "dragon power" into his genetic version of Chicano identity, conveniently glossing over other, less palatable parts of Chinese history. Carrying "Buddha in [his] heart," Anaya seems to have forgotten, for example, the brutal colonization of Tibet by China even though the Tibetan Buddhists have been historically committed to peaceful protest. And while Anaya does suggest that Mexico's 'dragon' Quetzalcóatl may be an "aspect of the Buddha" (48), it is hard to reconcile the Cultural Revolution of Mao, the border banditry of Pancho Villa, and the blood sacrifices of the Aztecs and the Mayans with Prince Siddhartha's vision of universal peace. It is even harder to accept Anaya's incorporation of Buddha into Southwestern mythology. By writing that "the Buddha is another Kachina we welcome into the pueblo," he orientalizes a religious icon in order to reterritorialize the imaginative space of Chicano writing. Just as Buddha "told the story of enlightenment and it spread to millions throughout Asia" (162), Anaya intends his Buddha-Kachina to enlighten the benighted Southwest. Anaya has become more than just a benign if excitable "Chicano Chinaman"; indeed, he has immersed himself in the very colonizing practices that he wishes to foreclose.

Not unlike the gendered alterity of his visions in *Bless Me, Ultima*, Anaya's imperialist fantasies in *A Chicano in China* repeatedly return to the figure of the woman, sometimes ravishing dominatrix, sometimes sly and slippery lover. A Chicano Andrew Marvell, Anaya exclaims that his "cruel mistress is not coy. She is direct, strong, a woman of the past that has not changed in hundreds of years. I revel in her love, her mystery" (83). China manipulates, controls her lover's psychic and spiritual dimensions. And Anaya reifies this imaginative love-making with the image of the dragon, frequently a male-marked dragon who must frequently grapple with China, his mysterious mistress. Anaya transforms the dragon into a colonialist metaphor *par excellence*, one in which the colonizer copulates with the colonized in reckless abandon. This tumultuous yet imperialist union has the effect of freezing history, of arresting social and cultural development. China cannot change socially, politically, or culturally because "she" orgasmically incarnates Anaya's imperialist designs. Not surprisingly, he dreams of dragon virility entering his body:

> "The dragon settles itself in me, its eyes breathing fire through my eyes, its breath the life in my lungs, its serpentine body settled along my spine and heart and liver and stomach. Each dragon scale touching and resting at one of the body's acupuncture points . . . The dragon sex now goes into my balls and penis" (46).

Interestingly, however, in some passages the image reverses trajectory: the Chinese dragon changes sex and becomes a powerful woman. In a proximate passage to the one cited above, Anaya writes: "I need this time of being alone and still to feel the thrashing dragon. China is entering me. I am absorbing China . . ." (45). Anaya intimates that China, consistently described as a woman throughout his narrative, is now the "thrashing dragon" that "enters" him, ravishes him. In another passage, Anaya exclaims, "China is a jealous woman-in-the-blood: a dragon, which once experienced will never let go" (79). Anaya also asks whether or not the "she-dragon" embodies the Jungian archetype of the "feminine principle" (100). Finally, he even wonders about his wife Patricia—"Has this woman beside me become a dragon-woman?" (192).

In part, the dragon's polymorphous and promiscuous androgyny can be explained by Anaya's dream of the two dragons. In this dream, he envisions two thrashing dragons. He recognizes that they are the carved bas-relief dragons of two rock stelae he has seen earlier at a museum in Xi'an. As part of an elaborate ekphrasis, the dragons represent the *yin* and the *yang*, the two opposing forces that engender human history. The dragons "entwine" but do not "swallow each other" (76), emphasizing both sides of the sexual divide and confirming the dragon as an androgynous image, becoming for Anaya a powerful locus of imperial desire. In his dreams, Anaya writes, "the two dragons are a union I will hold within my world, my castle, myself" (76).

In a later passage, an encomium on the Yangtze River, Anaya again makes China the figure of a woman: "The river and the life of the river embrace me. I have found the soul of China. I enter the blood of China and, like a woman who knows she has conquered a man, China spreads her arms and thighs . . . she allows me to enter into her bloodstream, her water, her history" (123). Swimming in the amniotic waters of the Yangzte, Anaya inverts the colonialist paradigm by imagining himself to be conquered by the woman China. In actuality, however, this temporary inversion still drives Anaya's colonizing ambitions since Anaya's submission to "China" permits the cultural appropriations that doom her separateness, the very independence for which Chicanos clamor in their attempts to forge a separate imaginative space.

In the introduction to *A Chicano in China*, Anaya informs the reader that he is a pilgrim making his way to China, "a traveler in search of symbols that speak the language of [his] soul" (vi). But he undercuts his proclaimed humility ("Communication, that's part of the key to the journey of a humble pilgrim" and "I was a humble pilgrim who went to communicate, to commune . . .") by orientalizing Chinese language and culture. His search for symbolic resonances leads not to respect for Chinese cultural difference, but to its assimilation within a fundamentally masculinist Chicano political ideology and discourse. He concludes early on in the narrative that "East is West—the two are one" (5). By collapsing the disparities between East and

West, Anaya can now enlist the aid of the Chinese in Chicano political causes. Arriving at the Beijing airport, Anaya exclaims "*¡El Tercer Mundo! He llegado, con una canción en mi corazón.* Peking, land of my grandfather's dreams. I rush to embrace the Chinese Brown brothers, Raza! Can you imagine a billion new souls for *La Raza?* We could rule the world" (17).

The intoxicating rush of enlisting a billion new citizens for a new Chicano utopia blinds Anaya to the colonialism within his idealistic fantasies. In his essay "Aztlán: A Homeland Without Borders," Anaya boldly advocates a new world order that obliterates the very existence of a Chicano identity: "The children of Aztlán are citizens of the world. We must move beyond the limitations of ethnicity to create a world without borders" (241). Eliminating borders, transcending ethnicities, and unifying disparate ideologies have always been the stock-in-trade of those who embrace colonizing principles, but colonizers have normally achieved their goals by extinguishing cultural difference, particularly when the colonized resist their efforts. Moreover, as one reviewer of Anaya's essay has cannily argued, events in the 1990s have demonstrated the necessity of reasserting, not eliminating, ethnicity:

> The re-balkanization of Eastern Europe, the violent dismembering of what the press now calls the 'former Yugoslavia,' the civil wars of Africa, the Los Angeles riots, identity politics, and the backlash against women, gays, and people of color in this country, and the English-only legislation—all point to a future where ethnicity, boundaries, and distinctions may well matter more than ever before. (Nigro 4)

In the context of the 1990s, therefore, Anaya's "world without borders" becomes what Said calls a "dominating framework" (Orientalism 40). And this "framework" insidiously assumes, as Fawzia Afzal-Khan suggests, that the "Orient" (in this case Anaya's China) "[is], if not definitely inferior to, then certainly in need of improvement by the West" (3). Although Anaya assumes the subject position of a citizen of the *Tercer Mundo* who automatically feels the pain and neglect of fellow Third World occupants, his insistence on the concept of Aztlán only reinscribes the very political and cultural boundary conditions from which he seeks to escape. In her review of Anaya and Lomelí's *Aztlán: Essays on the Chicano Homeland*, Nigro writes that for many Chicanos, "'Aztlán' has now been replaced with 'Nepantla,' the land 'in-between,' where signs are not so stable, where meaning is deferred, but which is all the richer because it is more problematic, less easy to be sure of" (4). Nigro's remarks can be taken as postmodernist glosses of Anaya's search for a chain of stable signification. His fundamental desire to crack the mysteries of China and his orientalist assimilations of China within a Saidian "framework" demonstrate his desire to control and fix the reach of Chicanismo's efforts.

Not content with a fantasy China, Anaya extends his Orientalism to the Japanese, reasserting the father/mother dichotomy that has so often structured his work:

> What a difference one sees immediately between these two neighbors, Japan and China. China is the sprawling rough-and-ready mother of a billion people—Japan, the strict orderly father of these wizards of high technology and business (186)

Anaya admits that this division may be an "oversimplification," but he continues the thread in asserting that the real difference between the two countries is "wealth." Japan is rich; China is poor. This is a very interesting distinction to make because the purveyors of Western capital (For Anaya, both Japan and America are "on the make"—178) can diffuse their wealth throughout an indigent China. The "strict orderly father of high technology and business" domesticates the "rough-and-ready" mother of a billion people, people waiting to serve the territorial ambitions of the imperializing father. Disturbingly, Anaya neglects a countermovement in Japanese culture that resists the Westernization of Japan and its capitalist encroachments. The writer Yukio Mishima commits *seppuku* to publicize precisely this point, a samurai suicide that shockingly calls into question the glossy renderings of a "Chicano Chinaman."[2]

Unreflexive, Anaya does not see how his criticism of Western imperialism and domination cuts its teeth (to use Achebe's phrase) on the very racism he ostensibly rejects. Ironically, he adopts a subject position that allows him to establish his own imaginative space; however, it is a space that enfolds and incorporates the same Orientalist fantasies that one finds in the works of Conrad, fantasies roundly criticized by Achebe and Said. Anaya's *Chicanismo* enshrines, therefore, a colonialist paradigm. Even José David Saldívar, who wisely argues for a new cultural and critical "cosmopolitanism" that does not diminish the "Américas" into "some homogeneous Other of the West" (4), still envisions "exploiting the possibility of canon expansion" (xii), of remapping the Borderlands and reconfiguring what was once only Anglocentric territory. Unavoidably perhaps, the unacknowledged danger in Saldívar's dream of postcolonial repositioning lies in the insidious reassertion of colonialist ambition, ambition that literally and figuratively reterritorializes Anglocentric space for Chicanos (and other Latinos). Likewise, Anaya envisions a New World Man whose world view is both "syncretic" and "encompassing" ("New World" 26). Anaya's trip home from China to Albuquerque amply illustrates this neo-colonial ambition, the expansiveness of the New World Man. Arriving at the San Francisco airport, Anaya marvels at imagined immigrant

Asians who, he believes, "will [now] call the United States their home" (191). He writes: "They are small, brown people from the jungles of Thailand or from the villages of Vietnam. How complete is everything if one only learns to expect the unexpected China in the blood—we return home" (191). Apparently because all Asians (except the Japanese who have betrayed the 'Orient' by "accept[ing] the West and its moneymaking ways" 186) have chosen to make America their "home," they can uncover "the unexpected China in the blood." Their "blood" assimilated into their new homeland, their genes reunited with, if controlled by, their "Chicano Chinese" relatives, these immigrant 'Orientals' can now be fully managed, contained, and employed. In short, they have been conscripted into the service of Anaya's new world order. In one passage, Anaya pointedly addresses Chicanos, succinctly formulating his Orientalist strategies. In a Machiavellian mode, Anaya advises: "Let us learn to adapt, Raza, take in, use, assimilate what we need . . ." (75).

At narrative's end, Anaya recounts a dream he has had in China of "building a wall to protect the front part of [his] house" (201). The contractor erects a wall that is "tiered, like a pyramid" (201). Pleased that visitors describe it as Aztec, Mayan, and Egyptian, Anaya writes that all these labels "fit" his intentions. The Great Wall of China, the "pathway to Aztlán", becomes the aboriginal and prelinguistic monument to Chicano hegemony ("The Great Wall calls. I am falling through my time in history to complete my destiny" 45). Anaya's private "Great Wall" safeguards his house by homogenizing all cultural difference—Aztecs, Mayans, Egyptians, Chinese are all housed and enclosed within Anaya's domain. Furthermore, Anaya's wall diminishes the cultural Other into a more manageable form. Writing that he "will not be afraid to walk in the land of the billion Chinese people, to share [his] love with them, and to take their love" (202), Anaya may sincerely wish to connect spiritually with the Chinese, but he does so only from a subject position that fantasizes control over the newly emergent Oriental Chicano.

NOTES

1. I would like to thank Rosaura Sánchez and Norma Cantú for their insight and commentary on earlier versions of this essay. I would also like to thank Dion Dennis who assisted me (as he always does) with the organization and expression of my ideas.

2. Jack Seward writes in his book *Hara-Kiri: Japanese Ritual Suicide* (Charles E. Tuttle 1968) that modern *seppuku* dates from the Meiji Restoration and represents the "pure pursuit of honor" (95). The pursuit of honor becomes the source of vital emotion for the samurai class. *Seppuku*, therefore, becomes the "spur for religious sentiment and to moral aspirations" (95). These were precisely the reasons behind Mishima's ritual suicide in 1970. He believed Japan had abdicated its martial honor to Western interests. See *Mishima* by John Nathan (Little, Brown, and Co., 1974).

Works Cited

Achebe, Chinua. "An Image of Africa: Racism in Conrad's Heart of Darkness." *Hopes and Impediments. Selected Essays*. New York, London: Doubleday 1988: 1–20.

Afzal-Khan. *Cultural Imperialism and the Indo-English Novel*. University Park, PA: The Pennsylvania State University Press, 1993.

Anaya, Rudolfo. *A Chicano in China*. Albuquerque, NM: University of New Mexico Press, 1986.

———. "Aztlán: A Homeland Without Boundaries." *Essays on the Chicano Homeland*. Eds. Anaya, Rudolfo and Francisco Lomelí, Albuquerque: University of New Mexico Press, 1989: 230–241.

———. *Bless Me, Ultima*. Berkeley, CA: Quinto Sol, 1972.

———. "The New World Man." *Without Discovery. A Native American Response to Columbus*. Ed. Ray González. Seattle: Broken Moon Press, 1992: 19–27.

Anzaldúa, Gloria. *Borderlands/La Frontera. The New Mestiza*. San Francisco: Aunt Lute Books, 1987.

Bruce-Novoa, Juan. "Charting the Space of Chicano Literature." *Retrospace. Collected Essays on Chicano Literature*. Houston: Arte Público Press, 1990: 93–113.

Nathan, John. *Mishima. A Biography*. Boston, Toronto: Little, Brown, and Co., 1974.

Nigro, Kirsten. "Looking Back to Aztlán From the 1990s." *Bilingual Review* 18 (1993). Internet. Four Pages.

Said, Edward W. *Orientalism*. New York: Random House, 1979.

———. "Two Visions in *Heart of Darkness*." *Culture and Imperialism*. New York: Alfred Knopf, 1993: 19–31.

Saldívar, José David. *The Dialectics of Our America. Genealogy, Cultural Critique, and Literary History*. Durham and London: Duke University Press, 1991.

Seward, Jack. *Hara-Kiri: Japanese Ritual Suicide*. Rutland, VT and Tokyo, Japan: Charles E. Tuttle, 1968.

JULIANA DE ZAVALIA

The Impact of Spanish-American Literature in Translation on U.S. Latino Literature

The presence, impact and influence of Spanish-American literature and culture in the United States are undeniable. Emily Hicks (1991) calls it "a cannibalizing pull" from America's "southern backyard." But today, this cannibalizing pull is coming from right within the U.S.—from the 27 million Puerto Ricans, Mexican Americans and Cuban Americans living there. And the Latino population in the U.S. is constantly growing with the influx of immigrants from all countries in Latin America. What happens when this somewhat culturally remote but geographically close area, labelled "exotic," "magical," "mysterious," is found to be "alive and kicking" within the geographical borders of the United States? The Americas are no longer separated by the Rio Grande, the river running between Mexico and the United States. Latino culture is now an inside phenomenon—hybrid, transculturated and more alive than ever.

Many U.S. Latino writers have been proclaiming "the increasing and inexorable latinization of the U.S.", what Gustavo Pérez Firmat refers to as a "rhythm" that sooner or later is going to get to everybody (1994, 1). Ilán Stavans (1995a) refers to the latinization phenomenon as the "Spanish accent" American (that is, U.S.) literature has acquired, while Chicana activist Gloria Anzaldúa proclaims the coming of "the new *mestiza*"—a racial, ideological, cultural and biological cross-pollination—the "*raza cósmica* . . . at the

Changing the Terms: Translating in the Postcolonial Era, edited and introduced by Sherry Simon and edited by Paul St. Pierre. Perspectives on Translation Series (Ottawa, O.N.: University of Ottawa Press, 2000): pp. 187–206. Copyright © 2000 University of Ottawa Press.

confluence of two or more genetic streams, with chromosomes constantly 'crossing over'" (1987, 77). Terms such as *transculturization, cannibalization, biculturization* are used to describe the cultural traffic between the U.S. and Latin America, between North and South, a traffic—no matter how imbalanced—that results whenever cultures meet and clash. Traffic is intensified when cultures share the same geographical space and boundaries become crucial in this situation. Here boundaries work in a twofold manner depending on the position of the speaker: they can be stigmatizing, homogenizing labels or empowering means of identity formation.[1]

Translation has played a major role in this process: witness the success of Isabel Allende's writing, films such as *Like Water for Chocolate* and *The House of the Spirits*, the proliferation of Mexican restaurants and Latin/ Caribbean music, bilingual street signs, TV stations, commercials, advertising in subways and buses, and most importantly, the Latino—and especially Latina (for women writers)—literary boom. For U.S. Latino writers, translation is a cultural phenomenon, a set of textual practices, a metaphor, an existential condition, a displacement, a *traslado*[2]—a site of both linguistic and topographic cultural difference.[3]

Rethinking the Interface Between Cultures

This paper attempts to explore the influence of contemporary Spanish-American literature in translation on the U.S. literary polysystem. I shall examine the ways in which the stronger host system refracts or constructs its image of Spanish America, and show how this corpus of translated literature and its U.S. refractions impinge on U.S. Latino literature. Spanish-American works in translation already interact among themselves in a separate literary system, but they also interact with(in) the U.S. literary polysystem in many ways. The existence within the U.S. literary polysystem of a large body of Latino writers, who, in some way or other, are related to and/or interact with Spanish-American culture (through descent roots, language, culture and traditions), makes the interface of the two polysystems problematic and complex. My approach emphasizes the importance of the Spanish-American component of U.S. Latino literature.[4] I will frame my analysis against the backdrop of Itamar Even-Zohar's theory of polysystems:

> [O]n the one hand, a system consists of both synchrony and diachrony; on the other, each of these separately is also a system. . . . [T]he idea of structuredness and systemicity need no longer be identified with homogeneity; a semiotic system can be conceived of as a heterogeneous, open structure. It is, therefore, very rarely a uni-system but it is necessarily a polysystem—a multiple system, a system of various systems which intersect with each other and partly

overlap, using concurrently different options, yet functioning as one structured whole, whose members are interdependent. (1990, 11)

Even-Zohar's theoretical framework is particularly useful for examining American literature(s)—an ambiguous term that I am deliberately using here to encompass not only Spanish-American literature and U.S. literature, but also U.S. Latino/Latina literature, a system combining the already multiple systems of both U.S. and Spanish-American literature. Even-Zohar's theory puts all the individual systems within a polysystem on an equal footing so that there is no hierarchical organization; rather, all the systems are organized around the notions of centre and periphery.[5] This tenet allows for full consideration of the heterogeneous and multiple literatures of the U.S., which are sometimes abandoned in the peripheries of the stronger Anglo-American literary system.

The Spanish-American Boom

In focusing on the Spanish-American influence on U.S. Latino literature, I shall centre my analysis on the literary boom of the 1960s and 1970s in Spanish America, which, it is important to point out, involved mainly the genre of the novel. For many novelists and critics, "*la nueva novela*" meant (rather pejoratively) commercial success, or bestsellerism. There resulted a plethora of definitions to describe this literary boom, and even recipes on how to write a boom novel.[6] But more importantly, the Spanish-American literary boom gave rise to a translation boom and international diffusion for the writers. The fact that this literary boom generated such translation activity into various European languages was taken as a sign of the maturity of Latin American culture, a coming into its own, as it were. Thus Sara Castro-Klarén and Héctor Campos (1986) wrote:

[E]ste fenómeno ha sido tomado como la prueba más eficaz de la madurez de la cultura latinoamericana. Se pensó, así, que la traducción en sí misma constituía el llamado "boom". La cultura latinoamericana habría pasado de ser una cultura de consumidores, consumidores de bienes intelectuales, a ser una cultura capaz de producir "civilización". Quiero decir que siendo leída en Europa, reseñada en *L'Express* o en la revista *Times,* había llegado a una paridad con la cultura metropolitana. (320)

[This phenomenon has been taken as the most effective proof of maturity of Latin American culture. Thus, it was thought that translation itself constituted the so-called "boom." From a consumer culture of intellectual goods, Latin American culture

became a culture capable of producing "civilization." Being read
in Europe and reviewed in *L'Express* and *The Times* meant parity
with metropolitan culture.]

In their opinion, translation into European languages, interviews of writers
in metropolitan media and the new superstar status of some of the writers
helped create the image of Latin American literature as a homogeneous
product. They see the literary boom as a market phenomenon that involved
only a few writers, and that was grossly misunderstood in the target systems
into which the works were translated.

But, the Spanish-American literary boom meant more to the writers
themselves. In the foreword to José Donoso's *The Boom in Spanish American
Literature: A Personal History,* Ronald Christ writes: "During the 1960s in
Latin America there appeared in different countries, and almost simultaneously, a number of novels and collections of short stories that by their vir-
tuoso technique and style dazzled a large reading public that no one had ever
guessed was there" (1977, viii). This statement stresses two very important
points: the Pan-American nature of the boom, and the appearance of a large
reading public unknown until then. As Christ points out, "This sudden flow-
ering of writers like Carlos Fuentes, Julio Cortázar, and Mario Vargas Llosa
won ever more attention because these same writers began, almost at once, to
be translated into foreign languages, and to put Latin America on the international literary map for the first time" (viii). José Donoso himself indicated
that in order to be recognized in their own countries, many Latin American
writers first had to achieve success in Europe and the United States. The
boom "conferred a unity where there may have been none, and a connotation
more powerfully economic than esthetic" (Christ 1977, viii).

Inherent in the concept of the Spanish-American literary boom was the
notion of internationalization, of movement beyond borders: geographical
borders, because the boom implied movement beyond national boundaries
into the rest of Latin America, Europe, the U.S.; linguistic borders, because
translation was a necessary and important factor in the internationalization
process; narrative borders, because the new novel implied going beyond traditional narrative strategies and seeking "foster parents" outside the writers' own
traditions, finally to coalesce into what Sarah Crichton calls "the hallmark of
Latin American literature—'magical realism'" (1982, 27).

This movement beyond borders, made possible through the translation
of Spanish-American works, effectively prepared the U.S. audience for the
U.S. Latino literary boom. Literary reviews especially played a major role in
this process because they create, feed and constantly reshape the U.S. construct of Spanish-American literature.[7] In addition, a wide gamut of rewrites
and refractions—in the form of translations, reviews, criticism, anthologies

and films—over the last twenty years helped shorten the cultural distance between the U.S. and its geographically close, yet culturally distant, southern neighbours. As André Lefevere wrote, "the interaction of writing and rewriting is ultimately responsible, not just for the canonization of specific authors or specific works and the rejection of others, but also for the evolution of a given literature, since rewritings are often designed precisely to push a given literature in a certain direction" (1984, 219). So, what triggers what? What feeds what? Does a successful translation trigger more translations? Does a successful film version of his/her book boost a writer's popularity and open new markets for his/her work? Is it a good review in a prestigious newspaper that brings success to a particular author? The position of publishing houses as canon formers and important means of refractions cannot be overlooked. In fact, the manipulation of literature in such a way that only a few Spanish-American writers dominate the market has created a situation in which "the search for stars has obscured the firmament" (Tritten 1984, 36).

García Márquez and Allende

Thus, a canon of Spanish-American literature in translation started to be formed. While the boom can be considered a landmark in the history of this process, two important milestones certainly boosted it: the publication of Gabriel García Márquez's *One Hundred Years of Solitude* in 1970 and the awarding of the Nobel Prize for Literature to García Márquez in 1982. The universe opened up by Gregory Rabassa's excellent translation of García Márquez's novel had far-reaching consequences: it stirred interest in Latin American culture, and set the mould for this literature, so much so that writers who did not fit into the mould were excluded from commercial success.[8] The popular success of García Márquez's novel fuelled interest in other Latin American writers, such as Carlos Fuentes and Mario Vargas Llosa, and promoted translation. As John Vinocur commented:

> [García Márquez] has been widely regarded as a leading figure of the recent Latin American literary renaissance, which in the United States is reflected in the recent publication of books by [several Latin American writers]. . . . But their books never approached the worldwide readership of *One Hundred Years of Solitude,* whose success opened publishing doors in foreign countries to many Latin American writers. (1982, A1)

The status of translation in the host polysystem is crucial to an analysis of canonicity. As Even-Zohar observed:

One might of course find sporadic references to individual literary translations in various periods, but they are seldom incorporated into the historical account in any coherent way. As a consequence, one hardly gets an idea whatsoever of the function of translated literature for a literature as a whole or of its position within that literature. Moreover, there is no awareness of the possible existence of translated literature as a particular system. The prevailing concept is rather that of "translation" or just "translated works" treated on an individual basis. (1990, 45)

In fact, the by-now classic *One Hundred Years of Solitude* illustrates Even-Zohar's point. García Márquez's novel has been part of the U.S. literary polysystem for more than twenty years by now. Can we still consider it a work isolated from U.S. literature, with no imprint whatsoever on the polysystem in which it moves? Within the frame of Even-Zohar's theory, it would be reasonable to say that García Márquez's work interacts with the U.S. polysystem in various ways. But what has become canonized in the U.S. literary polysystem is his particular mode of narration, which has become the model associated with Latin American writing. In distinguishing between two different types of canonicity, "one referring to the level of texts, the other to the level of models," Even-Zohar calls the establishment of a literary model in a system "dynamic canonicity"[9] (1990, 19). The new, revolutionary mode of narration—the model of which is embodied in García Márquez's *One Hundred Years of Solitude*—thus established itself as a "productive principle" in the U.S. polysystem, shaking up the dynamics of the existing system and proving to be very stimulating for the U.S. Latino novel as a genre. In the U.S., García Márquez's model has been used as the yardstick to compare and measure the work of other Spanish-American and Latino writers.

Reviews and critical articles of Spanish American writers began to appear in major U.S. magazines and newspapers. In her analysis of reviews of Latin American literature that appeared in various U.S. magazines between 1970 and 1984, Tritten reports:

the number of reviews during this period was surprising: approximately two to four reviews per year in the *New York Review* (each article frequently included several works); two in the *New Yorker* . . . Two to four reviews per year were published in *Time*. *Newsweek* printed the fewest with only one or two per year . . . (1984, 36)

It truly was the literary "discovery" of a continent ignored until then, for these reviews undoubtedly had an impact on a large segment of the U.S. readership, since the various magazines cater to different audiences. Between 1982 and 1994, there appeared in the *Book Review Digest* 259 entries under the heading "Latin American Literature": 122 for the period 1982–1989; 132 for 1990–1994. The year 1991 saw the most reviews. In many of the reviews, even if García Márquez is not the main subject, his style or mode of narration is evoked as a point of reference to introduce other works into the polysystem. One case in point is the review of Isabel Allende's *Of Love and Shadows* (Kakutani, 1987, C27): "Ms Allende is not mostly imitation García Márquez. Happily, Ms Allende is no longer the novice . . . [She] skillfully evokes both the terrors of daily life under military rule and the subtler forms of resistance . . ." Allende is truly a child of the sixties/seventies boom. Fifteen years after the publication of *One Hundred Years of Solitude,* she made her entrance on the U.S. literary scene with *The House of the Spirits,* a piece in the same mould as the greatest hits of the Spanish-American literary boom, a piece that brought her stardom overnight. But, if it was anticipation of revisiting the García Márquez's model that lured readers to Allende's novel, they soon discovered her own powerful voice.

"Magical realism" became the ready-made formula used to label anything produced by America's "southern backyard": a pot of milk falling spontaneously off a table, a green-haired woman . . . Is this sheer misunderstanding on the part of the host culture or is it depletion of a model? Depletion effectuated not only by critics and reviewers, but also by writers themselves seeking to fit the canonized and commercially successful model. Magical realism is what publishers and readers look for in this literature; anything that strays from the model is marginalized to smaller, more academic publishing presses, and branded as not Latin American enough. García Márquez's literary production exemplifies this attitude: *Of Love and Other Demons* (1995) has all the ingredients readers have come to expect in a García Márquez novel.[10] Not surprisingly, the novel sold very well, as did almost all his work in translation, except *The General in His Labyrinth,* which, even though it revisits the same historical period (independence from Spain to early twentieth century), does not quite fit the canonized model he himself created. As Tim Padget writes: "The author's own grandness is less on display . . . The sensuous detail that enchants such work as *Love in the Time of Cholera* is too often reduced to tedious historical minutiae" (1990, 70).

Modes of Translation

The stronger the host polysystem, the more fluent the translations and refractions. In Lawrence Venuti's opinion, it is difficult for a translator of a cultural other within a strong monolingual polysystem to try to practice translation as a "locus of difference," in an effort to avoid "an imperialistic domestication of a cultural other" (1992, 13). And referring specifically to the U.S. polysystem,

Carol Maier observed that there was such a preference among publishers for
readability, that an author's style is many times sacrificed "in the name of a
more appropriate version in English" (1990–1991, 20). Thomas di Giovanni's
English translations of Jorge Luis Borges's work is an interesting example of
how a writer's work can be sacrificed for the sake of readability and easier
understanding. Matthew Howard relates the "intimate collaboration" between
di Giovanni and Borges that would span over a period of four years:

> Indeed di Giovanni's translations tended to proceed from one
> underlying principle: to make Borges's writing clearer and less
> ambiguous for North American readers. He therefore saw one
> of his main tasks as explaining obscure regional references and
> providing historical details that Borges had omitted in writing for
> Argentine readers. (1997, 72)

He describes di Giovanni and Borges's method of translating, and suggests
that Borges himself acted as censor, attempting to create "a mirror, rival
'Borges,' Borges as an English writer" (76). At work in these translations,
therefore, is a domestication of the source text with the apparent consent of
the author.

In Latin America "the essentially literary quality—literarity truly made
manifest in certain works— . . . is 'mulattoed' by other functions." And the
reason for this, according to Roberto Fernández Retamar, is clear: "given the
dependent, precarious nature of our historical existence, it has fallen to literature to assume functions that in the metropolises have been segregated out
of it" (1989, 86).[11] But, when Latin American works are moved to another
polysystem, their instrumental nature, or "cultural difference," as Neil Larsen
(1990) terms it, loses its immediacy and the works are decontextualized[12]: in
the Latin American context, "local, historical circumstances . . . have generated the possibility of a literature that overcomes the traditional modern-
ism/realism duality by effectively being both modernist and realist at once"
(52). The coinage of the term "*real maravilloso*" enabled Alejo Carpentier [13] to
define "América's" cultural difference at the crossroads of history and culture.

> Cultural difference marks a clear, unmistakeable [*sic*] rift between the
> two worlds, whereas History, given its inherent universalizing concept,
> reduces difference, hence identity, to the point of disappearance . . .
> Here culture is, on the contrary, the point of entry into "a historical
> reality yet more real," which otherwise remains hidden from view.
> In proclaiming the cultural difference of "América" as the key to its
> historical identity, Carpentier, in effect, proclaims its *modernity* as
> both original and autonomous. (Larsen 1990, 54)

This emphasis on culture as "a point of entry into a historical reality" is crucial to understanding the import of *context*—the specific social and historical bearings—when discussing the cultural production of Latin America. The social responsibility of the majority of Latin American writers is even present in the experimentation of the boom novels, and as Doris Sommer writes: "even where [Jean Franco] sees social irresponsibility, for example, in the experimental 'Boom' novels of the 1960s and 1970s, a different reading would discern the novelists' social criticism in the form of impatience with standard social-narrative projects gone sour" (1988, 113). Thus it can be said that the literature that lays the greatest claim to modernity is that produced by the so-called *generación del boom:*

> Early attempts to trace the new Latin American literature to the influence of foreign models . . . have, especially since the Cuban revolution, tended to be de-emphasized in a more consciously nationalist or regionalist impetus to set forth the uniquely local sources of a literature that, if it does betray the superficial traits of outside influence, transforms the foreign element into a radical original compound. It is this complex, synthetic originality that, as this general line of thinking goes, lays proper claim to a modernity that would otherwise—if allowed to retain its privileged but alien metropolitan exemplarity—fall victim to its own intolerable unmodernity as a repetition. (Larsen 1990, 50)

Larsen seems to prefers this "regionalist and autonomizing" construct because it avoids distortion by "the worst kind of mechanical, colonizing pseudoclassification" (50). In his opinion, the most systematic and critical elaboration of this issue is provided by Ángel Rama's concept of transculturation, which Larsen describes as:

> A category of narrative composition and analysis [which] proposes that the Latin American narrative text . . . avoids the double bind in which one either settles for a direct imitation of metropolitan imports or seeks to expunge all "foreign" cultural differences. Instead, the narrative text must treat the local or regional culture itself as a species of language or code, with which to, as it were, speak or rearticulate or, in this sense, "transculturate" the exotic cultural dominant. (1991, xiii)

The "transcultural" and the "anthropophagous" are "two alternative paradigms of postcolonial oppositional culture" (xiii), which offer ways to cannibalize foreign models. Spanish-American literature is a transculturated, hybrid product, the synthetic operation of different referential codes, a contact zone for contending cultures. Thus, when moved to an alien polysystem, it is the code more familiar to the host polysystem that reviewers will emphasize. They will also tend to use stereotypes as the first step in learning about, and as a way of domesticating, the foreign product.[14] In the case of Spanish-American literature, "magical realism" became the stereotype by which to define a "peculiar reality," one that is "magical and exotic."

To combat decontextualization, some "North American critics of Latin American literature must realize that to continue to stress the 'magical' . . . is to deny the larger, broader understanding of reality that informs these texts" (Hicks 1991, xxvii). Hicks proposes a different metaphor that surpasses the binary opposition magical/real, that of "border writing": "Border writing emphasizes the differences in references codes between two or more cultures. It depicts a kind of realism that approaches the experience of border crossers, those who live in a bilingual, bicultural, biconceptual reality" (xxv). In the context of the Spanish-American literary boom, these border crossers were called "transculturators" (by Ángel Rama), writers who transformed the influence of foreign elements into a radically original compound, into a "border text," as Hicks defines it. Once Spanish-American literature is seen as having taken root in the U.S., the meaning of terms to express cultural traffic, such as transculturation and cannibalization, radically change. The questions raised are: Who cannibalizes whom?[15] How is cultural traffic constructed? How is the new territory charted?

The Latino Boom

The U.S. Latino literary boom gives visibility to a social group that maintains its shifting cultural borders within a "lived reality of colonial social conditions" and unequal power relations. Groups transculturate; new elements are added, contents may change, but boundaries still exist to preserve a group from being melted into the "multicultural pot," "euphemism for the imperializing and now defunct 'melting pot'" (Anzaldúa qtd. in Spitta 1995, 196).

How can we trace the history of this Latino literary boom, taking into account its colonial condition?[16] There are two forces at work: assimilation and resistance. And the Latino literary boom can be read in two ways: as a shift from magical realism to the reality of the *barrio*, the birth of "the up and coming" intellectual proclaiming the Latinization of the U.S., relishing a newly constructed Latino identity, trying to make it from the periphery to the centre of the polysystem; or as the commodification of a fashionable ethnicity, the birth of the "domesticated Latino"—a homogenized group where all Latinos are alike and interchangeable—who can provide "enlightenment without irritation, entertainment without confrontation" (Gómez Peña 1993, 51). The Latino boom bears such a striking resemblance to the Spanish-

American boom in the U.S. that it could be considered a child of the latter. The emergence of Spanish-American writers on the U.S. scene prepared the stage for the discovery of local Latino writers. And indeed, the exotization of Spanish America reverberates in the works of U.S. Latino writers; the mainstream readership had already framed these writers within a certain stereotype and expected them to write within the boundaries of magical realism. As for translation activity, Stavans[17] points out that after the Latino boom, the demand for translations of Spanish-American works diminished because the magical realism quota was now being filled by Latino writers.

Like the writers of the Spanish-American boom who sought fathers outside their own literary polysystems, U.S. Latino writers seek validation for their models outside the U.S. literary polysystem, in their Spanish-American forefathers, in their "descent roots." In *Dreaming in Cuban,* Cuban American writer Cristina García relates the Cuban revolution and exile through the story of the Del Pino family. In her review of the novel, Thulani Davis stated: "[i]t is perhaps [the] ordinary magic in Ms García's novel and her characters' sense of their own lyricism that make her work welcome as the latest sign that American literature has its own hybrid offspring of the Latin American school."[18] Chicana writer Ana Castillo dedicates her *Mixquiahuala Letters* to Julio Cortázar, "the master of the game." And indeed, the multiple readings that her novel offers point back to Cortázar's *Hopscotch.* In *How the García Girls Lost Their Accent,* Julia Álvarez exploits the family saga genre to recount the story of the García family under the dictatorship of Trujillo in the Dominican Republic, and their subsequent immigration to the United States. Puerto Rican writer Rosario Ferré, writing in English, offers *The House on the Lagoon,* which follows the history of the island through the saga of a prominent Puerto Rican family "in the manner of Gabriel García Márquez" (front cover comment). The elements of magical realism in these works attest to the adoption of a model that is still working for U.S. Latino writers. Critics claim these texts as belonging to both American and Latin American literatures.[19]

But if the sixties/seventies Spanish-American literary boom was an exclusively male phenomenon, the situation today is completely different. Interest is mainly centred on Latina and Spanish-American women writers; many anthologies of their work have come to light over the last years, as has a large amount of scholarly criticism. In the introduction to a recent anthology of women writers, Susan Bassnett (1990) laments the omission of many superb writers and adds: "We console ourselves with the thought that perhaps the very scale of omissions will lead to further books, to more translations, to new editions and re-publications of neglected materials . . ." (7). And, this is certainly happening. The large number of anthologies of women writings over the recent years shows that the long silence is finally over. We are witnessing a female boom. Spanish-American and U.S. Latina—for many anthologies place both groups in the same volume, thus blurring the boundaries between them—women's voices are surpassing those of their male counterparts. The success of the sixties/seventies boom novels in the U.S. also gave rise to the emergence of other Latin American masterpieces in the U.S. polysystem, such as the work of Ernesto Sábato, whose novel *Sobre héroes y tumbas* was not published in English translation in the U.S. until 1981—twenty years after its publication in Spanish.

The publication of Latino works by major U.S. publishing houses such as Vintage, Harper and Alfred Knopf attests to the mainstream success of some writers, and the push toward the centre of the U.S. polysystem. Traditionally, Latino and Spanish-American writers were handled by smaller publishing houses such as Curbstone, Bilingual Press and Ediciones del Norte, or by university presses.[20] The move from a small press to a major U.S. publishing house is therefore an indication of success. One case in point is Ana Castillo's first novel, *The Mixquiahuala Letters*, which was originally published by Bilingual Press in 1986, but which has recently been republished by Doubleday. This means more visibility and wider distribution in major bookstores, such as Barnes and Noble.

Translation becomes an important issue again when we consider that U.S. Latino writers who write in English are now being translated and published in Spanish in the United States. Moreover, classics of the boom generation are being relaunched (in Spanish) by divisions of major U.S. publishing houses, such as Harper Libros and Vintage en español, to meet the demands of a growing Spanish-speaking audience at home and south of the border. Puerto Rican writer Esmeralda Santiago wrote her first novel, *When I Was Puerto Rican*, in English, and later translated it herself into Spanish. Elena Poniatowska, a prestigious Mexican writer, translated Sandra Cisneros's English-language work into Spanish, in order to bring the Chicano writer into the Mexican polysystem, which has always cast a suspicious look at literature produced by Mexicans on the other side of the border. Could this trend mean an unofficial institutionalization of Spanish as the de facto second language of the United States?

Indeed, translation has become a highly significant activity and practice. But, in the case of Latino writers, the notion of translation needs radical redefinition: the rigid dichotomies target language/source language, original text/translated text seem quite inadequate in this hybridized context. In the introduction to the Spanish version of her novel *When I Was Puerto Rican*, Esmeralda Santiago explains:

> When I write in English I have to translate from Spanish, the keeper of my memories; when I speak in Spanish, I have to translate from the English that defines my present. And when I

write in Spanish, I find myself in the midst of three languages, the Spanish of my childhood, the English of my adulthood, and the Spanglish that constantly crosses over from one world to the other, just as we crossed from our neighborhood in Puerto Rico to the "barriadas" in Brooklyn. (xvii)

Translation is a way of life, a strategy for survival in the North. Some writers choose to write in English because it puts them in a better position to move from the periphery to the centre, and it offers access to a larger audience. In this case, Spanish becomes a touchstone, the locus of difference, the site of political and poetic imagination. Other writers have no choice in the matter: English was the language of schooling, and is therefore the language of writing; Spanish belongs to the private and more personal domain. However, sometimes the boundaries between English and Spanish no longer exist; a hybrid language is forged (as Esmeralda Santiago's "Spanglish") and attempts to use either English or Spanish exclusively create a feeling of being lost in translation.

Spanish-American Versus Latino Writing

The cultural difference between U.S. Latino and Spanish-American writings sometimes needs to be explained. Since culture is read differently by different audiences, cultural elements in these writings must be translated for certain audiences, and many Latino writers give a translation of the Spanish used in their texts, either weaving it into the fabric of the text or including a glossary. Silvia Spitta refers to this strategy as the "radical heterogeneity of those narratives," in terms of "the intercultural and transcultural dynamics of Latin American narratives" (1995, 198). Indeed, the stories move constantly between different cultural spaces that shape identities. There is a tension between deterritorialization and reterritorialization, and thus the risk of depoliticization of borders. But the stronghold of roots and tradition that comes across in these texts indicates that the majority of Latino writers are politically committed to their communities. In Castillo's *The Mixquiahuala Letters,* for example, Tere, the protagonist and writer of the letters, travels and translates back and forth between Mexico and the U.S., English and Spanish, Chicano traditions and her U.S. Latina self, as she negotiates her border identity.

At the core of many Latino writings is the tension to preserve that locus of difference—a difference that is sometimes erased in reading, depending on the audience—and thereby resist acculturation. On the other hand, there is also the need for consent, for visibility, for dialogue with the other component of their hyphenated identities—the stronger Anglo America—without being crushed by the imbalance of power. And, at the same time, there is the need to preserve the specificities of their own individual cultures (for Cuban culture is not the same as Chicano, Dominican is not the same as Puerto Rican). Preserving specificities is a way of avoiding depoliticization, and at the same time, it enables the writers to surpass the boundaries of stereotyping and the homogenizing labels that freeze groups into "emerging voices" or "exotic minorities," as Guillermo Gómez Peña says.

Interest in Latin America[21] has manifested itself in the proliferation of Latin American Studies programs throughout the U.S., programs that also include Latina (women) studies. The large critical output from these programs is such that some critics talk about "Latinoamericanism," which Enrico M. Santi compares to "Orientalism":

> Like Orientalism, then, Latinoamericanism would identify the corporate institution that frames both a systematic discipline . . . and the whole network of political, economic, and imaginary interests that underlie that discipline. To focus on the status of each as discourses would actually mean to deal principally with their own internal consistencies, not with their supposed correspondence with given cultural or geographical realities. (1992, 90)

The critical output from these programs is mainly produced in English, and in many cases does not take into account critical work produced over the years in Spanish, in Latin America. The fact that much of Latin American criticism in Spanish is only recently being translated accounts for its late incorporation into critical writing in U.S. academia. This lag allows, however, for late "discoveries," a fact that Fredric Jameson (1989) draws attention to in his foreword to the English translation of Roberto Fernández Retamar's essays.

The main goal of this paper was to discuss the cultural traffic in the Americas, and show how it affects the U.S. literary polysystem. I have been reluctant to frame this discussion within the concept of postcolonialism, which, in my opinion, mainly refers to the East-West cultural traffic. Here, in the Americas, there is rather a North-South traffic which has succeeded colonialism (by the Spanish) to a form of neocolonialism (by the U.S.), a more pervasive, yet more subtle phenomenon. The heavy cultural traffic in the Americas is constructed on a North-South/South-North plane. Spanish-American intellectuals, since their countries' independence from Spain (in the early nineteenth century, for the most part), have been trying to imagine and write their national states in relation—sometimes in opposition, at other times in apposition—to the northern giant, the United States. This trend can be observed not only in Domingo Sarmiento's conception of *civilización y barbarie* and José Martí's *nuestra América*, but also in Gloria Anzaldúa's *Borderlands/La Frontera*.

Translation is an important cultural vehicle in the Americas, a means of making it north along the Pan-American highway. This northbound cultural traffic is accompanied by successive waves of migration, especially from Central America and the Caribbean. These *traslados* opened the way for the recognition of the large Latino presence in the U.S., a force which is now expanding, within the U.S. borders, its own national borders in an attempt to rethink their "imagined communities." This cannibalization of the geographical borders of the U.S. forces us to rethink, from within these same geographical borders, the appropriation of (the concept of) America. America must be redefined so as not to reflect another appropriation from an imperial centre, but rather to consciously encompass the totality of the Americas.

NOTES

1. Suzanne Oboler (1995), xvi–xvii, explores the implications of ethnic labels, which she calls "social constructions," as both "strategic and referential."

2. Translation has become a favourite metaphor among Latino intellectuals and writers. Stavans and Pérez Firmat talk about the Latino as an individual "lost in translation." The concept of translation is deployed by many writers as they search for a mode of expression to transmit their bilingual experience, so much so that the boundaries between source and target language have become highly contested ground.

3. The concepts put forward in Sherry Simon's exploration of the ways in which "translation embodies paradigms of cultural difference" (1992), 160, are extremely helpful to our exploration of the import of translation in the context of U.S. Latino literature.

4. See Stavans (1995b), 32, who raises the question "What happens when Latinos are seen as a Hispanic American branch reaching beyond the spiritual and geographical limits of a U.S. minority?" Oboler (1995), 159, stresses the need to recognize and study the "cultural, linguistic and historical ties to various nations in Latin America," as well as to research and study the "histories, cultures and experiences that have shaped the various and multiple meanings and social values of being Latinos and Latinas in the U.S."

5. In a way, this organization can be seen as hierarchical in that the stronger system(s) are always as the centre of the polysystem, setting the boundaries of what is peripheral in relation to them.

6. See R. Avilez Fábila, "Cómo escribir una novela y convertirla en bestseller," *Mundo Nuevo* (Oct. 1970): 41–52.

7. Susan Tritten (1984) and Carol Maier (1990–1991) both comment on the implications of reviews of Latin American literature in the United States.

8. It seems to me that the characteristics attributed by critics to the Spanish-American literary boom—bestsellerism, homogenization, exclusion of writers—are reinforced when the works are translated and reviewed in an alien polysystem.

9. Even-Zohar (1990), 19, refers to the establishment of a specific text in a literary canon as "static canonicity."

10. See Stavans (1995c), 149–171, for a reassessment of Gabriel García Márquez's imprint in the literary world.

11. See also Riding (1983) for a discussion of the role of Latin American intellectuals.

12. Gustavo Pellón (1992), 82, warns against socio-historical decontextualization "that is brought to bear on a literary corpus such as that of Latin America, which one could argue is consciously defined by its problematic discourse with its society and history."

13. See "De lo real maravilloso" in Carpentier (1964).

14. Partha Mitter (1987) discusses the role of stereotypes in understanding alien cultures.

15. The terms *cannibalization* and *domestication* are used to express a two-way cultural traffic. Both concepts presuppose a power relation. Whereas cannibalization is taken as a strategy of resistance, domestication implies colonization. Both terms, however, point to the same direction. The question is when and how does cannibalization become domestication, and vice versa.

16. I am reluctant to use the term *postcolonial* here. In an essay contextualizing the use of the term *postcoloniality*, Ruth Frankenberg and Lata Mani (1996), 274, propose: "the particular relation of past territorial domination and current racial composition that is discernible in Britain, and that lends a particular meaning to the term 'postcolonial' does not, we feel, obtain [in the U.S. context]." They suggest using the term "'post-Civil Rights' broadly, to refer to the impact of struggles by African American, American Indian, La Raza, and Asian American communities that stretched from the mid-1950's to the 1970's," 274.

17. In a conversation at Amherst College, October 1995.

18. Gladys M. Varona-Lacey (1994), 126, in her review of the Spanish version, *Soñar en cubano*, writes: "*En Soñar en cubano* Cristina García ofrece descripciones que lindan con el surrealismo y el realismo mágico" [In *Soñar en cubano* Cristina García offers descriptions that verge on surrealism and magical realism].

19. For example, Stavans (1995b), 19, questions: "Is Oscar Hijuelos possible without José Lezama Lima and Guillermo Cabrera Infante? Or is he only a child of Donald Barthelme and Susan Sontag?"

20. The University of Texas at Austin is very active in this field.

21. By the 1960s, U.S. interest in Latin America had become part of the *Zeitgeist*. If the U.S. looked upon Latin America as its "backyard," the Cuban revolution in 1959 dealt a blow to the neighbourhood. It fuelled strategies and policies to prevent the spread of Communism in America, such as international development programs (IDPs), the Peace Corps, the Alliance for Progress, military threat and/or military intervention. IDPs included financing Latin American studies which would cover a wide range of activities, including the translation and diffusion of authors from and topics on Latin America. This was reinforcement of the Cold War without being overtly political.

Works Cited

Theory and Criticism

Anzaldúa, Gloria. 1987. *Borderlands/La Frontera: The New Mestiza.* San Francisco: Aunt Lute Books.

Bassnett, Susan. 1990. Introduction to *Knives & Angels,* ed. Susan Bassnett. London: Zed Books.

Carpentier, Alejo 1964. *Tientos y diferencias.* Mexico: U Nacional Autónoma de México.

Castro-Klarén, Sara, and Héctor Campos. 1986. "Traducciones, tirajes ventas y estrellas: El boom." *Ideologies and Literatures* 4, no. 17: 319–338.

Christ, Ronald. 1977. Foreword to *The Boom in Spanish American Literature: A Personal History*, by José Donoso. New York: Columbia University Press.

Crichton, Sarah. 1982. "El boom de la novela latinoamericana." *Publishers Weekly* (Dec. 24): 29–33.

Davis, Thulani. 1992. Rev. of *Dreaming in Cuban*, by Cristina García. *The New York Times* (May 17).

Donoso, José. 1977. *The Boom in Spanish American Literature: A Personal History.* New York: Columbia University Press.

Even-Zohar, Itamar. 1990. "Polysystem Studies." *Poetics Today* 11, no. 1, Special Issue.

Fernández Retamar, Roberto. 1973. *Calibán. Apuntes sobre la cultura de nuestra América.* Buenos Aires: Editorial La Pléyade.

———. 1989. *Caliban and Other Essays.* Trans. Edward Baker. Minneapolis: University of Minnesota Press.

Flores, Juan. 1996. "Puerto Rican and Latino Cultures at the Crossroads." In *Latinos in New York: Communities in Transition,* ed. Gabriel Haslip-Viera and Sherrie L. Bauer. Indiana: University of Notre Dame Press.

Frankenberg, Ruth, and Lata Mani. 1996. "Crosscurrents, Crosstalk: Race, 'Postcoloniality' and the Politics of Location." In *Displacement, Diaspora, and Geographies of Identity,* ed. Smadar Lavie and Ted Swedenburg, 273–293. Durham: Duke University Press.

Gómez Peña, Guillermo. 1993. *Warrior for Gringostroika.* Saint Paul: Graywolf Press.

Hicks, Emily. 1991. *Border Writing. The Multidimensional Text.* Theory and History of Literature 80. Minneapolis: University of Minnesota Press.

Howard, Matthew. 1997. "Stranger than Ficción." *Linguafranca* (June–July): 71–78.

Jameson, Fredric. 1989. Foreword to *Caliban and Other Essays,* by Roberto Fernández Retamar, trans. Edward Baker. Minneapolis: University of Minnesota Press.

Kakutani, Michiko. 1987. *New York Times* (May 20): C27.

Larsen, Neil. 1990. *Modernism and Hegemony: A Materialist Critique of Aesthetic Agencies.* Theory and History of Literature 71. Minneapolis: University of Minnesota Press.

———. 1991. Foreword to *Border Writing: The Multidimensional Text,* by Emily Hicks, xi–xx. Minneapolis: University of Minnesota Press.

Lefevere, André. 1984. "Why Waste Our Time on Rewrites? The Trouble with Interpretation and the Role of Rewriting in an Alternative Paradigm." In *The Manipulation of Literature,* ed. Theo Hermans, 215–243. New York: St. Martin's Press.

Maire, Carol. 1990–1991. "Rewriting Latin American Literature in Translation: Time to 'Proceed to the Larger Question.'" *Translation Review* 34–35: 18–24.

Mitter, Partha. 1987. "Can We Ever Understand Alien Cultures? Some Epistemological Concerns Relating to the Perception and Understanding of the Other." *Comparative Criticism* 9: 7–14.

Oboler, Suzanne. 1995. *Ethnic Labels, Latino Lives: Identity and the Politics of (Re)Presentation in the United States.* Minneapolis: University of Minnesota Press.

Padget, Tim. 1990. Rev. of *The General in His Labyrinth*, by Gabriel García Márquez. *Newsweek* (Oct. 8).

Pellón, Gustavo. 1992. "The Canon, the Boom, and Literary Theory." *Latin American Literary Review* 20, no. 40: 80–82.

Pérez Firmat, Gustavo. 1994. *Life on the Hyphen: The Cuban-American Way.* Austin: University of Texas Press.

Rama, Ángel. 1982. *Transculturación Narrativa en América Latina.* México D.F.: Siglo XXI Editores.

Riding, Alan. 1983. "Revolution and the Intellectual." *The New York Times* (Mar. 13): 6–28.

Santi, Enrico M. 1992. "Latinamericanism and Restitution." *Latin American Literary Review* 20, no. 40: 89–96.

Simon, Sherry. 1992. "The Language of Cultural Difference: Figures of Alterity in Canadian Translation." In *Rethinking Translation: Discourse, Subjectivity, Ideology,* ed. Lawrence Venuti, 159–176. London/New York: Routledge.

Sollors, Werner. 1986. *Beyond Ethnicity.* New York: Oxford University Press.

Sommer, Doris. 1988. "Not Just a Personal Story: Women's Testimonies and the Plural Self." In *Life/Lines: Theorizing Women's Autobiography,* ed. Bella Bozki and Celeste Schenk, 107–130. Ithaca, N.Y.: Cornell University Press.

Spitta, Silvia. 1995. *Between Two Waters: Narratives of Transculturation in Latin America,* 159–176. Houston: Rice University Press.

Stavans, Ilán. 1993. "Lust in Translation: Notes sobre *el boom* narrativo hispánico-norteamericano." *Revista Hispánica Moderna* 46, no. 2: 384–393.

———. 1995a. "American Lit Takes a Spanish Accent." *Boston Sunday Globe* (Jan. 8): A31.

———. 1995b. *The Hispanic Condition: Reflections of Culture and Identity in America.* New York: HarperCollins Publishers.

———. 1995c. "The Master of Aracataca." *Michigan Quarterly Review* 24, no. 2: 149–171.

Tritten, Susan. 1984. "Reviews of Latin American Literature in United States Magazines: Aid or Impediment to Understanding?" *World Literature Today* 58, no. 1: 36–39.

Varona-Lacey, Gladys M. 1994. Rev. of *Soñar en cubano,* by Cristina García, trans. Marisol Palés-Castro. *Hispamérica* 23, no. 68: 125–126.

Venuti, Lawrence. 1992. Introduction. *Rethinking Translation: Discourse, Subjectivity, Ideology,* ed. Lawrence Venuti, 1–17. London/New York: Routledge.

Vinocur, John. 1982. "García Márquez of Colombia Wins Nobel Literature Prize." *The New York Times* (Oct. 22): A1, A31.

West, Paul. 1985. Rev. of *The House of the Spirits,* by Isabel Allende, trans. Magda Bogin. *The Nation* (July 20).

Novels

Allende, Isabel. 1982. *La casa de los espíritus.* Barcelona: Plaza and Janes.

———. 1985. *The House of the Spirits.* Trans. Magda Bogin. New York: A.A. Knopf.

———. 1984. *De amor y de sombras.* Barcelona: Plaza and Janes.

———. 1987. *Of Love and Shadows.* Trans. Margaret Sayers Peden. New York: A.A. Knopf.

Álvarez, Julia. 1991. *How the García Girls Lost Their Accent.* Chapel Hill, N.C.: Algonquin Books.

Castillo, Ana. 1992. *The Mixquiahuala Letters.* New York: Anchor Books.

Cisneros, Sandra. 1986. *The House on Mango Street.* Houston: Arte Público Press.

———. 1994. *La casa en Mango Street.* Trans. Elena Poniatowska. New York: Vintage Books.

Ferré, Rosario. 1996. *The House on the Lagoon.* New York: Plume/Penguin.

García, Cristina. 1992. *Dreaming in Cuban.* New York: Ballantine Books.

———. 1994. *Soñar en cubano.* Trans. Marisol Peles Matos. Madrid: Espase-Calpe.

García Márquez, Gabriel. 1967. *Cien años de soledad.* Buenos Aires: Editorial Sudamericana.

———. 1970. *One Hundred Years of Solitude.* Trans. Gregory Rabassa. New York: Harper & Row.

———. 1989. *El general en su laberinto.* Buenos Aires: Editorial Sudamericana.

———. 1990. *The General in His Labyrinth.* Trans. Edith Grossman. New York: A.A. Knopf.

————. 1994. *Del amor y otros demonios.* Barcelona: Mondadori.

————. 1995. *Of Love and Other Demons.* Trans. Edith Grossman. New York: A.A. Knopf.

Sábato, Ernesto. 1961. *Sobre héroes y tumbas.* Buenos Aires: Fabril Editores.

————. 1981. *On Heroes and Tombs.* Trans. Helen R. Lane. Boston: Godine.

Santiago, Esmeralda. 1993. *When I Was Puerto Rican.* Reading, Mass.: Addison-Wesley.

————. 1994. *Cuando era puertorriqueña.* New York: Vintage Books.

SILVIA SPITTA

Of Brown Buffaloes, Cockroaches and Others: Mestizaje *North and South of the Rio Bravo*

What is Chicano theatre?
It is theatre as beautiful, rasquachi, human, cosmic, broad, deep, tragic, comic as the life of La Raza itself.

Luis Valdez, Early Works

Nos hallamos entonces en una de esas épocas de palingenesia, y en el centro del maelstreón universal.

José Vasconcelos, La raza cósmica

In downtown Mexico City there is an important central square known as Tlatelolco or Plaza de las Tres Culturas where a small plaque commemorates 500 years of colonialism. "1492" the plaque reads, "was neither triumph nor defeat, it signaled the painful birth of the *mestizo* nation that Mexico is today." According to this version of history, *mestizaje* is seen not as defeat, nor as the vanquishment of great American indigenous cultures, but as the birth of a new people. In line with this thinking, in Latin America the 12th of October is celebrated as "El Día de la Raza" while in the US and Canada the 12th of October is Columbus Day (hence the birth of imperialism and the expansion of the West).

While both the plaque in Tlatelolco and El Día de la Raza are celebratory versions of 500 years of colonialism and the *mestizaje* to which they

Revista de Estudios Hispánicos, Volume 35, Number 2 (May 2001): pp. 333–346. Copyright © 2001 Silvia Spitta.

gave rise, the underside of this triumphalist ideology can perhaps best be illustrated by the contradictions embodied in José Vasconcelos's 1925 *La raza cósmica*—one of the most influential essays written about this process—and in the many different versions of *mestizaje* which have been adopted by Chicanos north of the Rio Grande.

In *La raza cósmica* Vasconcelos creates neologisms such as "universolópolis" to refer to the utopian capital of a new world situated on the shores of the Amazon River; he resuscitates old-fashioned ideas about an Atlantis as the site of a magnificent civilization point of origin of the "red" race of America; he assumes without question the European division of the races into white and the others (red, black, and Mongol); he inverts eugenicist belief in race mixture as degeneration by proposing an inexplicable and sudden superlative *mestizaje;* he formulates a mysterious "eugenics of aesthetic taste" ("del gusto estético") where the poor and ugly bodies that invariably belong to non-whites—monstrous bodies—(he calls them monstrous), deformed by ignorance and poverty will become conscious of their own ugliness and opt to disappear from the face of the earth. Full of other equally extravagant, eccentric, and contradictory claims, *La raza cósmica* is a text marked by the deep ambivalence that permeates ideologies of *mestizaje* and today reads more like science fiction than the American and *mestizo* manifesto Vasconcelos proposed to write (*La raza* 42).

In his magnificent biography of Vasconcelos, José Joaquín Blanco tracks the political trajectory that led him from a progressive politics to embrace nazism; from Vasconcelo's first self-characterization in *Indología* (1926) as a *mestizo* to his declarations ten years later of being "Hispanic" and a pure Creole in *Ulises criollo* (Blanco 17). Blanco situates the changes in Vasconcelos's position that led him to swing radically from a liberal political stance to that of an advocate of fascism under the sign of the contradictory and the dissonant (Blanco 9). Vasconcelos has to be read the other way around: the dissonant and the contradictory in his thinking and political posture cannot be used as some sort of lack of academic and political rigor, or of some mental lapse, but rather *La raza cósmica* should be read as one of the most eloquent documents regarding the difficulty and virtual impossibility Vasconcelos and so many other Latin American thinkers before and after him face(d) trying to extricate themselves from Latin America's colonial past.[1]

Vasconcelos is radical when he points out the evident: that in no continent other than in America have all the races come face to face and mixed and that this great racial and cultural mixing took place largely thanks to the whites and their respective empires that served as bridges between Europe and America and facilitated the vertiginous process of American *mestizaje*. As part of the discourse that opposed the Latin to the Anglo-Saxon worlds, characteristic of his time and connected to the War of 1898,

Vasconcelos feels the need to explain the contrast between North and South and, more specifically, between the prosperity of the North and the relative backwardness of the South. He finds the answer in eugenics and in the legacy of two very different colonial policies: while in the United States the Anglos exterminate indigenous populations and marginalize African-Americans, in Latin America there has been *mestizaje* of races that is laudable. However, the races that have mixed have been too "dissimilar." Such dissimilarity—as it was commonly accepted in Vasconcelos's time—invariably led to a degenerative *mestizaje* because only the base elements of each race intermixed with one another. Hence he concludes matter-of-factly: "Sucede que el *mestizaje* de factores muy disímiles tarda mucho tiempo en plasmar" (*La raza* 11) Despite these reservations, Vasconcelos proposes—indeed decrees—that *mestizaje* would henceforth be a mixing of the superlative elements of each race and no longer that of the most base ones.

The overlap of the concept of race and culture in regards to questions of colonization is so prevalent that even though Vasconcelos is conscious of it, he cannot relinquish it. Thus he criticizes nineteenth century European ideas in the following manner:

> Nosotros nos hemos educado bajo la influencia humillante de una filosofía ideada por nuestros enemigos, si se quiere de una manera sincera, pero con el propósito de exalter sus propios fines y anular los nuestros. De esta manera nosotros mismos hemos llegado a creer en la inferioridad del *mestizo*, en la irredención del indio, en la condenación del negro, en la decadencia irreparable del oriental. (*La raza* 45)

To counter the colonizing manipulation of racial ideas deployed to subordinate Latin American populations, Vasconcelos finds no other way out than merely to invert the terms of the debate: *mestizaje* will no longer be a degenerative mixing of races, it will be the miscegenation of the superior elements of all the races.

He understands his essay *La raza cósmica* as an attempt to reconstruct "nuestra ideología y organizer conforme a una nueva doctrina étnica toda nuestra vida continental" (*La raza* 46). In other words, his position incorporates an essential anti-colonial gesture. Despite the best intentions however, his inability to theorize using mixture and *mestizaje* as starting points forces him to always seek the "purity" of originary cultures and to go back to an unadulterated and ideal version of the "Spanish" or the "African." Hence Vasconcelos merely inverts the terms of the debate and grants a positive value to racial categories charged with negativity until then. In the end he is unable to overcome the racism inherent in such thinking. For, as Latin American critics have shown time and again, *mestizaje* is "an ideological discourse whose purpose [was] to justify the hegemony of 'national' Creole groups who assumed power when the colonial system fell apart" (Lienhard 189).

To be sure, national consolidation depended on the peaceful intermarriage and co-existence of two cultures, races, and genders. The violence at the root of modern Latin American nations, inscribed in the Malinche myth, was erased from national imaginaries. As Norma Alarcón puts it:

> It is worthwhile to remember that the historical founding moment of the construction of *mestiza(o)* subjectivity entails the rejection and denial of the dark Indian Mother as Indian, which has compelled women to often collude in silence against themselves and to actually deny the Indian position even as that position is visually stylized and represented in the making of the fatherland. Within these blatant contradictions, the overvaluation of Europeanness is constantly at work . . . Thus, Mexico constructs its own ideological version of the notorious Anglo-American "melting pot" under the sign of *Mestizo(a)*. (377)

While it may be debatable which came first, the ideology of the melting pot or that of *mestizaje*, it is clear that Alarcón makes this point in order to underscore the fact that both ideologies, regardless of their grounding in two very different cultures and national formations, equally erase the indigenous constituent at the base of their culture.

Consequently, what we have is a split between utopian-sounding constructions of *mestizaje*—such as Vasconcelos's "cosmic race"—and the experiences of real *mestizos*. However, despite Vasconcelos's vertiginous oscillation between the cosmic and the comic, between his liberatory political praxis and his problematic adherence to the tenets of the pseudo science of eugenics, "la raza cósmica" has not only become a foundational concept in Mexico and all of Latin America, but it has also been adopted by Mexican-Americans North of the Rio Grande.

In the "Plan Espiritual de Santa Bárbara"—a Chicano manifesto of the 60s—the university policies that Vasconcelos proposed in Mexico in the 20s are adopted as a radical cry: "No venimos a trabajar *para* la universidad sino a pedir que la universidad trabaje para nuestro pueblo." This political program of radicalization of the universities ends with the Vasconcelian motto inscribed at the main entry of Mexico's most important university: "Por la raza habla el espíritu." Yet another foundational manifesto, the "Plan Espiritual de Aztlán" (Denver 1969), substitutes Vasconcelos's Atlantis with an Aztlán vaguely situated in an indeterminate space of the Southwest, which serves as a mythical point of origin and return. Chicanos are then seen as a people whose forefathers migrated South to Tenochtitlán from Aztlán and now—completing a migratory circle—are migrating back. The creation of Aztlán as foundational myth allows Chicanos in the 60s to abolish and/or critique national boundaries as arbitrary, i.e., to postulate a pre- or post-national migratory space as the basis of their culture. Chicanos then affirm their unique migratory and geographical position with respect to the United States as well as the rest of Latin America:

> Con el corazón en las manos y las manos en la tierra, Nosotros Declaramos la Independencia de nuestras Naciones *Mestizas*. Somos la Raza de Bronce con una Cultura de Bronce. Frente al mundo, frente a toda América del Norte, frente a nuestros hermanos del Continente de Bronce, Somos una Nación, Somos una Unión de pueblos libres, Somos Aztlán. (Valdez, Steiner 403)

Aztlán then becomes a great *mestizo* nation alike in spirit yet different from other *mestizo* nations in Latin America.

Years later, Gloria Anzaldúa in her foundational *Borderlands/La frontera* will simply assume Aztlán as a given fact. In her works Aztlán forms a closed circuit point of both origin and return to a homeland of Chicanos. Through Aztlán, then, Chicanos regain—at least in imaginary terms—the land they lost in 1848 with the Treaty of Guadalupe Hidalgo. Aztlán also serves Chicanos to put US ideology on its head: the "invaders" are Anglos and not Mexican "wetbacks"; the border is posited as a fluid and open border (like the daily reality of so many border towns) and not the rigid and impassable barrier that Washington is trying to build along two thousand miles.

At once appealing to yet deviating from Vasconcelos's inclusiveness in *La raza cósmica,* these early manifestos establish a rigid dichotomy between whites and *mestizos*. While Anglos are characterized as materialists, lacking in humanity, aggressive, racist, individualists, and arrogant exploiters, Latins are humanists united by strong family, community, and land ties. This early Manicheanism turns against itself and creates a series of divisions within the Chicano Movement. It marginalizes Chicanos who are not part of the Movement, who are not politically involved and who do not form bonds of solidarity with the working classes and migrant workers. It also labels middle-class Chicanos as acculturated and "sell outs"—which is the main reason why so many Mexican-Americans violently refuse the label Chicano.

In the philosophical poem "Pensamiento serpentino: A Chicano Approach to the Theatre of Reality," Luis Valdez attempts to overcome this early Manicheanism. He writes:

To be CHICANO is not (NOT)
to hate the gabacho or the
gachupín or even the pobre
vendido . . .

To be CHICANO is to love yourself
your culture, your
skin, your language (175)

The problem with his formulation is not his conciliatory intention but rather
determining what the "your culture" of the poem refers to when in fact he is
writing about an uprooted, deterritorialized culture—geographically, socially,
and politically. It is perhaps for this reason that Valdez, as many Chicanos
before and after him, turns his back on US history and adopts an indigenist
position reinventing a glorious pre-Columbian indigenous past. He adopts the
Maya concept of the "can" as synonym of the "cosmic race" in order to establish an unbroken continuity between pre-Columbian and Chicano culture:

Para el hombre cósmico
el CAN de los mayas antiguos
la muerte no existe
Racial distinctions
no existen
límites materiales
no existen
nation, wealth, fashions,
hatreds, envidias, greed,
The lust for power
no existen,
not even the lust for
CHICANO POWER

Como los curanderos
abusados
El hombre CAN
se vuelve pájaro
o animal o pescado
y se mete al río a descansar.

He can be everything
because he LOVES everything
(menos el diablo)

he identifies with TODO
So he IS todo
And that, carnales
is truly being

Chi-CAN-o
Mexico, after all, means
feathered serpent
or, if you are mathematically
trucha, it means
$E=MC^2$ (Valdez 179–181)

Overlooking the glibness of the 60s evident in this poem, the adoption of the "cosmic race" as ideal allows Chicanos to muddy and complicate the rigid black/white racial and cultural dichotomy operative in the US and to counter it with a much more open and fluid understanding of culture. Indeed, as the results of the most recent census demonstrate, *mestizaje* is increasingly becoming a reality as the one-drop rule fast recedes under the impact of a more inclusive understanding of racial and cultural mix. Like the writings of many Latinos, Valdez's poem then, with its mixture of languages (the use of "Spanglish"), is another way of performing the fluidity of the border and putting into question the US national imaginary based on the identity between race, language culture, and space.

However, even though *mestizaje,* when it is transferred north serves as a critical weapon, some, if not all, of its negative connotation arc transferred north as well. In *Borderlands,* for example, Anzaldúa takes up Vasconselos's idea of a cosmic race as a theory of generous inclusiveness of differences opposed to "the theory of the pure Aryan, and to the policy of racial purity that white America practices" (77). At the same time, however, she assumes all the negativity associated with the term *mestizo* and writes that when she looks at herself in the mirror all she sees is "pena. Shame" (*Borderlands* 140). The cosmic *mestiza* only appears in the lyrics used as epigraph to her chapter on "La conciencia de la *mestiza.*" They are from the *conjunto* Los Tigres del Norte and echoing Vasconcelos's motto they read "Por la mujer de mi raza / hablará el espíritu" (*Borderlands* 99).

An even more problematic formulation is Cherríe Moraga's recent poem "Halfbreed." Adopting the term "halfbreed" (applied to mixed US Indians) to write about her *mestiza* condition, Cherríe Moraga equates her *mestizaje* with her mother's brown head reflected in a toilet bowl:

the difference between you and me
is as I bent

over strangers' toilet bowls,
the face that glared back at me
in those sedentary waters
was not my own, but my mother's
brown head floating in a pool
of crystalline whiteness (95)

The importance of the adoption of Vasconcelos's thinking north of the Rio Grande stems from the effect it has when it is confronted with the black/white divide that dominates the national imaginary in the US. Indeed, it is no accident that Vasconcelos grew up on the US-Mexico border subjected to violence from both Anglos and Apaches. However, despite *mestizaje's* problematic theoretical underpinnings and history, when it crosses the Rio Bravo it performs a critique of the melting pot as intrinsically an ideology of whitening. Although *mestizaje* itself operates in a similar way—as is evident in Vasconcelos's complete disregard for Mexico's indigenous roots—in the United States it tends to function as an ideal of political union of all third world peoples.[2] However, the eugenicist underpinnings of the whole theorization of *mestizaje* do not get lost in translation. They resurface time and again almost as if the history embedded in words invariably burdens—if not shackles—contemporary intentions. In fact, in Latin America since Columbus, *mestizos* have elicited deep resentment and suspicion. While I will not elaborate on this point here, suffice it to say that the earliest recorded usage of the term is already negative. Only sixty or so odd years after Columbus's landfall one chronicler reported to the Crown in 1563 that "la tierra está llena de *mestizos,* que es una maldita gente" (Boyd-Bowman 585).

The notorious lawyer and Chicano activist Oscar Zeta Acosta is perhaps the clearest example of the uneasy coupling between utopian intent and abjection embodied by the split that separates ideologies of *mestizaje* from the reality of being *mestizo* in our America. Already in his 1972 autobiographical novel *The Autobiography of a Brown Buffalo* he writes: "I am the nigger after all" (95). A Chicano *Bildungsroman, Autobiography of a Brown Buffalo* echoes Jack Kerouac's programmatic *On the Road* (1957)—a manifesto of the Beat Generation that describes the increasing destabilization of our society under globalization and its mobilization on all the roads, freeways, trains and other means of communication. Like Kerouac, Zeta situates the narrator on the road: between his childhood in El Paso; his adolescence spent in an agrarian valley of the San Joaquín; his college years as a student (of literature, music, mathematics); his years in Panama as an evangelizers; his work as a lawyer in San Francisco; and finally his decision to assume an activist Chicano identity. This history of mobility, lack of roots, and deterritorialization translates into a sense of identity that coincides with the historical association of *mestizo* with *métis* and a particular kind of sly and negative cunning: "I am too tricky," writes Zeta, "I can make any kind of face you ask. After all, I've been a football man, a drunk, a preacher, a mathematician, a musician, a lawyer . . . and a brown buffalo" (197).

It is only upon crossing the border from El Paso to Juárez that Zeta comes to the realization that Mexico can never be the "home" he is searching for as a son of an "Indian from Durango" simply because he does not speak Spanish. Hence, language and place go together—when he lost the mother tongue he lost the motherland. And yet, as a *mestizo* in the US, he also has no place. As a symbol of his *mestizaje* he adopts the American bison or buffalo (an animal characterized simultaneously by strength and extreme vulnerability given the fact that it was brought to near extinction). Zeta travels back across the border to Los Angeles where he assumes the radical chicanismo of the 60s. He recounts his experiences there in his second novel, *Revolt of the Cockroach People*, where he becomes the buffalo and changes his name from Oscar Zeta Acosta to Buffalo Zeta Brown.[3] Picking up on the negative connotations of the term *mestizo*, Zeta now adopts the cockroach—an insect that we consider abject and mercilessly try to eradicate from the face of the earth, yet which is now stronger than ever—as yet another symbol for *mestizaje*.

In the end all of Zeta's work revolves around himself, his unstable on-the-road identity, his life as a series of interminable journeys (both psychedelic and not), his transformations into something or other (from Samoan to Chicano lawyer; from Latino activist to writer; from buffalo to cockroach) and his debasement and abjection. They remind us of one of the most eloquent passages in Kerouac about identities on the road where the protagonist wakes up late one afternoon in a cheap hotel in front of the train station and where, unlike some of us who while traveling wake up and for a moment feel disoriented because we don't know where we are, Kerouac's protagonist wakes up and does not know *who he is:*

> I woke up as the sun was reddening; and that was the one distinct time in my life, the strangest moment of all, when I didn't know who I was—I was far away from home, haunted and tired with travel, in a cheap hotel room I'd never seen, hearing the hiss of steam outside, and the creak of the old wood of the hotel, and footsteps upstairs, and all the sad sounds, and I looked at the cracked high ceiling and really didn't know who I was for about fifteen strange seconds. I wasn't scared; I was just somebody else, some stranger, and my whole life was a haunted life, the life of a ghost. I was halfway across America, at the dividing line between the East of my youth and the West of my future, and maybe that's why it happened right there and then, that strange red afternoon. (17)

Kerouac, like Zeta, was a son of immigrant parents; both learned English in public schools and for both identity is something transitory. Their successive shedding of identities perhaps tells us that identity, as we traditionally have come to think of it, is a quality, a characteristic, an ineffable something actually anchored in a specific nation state and language and that when that nation state and language are lost identities are lost as well. Zeta's writings bespeak the fact that once that relation to a specific space and language is broken, it actually becomes impossible, if not irrelevant, to speak of identity. It is no accident then that both Kerouac and Zeta work their way out of this dilemma by ultimately defining themselves as writers. The word becomes their mark of identity better than any other cultural marker. Thus, on the border, trying to get back to the US after having lost all his documents in Mexico, Zeta tells the immigration officer: "I've got nothing on me to prove who I am . . . just my word" (195).

Within the spatial logic which dominates the town, Riverbank, where Zeta grew up and which he finds reproduced everywhere he goes, he is the stranger, the other, the Negro, the cockroach, the man who fears extermination and extinction. Throughout his life all the houses he lives in and places where he works are cheap hotels, whorehouses, apartments right next to skid row etc. reminding us of Madan Sarup's words who, taking Julia Kristeva a step further, claims that migrants, immigrants, strangers, and foreigners of the modern world have replaced those who were considered aberrant before (the madman, the eccentric, the pervert) (12).

What is radical about Zeta is that, instead of letting himself be named and made abject by a national imaginary for which he is forever the outsider and suspect, he takes abjection to its extreme, he revels in and glorifies abjection transforming it into an aesthetic and a powerful means of rebellion and self-labeling. Within his eschatological un-politically correct imaginary, he describes everyone in absolutely pejorative terms and deploys the worst racist and homophobic epithets. Even though he is presumed to have been homosexual, he writes that homosexuals are "fancy assed fags" that can be readily spotted because their eyes are too close together. Chinese are "Chinks,"; Japanese are either "rich Japs" or "sneaky Japs,"; Jews are "bastards,"; blacks are "niggers," etc.

The same dichotomy between "pure" identities and abject identities overwhelmed Vasconcelos's thinking in *La raza cósmica* when he wrote that the Chinese should not be allowed to immigrate to Latin America because they come to "degradar la condición humana [porque] se multiplican como ratones" (29); blacks and Asians (he writes blacks and yellows) "tienen su tufo;" and blacks are "ávidos de dicha sensual, ebrios de danzas y desenfrenadas lujurias" (31). In another quote that I cannot leave aside because it is so far from the cosmic that it is almost comic Vasconcelos writes that "el mogol con el misterio de su ojo oblicuo . . . toda cosa la mira conforme a un ángulo extraño [y] descubre no sé qué pliegues y dimensiones nuevas" (31). He also writes about the melancholy and sick Muslim sensuality and of "estrías judaicas." No one is exempt from this merciless labeling except, of course, Anglo-Saxons who possess "la mente clara . . . parecida a su tez" and "ideales superiores" (35) and Latins who enjoy "mayor facilidad de simpatía con los extraños" (26) and a lesser degree of repulsion than Anglos to people with strange blood (29).

Like Vasconcelos, who felt "asco de su cuerpo feo y deserotizado" (Blanco 51) Zeta describes himself as irascible, fat, big bellied, with sagging breasts, hairless, the greatest barfer in the world, and parodying his exaggerated machismo he describes himself as the greatest macho in the world with "the smallest prick in the world" (82). He also calls his penis "the thing" (46), "my dead vine" (46), "my abandoned lily" (52), and is unable to have sex other than with prostitutes or with women under terrible and abject circumstances. Anglo girls and women with whom he tries to have sex tell him not to "get that dirty stuff" inside of them (154). "I am the nigger after all," he concludes after his mother has accused him of rejecting his Latina school companions in favor of Anglo girls:

> I am nothing but an Indian with sweating body and faltering tits that sag at the sight of a young girl's blue eyes. I shall never be able to undress in front of a woman's stare. I shall refuse to play basketball for fear that some day I might have my jersey ripped from me in front of those thousands of pig-tailed, blue-eyed girls from America. (94–95)

Despite these contradictions and personal failures that make Zeta so hard to read today, there is an important moment in his thinking that is worth rescuing and that echoes with the utopian moments in Vasconcelos's thinking. It happens in Juárez when he has hit bottom and no longer knows what identity to assume. His brother tells him about the Chicano Movement and Zeta, who hears the designation for the first time, immediately decides to join the Chicano Movement and move to Los Angeles. In his mind he practices how he is going to address the movement at a rally and calls for brown buffalo unity: "Unless we band together, we brown buffaloes will become extinct. And I do not want to live in a world without brown buffaloes" (199). He finally gives this talk when he runs for Sheriff of L.A. and during other rallies in the 60s. But most importantly, this illumination is transformed into significant political action when at a trial recounted in *The Revolt of the Cockroach People,* he manages to disqualify one hundred judges on the basis of racism by arguing that Chicanos until then, being neither black nor white, had lacked a racial classification (many marked "white" in census reports and if lower class they marked "black").[4] Zeta claimed that Chicanos had to be considered a third—actually fourth, after Asian—minority group subjected to systemic forms of discrimination.[5]

While Zeta's accounts can be criticized as so many attempts at self-promotion, the great achievement of the Chicano Movement was to incorporate *mestizaje* as a legal—if still problematic—category. The proliferation of "hyphenated Americans" so bemoaned by the Right, may in fact be an index of how much the US has changed in the past forty years, and, twenty years away from Latinos becoming the largest "minority" in the US, a sign of how much "*mestizaje*" is becoming an operative principle and liberatory ideal.

NOTES

1. Jorge Klor de Alva goes so far as to affirm that we cannot talk of decolonization in Latin America given the intensity of the *mestizaje* that shaped Latin America and hence the difficulty of establishing radical differences between the colonized and the colonizers.

2. Latina feminism especially reads *mestizaje* as a union of third world women within and without the US. See Sonia Saldívar-Hull, "Feminism on the Border: From Gender Politics to Geopolitics" (95).

3. Apparently inspired by the 1921 film *The Mark of Zorro* with Douglas Fairbanks. As Ilan Stavans points out, it is ironic that Zeta Acosta would choose precisely a movie in which "Zorro" confronts a Mexican scoundrel in an effort to reconstitute Anglo power. Moreover, the film depicts the people as a "*mestizo* mobocracy." Zeta was also inspired by Costa Gavras's *Z* and the film *La cucaracha* where the protagonist is a General Zeta—a blending of Zapata and Pancho Villa (Stavans 59–60).

4. See my colleague Christina Gómez's dissertation and book (in progress) *The Significance of Race for Latinos in the 1990's*.

5. See Carl Gutiérrez-Jones, *Rethinking the Borderlands* and Ramon Saldívar, *Chicano Narrative: The Dialectics of Difference* (90–98).

WORKS CITED

Alarcón, Norma. "Chicana Feminism: In the Tracks of 'The' Native Woman." *Living Chicana Theory*. Berkeley: Third Woman Press. 1998. 371–382.

Anzaldúa, Gloria. *Borderlands/La frontera: The New Mestiza Writes*. San Francisco: Aunt Lute, 1987.

Blanco, José Joaquín. *Se llamaba Vasconcelos: Una evocación critica*. Mexico: Fondo de Cultura Económica, [1977] 1983.

Boyd-Bowman, Peter. *Léxico hispanoamericano del siglo XVI*. London: Tamesis Books, 1971.

"El Plan Espiritual de Santa Bárbara (compiled)" *El sexto sol de MeCHa Library* (Netscape: http://www.hiline.net/~juancv/library.htm. 1996).

Gutiérrez-Jones, Carl. *Rethinking the Borderlands*. Berkeley: University of California Press, 1995.

Kerouac, Jack. *On the Road*. New York: Penguin, 1991.

Klor de Alva, Jorge. "Postcolonization of the (Latin) American Experience: A Reconsideration of 'Colonialism,' 'Postcolonialism,' and 'Mestizaje'." *After Colonialism: Imperial Histories and Postcolonial Displacements.* Ed. Gyan Prakash. Princeton: Princeton University Press, 1994. 241–275.

Lienhard, Martin. "Of Mestizajes, Heterogeneities, Hybridism and Other Chimeras: On the Macroprocesses of Cultural Interaction in Latin America." *Journal of Latin American Cultural Studies* 6 (1997): 183–199.

Moraga, Cherríe. "Halfbreed." *Chicana Lesbians: The Girls Our Mothers Warned Us About.* Ed. Carla Trujillo. Berkeley: Third Woman Press, 1991. 95.

Saldívar, Ramón. *Chicano Narrative: The Dialectics of Difference.* Madison: University of Wisconsin Press, 1990.

Saldívar-Hull, Sonia. "Feminism on the Border: From Gender Politics to Geopolitics." *Criticism in the Borderlands: Studies in Chicano Literature, Culture, and Ideology* Ed. Hector Calderón and José David Saldívar. Durham: Duke University Press, 1991. 203–220.

Sarup, Madan. *Identity Culture and the Postmodern World.* Athens: University of Georgia Press, 1996.

Stavans, Ilan. *Bandido: Oscar "Zeta" Acosta and the Chicano Experience.* New York: Icon Editions, 1995.

Valdez, Luis. *Early Works: Actos, Bernabé and Pensamiento Serprentino.* Houston: Arte Público Press, 1990. 170–185.

Valdez, Luis, and Stan Steiner, eds. "El plan espiritual de Aztlán." *Aztlán: An Anthology of Mexican American Literature.* New York: Alfred Knopf, 1972.

Vasconcelos, José. *La raza cósmica: Misión de la raza iberoamericana.* México, DF: Espasa Calpe, [1948] 1992.

Zeta Acosta, Oscar. *The Autobiography of a Brown Buffalo.* New York: Vintage, 1989.

ANNE CONNOR

Desenmascarando a Ysrael: The Disfigured Face as Symbol of Identity in Three Latino Texts

There's no art
To find the mind's construction in the face

(*Macbeth, I, iv*)

With its features and expressions that are impossible to duplicate artificially, the face can be construed as a sort of large-scale fingerprint. Unlike animals, who use their sense of smell to recognize each other, we humans identify one another primarily by our faces, and the immense variety in this distinguishing feature is certainly enough to inspire awe. Such was the attraction during the 18th and 19th centuries, for example, that physiognomy, the science of reading a person's psychological traits and character type through the study of the structure of the face, came into vogue (Hollington 6). Although this discipline was later discredited with the growth of modern anatomical knowledge, we still tend to think of the face as the sign of humanity par excellence.

Perhaps due to the power behind this sign, the importance of the face as literary symbol has been underlined in three works by authors of Latinamerican descent living in the United States. Junot Díaz, Dominican-American, paints the picture of a boy with a disfigured face in two of his short stories in the collection *Drown* (1996). More than ten years earlier, Cecile Pineda, Chicana playwright and novelist, wrote her first novel, *Face* (1985). This work

Cincinnati Romance Review, Volume 21 (2002): pp. 148–162. Copyright © 2002 Cincinnati Romance Review.

narrates the experience of a very poor Brazilian man who must reconstruct his face after it has been completely destroyed in an accident. And even more recently, Cristina García, of Cuban-American descent, includes two characters who suffer through a "change of face" in her novel *The Agüero Sisters* (1997). In spite of the cultural differences between these three authors, for all of them the face symbolizes, in one way or another, the identity of their characters. In this study I will first analyze the ways in which the writers construct their characters' identity through the representation of the deformed face, and then we'll explore some possible reasons such constructions appeal in particular to the experience of the Latinos in the United States.

In *Drown*, we find many indications that the two short stories about a boy with a disfigured face are essential toward an understanding of the collection as a whole. The first, entitled "Ysrael," stands out due to its privileged position as the first story in the book. The second, "No Face," is conspicuous in the collection as the only story narrated completely in third person. Moreover, "No Face" distinguishes itself from the others because Yunior, the protagonist and narrator of the collection, does not appear in this story.

The plot of "Ysrael" is deceptively simple. Two brothers, Rafa and Yunior, are forced to leave the city to live with their aunt and uncle when their mother is unable to take care of them due to economic hardship. Bored with country life and anxious for adventure, when the siblings hear about the mysterious boy in a nearby town who must wear a mask because his face was eaten by pigs, they set off on a journey to see the legendary monstrosity with their own eyes. From the beginning of the story, the plot foreshadows the important themes in the rest of *Drown*. The displacement from the city to the countryside in order to improve their economic situation prefigures the children's posterior move to the United States. Also, on the bus trip, a man fondles Yunior without the boy's consent, which serves as a prelude to Yunior's first homosexual encounter that occurs later in the story "Drown." These previews of major events in the narrator's life underline the importance of "Ysrael" in relation to the rest of the short story collection. When the boys finally meet Ysrael, instead of the image of complete marginalization that they had expected, they are confronted with the fact that the disfigured boy's family is evidently better off economically than they are: "Ysrael's sandals were stiff leather and his clothes were Northamerican." Furthermore, Yunior even notices the similarity between his own situation and Ysrael's:

> . . . the kite was no handmade local job. It had been manufactured
> abroad.
> Where did you get that? I asked.
> Nueva York, he said. From my father.
> No shit! Our father's there too! I shouted.

I looked at Rafa, who, for an instant, frowned. Our father only sent
us letters and an occasional shirt or pair of jeans at Christmas. (16)

Rafa is already bothered by any indication of Ysrael's humanity, but the
discovery that this boy, whose condition should emblematize complete alien-
ation, receives more attention from his father than the brothers themselves
do, proves to be totally unbearable. The similarities between the children don't
stop there. A close reading of the text reveals an intimate identification between Yunior and Ysrael. To begin with, before they set off on their quest to
find Ysrael, Rafa utilizes Yunior's face as a model for his imagination of what
the other boy's face would took like:

My brother kept pinching my face during the night, like I was
a mango. The cheeks, he said. And the chin. But the forehead
would be a lot harder. The skin's tight.
All right, I said. Ya. (9)

In addition, Ysrael isn't the only one who had suffered insults due to his
abnormal countenance. In the city, Yunior was used to being the victim of his
brother's taunting:

Back in the Capital he rarely said anything to me except,
Shut up, pendejo.
Unless, of course, he was mad and then he had about five hundred
routines he liked to lay on me. Most of them had to do with my
complexion, my hair, the size of my lips. It's the Haitian, he'd say
to his buddies. Hey Señor Haitian, Mami found you on the border
and only took you in because she felt sorry for you. (5)

The color of his skin and his African features situated Yunior as the
"Other," much like Ysrael, though to a lesser degree. Besides, Rafa not only
abused his younger brother verbally but also "pounded the hell" (5) out of
him, which ends up being exactly what he does to Ysrael. The tragic aspect
of this assault on Ysrael is heightened by the fact that just moments before, Yunior seems to make an authentic connection with Ysrael: "The mask
twitched. I realized he was smiling, and then my brother brought his arm
around and smashed the bottle on top of his head" (18). Another key identification between Yunior and Ysrael occurs in "No Face," which constitutes a
sort of complementary story to "Ysrael," since this time the narrative presents
the action from the point of view of the boy without a face. Although the
name of the protagonist is never mentioned, there can be little doubt that he
is Ysrael, since his face had been eaten by pigs and his day transpires between

the preparations of going North to receive the long-awaited operation, and the constant fleeing from boys who want to beat him up. In this story, Ysrael lives in a completely solitary world. He sleeps not in his parent's house, but rather in a shack behind it, as if he were an animal. The accident with the pigs has erased his own identity as member of the family. When his mother sees him playing with his brother without his mask on, she immediately brings him the cloth to cover his face and warns him that he should leave before his father sees him. The abuse and or complete rejection from his father is left implicit: "Go, she says. Before your father comes out. / He knows what happens when his father comes out" (160).

The only positive moment of physical contact for the boy occurs during his monthly check-up: "The doctor smiles and makes him remove his mask and then massages his face with his thumbs" (158). Interestingly enough, this scene bears a striking resemblance to one of Yunior's fantasies, in which he envisions his father's reaction when he sees his youngest son for the first time after years of absence in the United States: "Squatting down so that his pale yellow dress socks showed, he'd trace the scars on my arm and on my head. Yunior, he'd finally say, his stubbled face in front of mine, his thumb tracing a circle on my cheek" (88).

Yunior's scars, besides representing the pain that the young boy carries inside due to his longing for his absent father, and for human contact in general, establish without a doubt the identification between himself and Ysrael. It is important to note that both Yunior and Ysrael hold on to the hope that the solution to all of their problems lies in the North. While Ysrael hopes to receive miraculous plastic surgery there, Yunior has faith that one day his father will send for his family and they will all move to the country of "endless opportunities." Another indicator of the connection between these two characters lies in the graphic similarity in the spelling of their names: the fact that both boys' names start with a Y stands out on the written page, since both Yunior and Ysrael are orthographic adaptations of two names traditionally spelled differently: Junior and Israel. The more traditional orthography reveals that the symbolic importance of the names goes beyond linking the two characters. "Junior" graphically and orally is similar to the first name of the author, "Junot." And Díaz has certainly never hidden his identification with the protagonist of his short story collection, as the autobiographical character of the work has been emphasized by reviewers such as Samuel Freedman: "Mr. Díaz's characters live, as his actual family did, in a low-income apartment complex surrounded by the malls, cineplexes and municipal pools of the middle class" (2.1).

As we have already established the close, symbolic bond between Yunior and Ysrael, and later the relation between Junior and Junot, the next obvious step is the study of the identification between Junot and Ysrael. However, Israel also alludes to the country of the Israelites and we should first explore the significance of the Biblical name of the disfigured boy. The kingdom of Israel was overthrown in 722 BC by the Assyrians and consequently, the twelve Israelite tribes were either destroyed or scattered. With only this information, we can read the story "Ysrael" as an allegory of the suffering of an entire people due to their face, or racial or ethnic identity. However, an analysis of "Ysrael" in relation to the modern country which bears the same name proves to be even more revealing. Founded in 1948 as country of refuge for the Jews after the holocaust, Israel's history has been dramatically turbulent. As the holy land for both Jews, Christians, and Muslims, this relatively small territory symbolizes not only a confluence of cultures but also the site of religious and cultural battles that continue today. Consequently, the character Ysrael not only refers to Junior/Junot but also to the experience of the exiled whose hope of refuge ends up being as problematic as his previous reality. Ysrael's monstrous face expresses the experience of being a minority, of not fitting in a given culture, and even worse, of suffering complete rejection by the dominant culture. As a face without recognizable characteristics, Ysrael's countenance can be understood as representing the identity of someone displaced from his roots; or simply, the lack of a fixed identity due to the circumstances of being an immigrant. It is certainly plausible, then, to relate the author's situation with that of his character Ysrael. In fact, the difficult state of not belonging completely to any culture is expressed in the opening lines of *Drown*, in the epigraph, a quote from a poem by Gustavo Pérez Firmat:

> The fact that I
> am writing to you
> in English
> already falsefies what I
> wanted to tell you.
> My subject:
> how to explain to you that I
> don't belong to English
> though I belong nowhere else.

In order to survive his own displacement, Ysrael creates a fantasy universe, in which he combats injustice throughout the world and is able to escape the difficult reality he confronts day to day. In "No Face", for example, the powers of "FLIGHT," "STRENGTH," and INVISIBILITY," all written in capital letters, refer to the vocabulary of the superheroes in his comic books, and they help him survive the attacks from the other boys. Similarly, the creative act of literary expression, and in particular the writing of *Drown*, can be seen as an escape valve for Yunior/Junot.

The difficulty of not "belonging" anywhere is also explored in detail in the novel *Face*. The protagonist, Helio Cara, whose name indicates that he is more of an emblematic character than an individual one, falls off a cliff and his face is left unrecognizable. So extreme is his deformity that Helio seems to have lost much more than his normal features. For example, after asking Helio to take off his mask so that he can inspect the scars, his boss' reaction is a typical expression of rejection: "He watches the boss' eyes narrow, sees them falter, hears the low whistle escape him. / 'God!' The boss turns away. 'It's not. . . .'" (53)

Although David E. Johnson has pointed out that the ellipsis at the end of this exclamation allows for multiple possibilities of ending the sentence, the most probable word would be "human" (81). Without the financial means to afford plastic surgery, Helio becomes a social outcast, since his lack of face denies him of his humanity. And since society treats him like a monster, he begins to act accordingly. For example, when his girlfriend says to him, "I'm afraid to look at you. [. . .] I can't make love to a monster," he loses control, rapes her, and pulverizes her face:

> His hands become separated from the rest of him. He watches
> them hit her face, her neck, smashing at her cheekbones, whipping
> her head from this side to that. The bones crunch under his blows.
> Again and again. He feels nothing as the small white teeth shatter
> against his knuckles. (77)

After leaving in tears, he reproaches himself, asking why he had hit her when it was his boss who really deserved it: "Had he hit her like that because he wanted someone to share in his ugliness? Because the monster he had become wanted company?" (79). This act of violence without any real provocation allows us to re-examine the assault Rafa and Yunior committed against Ysrael. While they obviously don't have to provoke Ysrael's disfigurement, it is likely that, precisely because of his disfigurement, the boys identify with him. Since they had lost their own identity when their father abandoned them (especially Yunior, whose name points to the fact that his identity is a continuation of his father's), they see themselves reflected in Ysrael, the boy without identity by definition. Attacking Ysrael, then, implies a self-loathing, much like that manifested in the character of Helio Cara.

However, Helio doesn't let hate consume him completely. With only the help of a book on plastic surgery and some novocaine, he undertakes the arduous work of reconstructing his face. I believe that Juan Bruce-Novoa (76) is correct in pointing out the metafictional character of the novel at this juncture. Pineda herself indicates the connection between written and facial expression in the novel's epigraph:

Like a novel, the face is a web of living meanings, an inter-human event, in which the thing and its expression are inextricably joined.

Maurice Merleau-Ponty, *Phenomenologie de la Perceptión*

The reconstruction of the face as an artistic feat becomes an act parallel to Pineda's own work, for in writing she constructs another face: that is, *Face* the text. Bruce-Novoa summarizes this process: "What the novelist really creates, finally, is herself as novelist" (77). In my view, however, the writing of *Face* goes beyond the production of a novelist. Pineda's personal identification with the theme of losing face, or identity, comes to light in a commentary from her essay, "Deracinated: The Writer Re-Invents Her Sources":

When *Face* was published, my editor [. . .] burbled at me brightly: I think it's wonderful how writers—meaning me, I suppose—are beginning to write about things they don't know.
Her remark implied I knew nothing about the loss of face, the disenfranchisement that comes of marginalization. Perhaps she thought I had not confronted loss. Or that writers are not capable of transfiguring the quotidian, unequal to the metaphoric transmutations required by art. (64)

Given this information, it seems quite clear that Helio Cara's struggle to reconstruct his face serves as metaphor for the suffering of those marginalized by society. However, the same figure indicates the possibilities of liberation through one's own creativity. As Pineda identifies herself as Chicana, we can infer that her own experience as a minority in the U.S. served as a source to create this allegory of loss of identity in *Face*. In this way, the writing of *Face* can imply not only the creation of a novelist but also an attempt to express metaphorically the experience of being the "Other."

Some, however, have been bothered by the fact that Pineda doesn't deal directly with Chicano themes and that her ethnicity was not mentioned in the first edition of *Face*. They even accuse her of having assimilated the dominant culture as her own. For example, Johnson proposes that the way in which *Face* was published denotes a calculated rejection of the Chicano community: "We would argue that Viking Penguin publishes *Face* within the traditionally 'white' category, 'American Fiction', precisely in order to homogenize its face, to defuse beforehand questions of ethnicity and, therefore, to create for it a potentially larger market" (74). Similarly, in his reading of the text, Johnson perceives Helio's efforts not as a creative act in order to recover his identity, but rather as an act of assimilation:

Face posits that society constitutes itself of the faceless, not the literally faceless but the culturally faceless: it demands the normativity of the average face. Society reaches for the homogeneity of the unremarkable. Thus, *Face*'s paradox: in order to be human one must have a face, but the face is a cultural construct, therefore, one must have an acceptable face. Which means, because society requires uniformity, one must be faceless, indistinguishable, unremarkable. (80)

This reading may appear quite suggestive, especially when Johnson reminds us of Helio's reaction after finishing a series of surgeries and observing what he wanted to achieve in the mirror: "It is a face; it is not particularly striking, certainly not attractive or handsome. It evokes neither origins nor class. It is unremarkable—like anyone else's" (191–192). Johnson goes on to relate Helio's conformity with Pineda's identity as author: "*Face* as such displaces Pineda's Chicanicity. As we noted above, nowhere does *Face* announce that it is Chicano writing. Thus it is a thoroughly assimilated—unremarkable—*Face*" (88).

However, in my opinion, this reading ignores the fact that Helio's actions place him, above all, as a rebel against the society he lives in. First of all, he rejects the mask the government issues him. This mask *does* emblematize all of the negative aspects associated with assimilation. As Johnson rightly points out: "[The mask] manifests the technologization and standardization of the face: it is rubber; 'it is neither brown nor orange, but the clinical color of ice bags, of hot water bottles'" (82). Helio doesn't use the mask they have assigned him for many reasons. First of all, the material does not let his skin breathe. And secondly, the mask eliminates his individuality, making it impossible for his friends and acquaintances to recognize him. But when he goes to the clinic to receive "rehabilitation" from the government, the clerk admonishes him for having fabricated his own mask out of cotton, explaining:

> It's not supposed to make you feel comfortable. It's designed to give people seeing it immediate recognition that the wearer is . . . (he lowers his voice) . . . *facially impaired.* [. . .] The program already spent millions educating the public. Now it wouldn't do, would it, if everyone wore what he liked? (70)

It's quite evident that Helio is not seeking to blindly assimilate what the government has determined to be "correct." We can also observe his rebellion against the system in the very act of operating on himself. Before undergoing this formidable task, he must commit small acts of vandalism against the government, such as robbing a plastic surgery manual from the public library. In addition, there can be no doubt that Helio, through his do-it-yourself approach to surgery, defies the entire medical system (whose omnipotent power is manifest in the double reference to god found in the plastic surgeon's name, Teofilho Godoy). But above all, it seems to me that the creative act of reconstructing one's face constitutes a powerful image in regards to our ability to formulate our own identities. Let's return to the quote Johnson uses to demonstrate that Helio, in spite of everything, is a conformist: "It is a face; it is not particularly striking, certainly not attractive or handsome. It evokes neither origins nor class. It is unremarkable—like anyone else's." What is missing from this quote are the following sentences: "But no. Not like anyone. It is his, his alone. He has built it, alone, sewn it stitch by stitch, with the very thin needle and the thread of gossamer. It has not been given casualty by birth, but made by him, by the wearer of it" (192). Contrary to the textual manipulation offered by Johnson, here we are presented with an image of pure originality. Ultimately, Johnson, by refusing to accept literary diversity in Latino writing, pigeonholes Pineda as an assimilationist.

The face as symbol of identity also presents itself in *The Agüero Sisters* by Cristina García. Both Reina and Constancia go through a metamorphosis, an about-face, if you will, which modifies the direction of their lives. However, the changes in the faces of the two sisters point toward opposite directions.

Reina, after having been struck by lightning, miraculously receives a number of skin grafts from a wide variety of people, both dead and alive. This change seems to point towards the future, as some of her body parts are completely rejuvenated after the operation: "Most of Reina's nutmeg color is gone, replaced by a confusion of shades and textures. A few patches of her skin are so pink and elastic, so perfectly hairless, they look like a newborn pig's" (66). With her new skin, Reina turns her back on her past in Cuba and decides to move to Florida and live with her sister Constancia. The reasons for this sudden decision are never explicitly revealed. Reina, who seems to be the perfect revolutionary before the accident, doesn't even think twice about her determination to abandon her native country. What is apparent is the stark contrast between her new skin and her surroundings. The apartment that she had inherited from her father (or stepfather, as we later discover), consisted of the well-known ornithologist's old office, and it was full of objects and books of time past. The new Reina simply no longer belongs to this environment. Her change of skin reflects her change of self:

> Reina doesn't particularly mind her skin, mismatched and itchy as it is, but she cannot tolerate its stench. No one else seems to notice, but to her it reeks of dry blood and sour milk. She recalls hearing of animals in the wild spurning their own kind when touched by an unknown odor. Now Reina understands why. (66)

So dramatic is her change of identity that not even her distinctive scent remains. Instead of waiting for it to return, she decides to adopt a life that will reflect her new being, and moves to the United States.

Constancia, on the other hand, had already adapted completely to the culture of the United States, where whatever is "new" is valued over everything else, and she had even created her own line of beauty products. One night, however, she dreams she is undergoing plastic surgery: "The surgeon severs roots and useless nerves, reinvents the architecture of her face" (104). When Constancia wakes up from this nightmare, it is as if she has become the protagonist of a fantastic short story:

> She switches on her vanity mirror, and finds her face in disarray, moving all at once like a primitive creature. Her neck and temples itch furiously, erupting with bumps each time she attempts to scratch.
> [. . .] Then she checks the mirror again. Her face has settled down, but it appears different to her, younger, as if it truly had been rearranged in the night. She rubs her eyes, pinches her cheeks. Her eyes seem rounder, a more deliberate green. Then it hits her with the force of a slap. This is her mother's face. (104–105)

In contrast with Reina's experience, Constancia's change of face points toward the past. The fact that her mother's face has unexpectedly usurped her own, seems to indicate the need for Constancia to return to her roots in order to find out the truth about her origins, which up until then she had ignored. Here the face symbolizes an important aspect of identity: physical inheritance. When a child is born, it is this aspect of the face which we first try to decipher: Who does he or she most resemble? Similarly, physical inheritance has the mysterious capacity to reveal to us the presence of our ancestors without our knowing they exist. For example, Reina's daughter, Dulce, who had never met her father, has no difficulty recognizing him in a photo at the museum: "The odd thing was that he seemed very familiar to me, even though I'd never seen him before. Then I realized it was because I'd inherited his face" (53). The features that point out her origin cannot be erased. In a similar vein, Constancia, who was physically rejected by her mother, has to face the maternal image every time she looks at herself in the mirror. Curiously, although sometimes she wants to scratch her face and return to her original features, Constancia also "finds the soft stretch of Mama's face over hers oddly sustaining, as if she were buoyed by a warm tidal power" (130). In spite of the fact that her mother refused to take care of her daughter while she was living, her physical presence in Constancia's features helps to calm the daughter, as it constitutes a permanent indication of her roots. This connection, which Constancia had previously denied, obliges her to return to Cuba, unearth her father's diaries, and in this way discover, although only partially, her own origins.

Unlike the characters in *Face* and *Drown*, the changes experienced by Reina and Constancia constitute *re*figurations of the face instead of *dis*figurations. For these women, their physical appearance serves to indicate the next necessary step in their lives—toward the future or the past—in order to adjust to their new identity. What *The Agüero Sisters* shares with the other texts studied is the importance of physical heredity through the use of the face as symbol. When Reina loses the features of her genetic inheritance, she can finally abandon the majority of her father's relics, which she had preserved so religiously in the past. On the other hand, Constancia sets off on a search for her own origins after recovering the features of her dead mother. Similarly, Helio is only able to remember the details of his father's assassination after he has successfully reconstructed his own face. On the other hand, the brothers in *Drown* are able to identify with Ysrael precisely because their father abandoned them and they find themselves "faceless."

To conclude, we have seen that the face, linked to physical heredity, functions as a powerful symbol of identity for three Latino writers. In *Drown* and *Face*, we note that disfigurement emblematizes the experience of being marginalized in society. The mask in both texts has a definite negative connotation. While Helio's mask doesn't allow him to breathe, Ysrael's is described as being infested with fleas. The mask, then, may represent a false identity, or the identity imposed by an outside force; in other words, by the dominant society. In both texts, the only way to rise above the condition of having a deformed face is through artistic refiguration, or creativity. The use of the face in *The Agüero Sisters* adds the genealogical aspect of identity to this construction. The identity represented in our faces has in part been inherited, and therefore serves as a physical reminder of our past. In spite of the cultural differences between these three authors, for all of them, the face constitutes a very suggestive symbol of identity. This sign of humanity allows them to explore their own marginalization as "Latinos" in the U.S. and at the same time (or as a consequence) offers a symbolic way of expressing the constant process of re-construction of identity, a process which arises when one does not belong completely anywhere.

Works Cited

Bruce-Novoa, Juan. "Deconstructing the Dominant Patriarchal Text: Cecile Pineda's Narratives." *Breaking Boundaries: Latina Writing and Critical Readings.* Ed. Asunción Horno-Delgado. Amherst: University of Massachusetts Press, 1989: 72–81.

Díaz, Junot. *Drown.* New York: The Berkeley Publishing Group, 1996.

Freedman, Samuel G. "Suburbia Outgrows Its Image in the Arts." *New York Times* 28 Feb. 1999, late ed.: 2.1

García, Cristina. *The Agüero Sisters*. New York: The Ballantine Publishing Group, 1997.

Hollington, Michael. "Monstrous Faces: Physiognomy in *Barnaby Rudge*." *Dickens Quarterly* 8:1 (1991): 6–15.

Johnson, David E. "Face Value (An Essay on Cecile Pineda's *Face*)." *The Americas Review, A Review of Hispanic Literature and Art of the USA* 19:2 (1991): 73–93.

Pineda, Cecile. *Face*. New York: Penguin, 1985.

———. "Deracinated: The Writer Re-Invents Her Sources." *Máscaras*. Ed. Lucha Corpi. Berkeley: Third Woman Press, 1997: 57–70.

MIRIAM DECOSTA-WILLIS

Martha K. Cobb and the Shaping of Afro-Hispanic Literary Criticism

For My Friend and Former Colleague (1917–2002)

Martha Kendrick Cobb, professor of Spanish and comparative literature at Howard University and chair of the Department of Romance Languages from 1976 to 1981, was one of the early theorists in the emerging field of Afro-Hispanic literary criticism. Educated at historically black institutions and stimulated by the racial aesthetics of Negritude, the New Negro and Black Aesthetic movements, she helped to shape critical discourse on the literature of blacks in Africa and the Americas. For more than a decade, she created courses and programs, developed pedagogical materials, presented scholarly papers, and published twenty groundbreaking essays, reviews, and profiles. Her work culminated in the publication of a seminal text in comparative diasporic literature, *Harlem, Haiti, and Havana: A Comparative Critical Study of Langston Hughes, Jacques Roumain, and Nicolás Guillén*, which won the College Language Association Award for Outstanding Scholarship in 1983. In this study, which would serve as the paradigm for other publications in the field, she identifies and analyzes the thematic, stylistic, and structural parallels in the works of black writers.

In 1969 Cobb joined the faculty of Howard University as a lecturer in the Department of Romance Languages at the height of the Black Arts and

CLA Journal, Volume 45, Number 4 (June 2002): pp. 523–541. Copyright © 2002 College Language Association.

Black Aesthetic movements, when activist writers and scholars developed an aesthetic that would serve as the critical base for black cultural nationalism. It was in the midst of this intellectual and cultural fervor that Cobb returned, this time as a faculty member, to Howard University, which had become a center of black nationalist ideology, of Africancentric scholarship, and of social, political, and artistic revolution. The campus was alive: students in thick Afros and colorful dashikis gave the Black Power salute at graduation; sociologist Andrew Billinsley was named vice president; Sterling Brown gave poetry readings before standing-room-only crowds; Tony Brown and Samuel Yette taught in the School of Communications; writers-in-residence John Oliver Killens and Haki Madhubuti offered classes in creative writing; student Debi Allen performed on the stage of the Ira Aldridge Theatre; francophone poet Léon Damas autographed books in Founders Library; Sonia Sanchez and Amiri Baraka lectured in Douglass Hall; O. R. Dathorne published anthologies of Caribbean literature; Stephen Henderson organized national conferences of black writers; and in the Moorland-Spingarn Research Center, Dorothy Porter ordered books by black authors from Cuba, Colombia, and Costa Rica. Many students and professors were committed to recovering and redefining the history and culture of African-descended people.

Cobb was stimulated by Black Aestheticians such as Stephen Henderson, who developed a new approach to literary criticism. His anthology and the seminal texts of Hoyt W. Fuller, Larry Neal, and Addison Gayle advocated a Blackcentric theory of cultural production and reception.[1] According to Sandra Adell, "The Black Aesthetic . . . helped to define the contours of the African-American literary tradition. It also helped to elaborate and refine the theories of black literary criticism received from an earlier generation of black writers."[2] In the bibliography of *Harlem, Haiti, and Havana*, Cobb cites the studies of LeRoi Jones, Larry Neal, and George Kent, but it is Stephen Henderson's "The Forms of Things Unknown," the introduction to his *Understanding the New Black Poetry: Black Speech and Black Music as Poetic References*, that contributed to her thinking in the 1970s. Although Henderson's anthology was not published until 1973, he showed the manuscript of "Forms" to Howard colleagues such as Cobb, who shared his views on literature and who had offices, as he did, in Locke Hall. In the first chapter of *Harlem, Haiti, and Havana*, Cobb acknowledges her indebtedness to Henderson, particularly his "call for a critical frame based on black speech and black music as poetic reference" (*Harlem* 7), as well as his emphasis on the continuity and integrity of the African-American—and, by extension, African-Diasporic—poetic tradition. Edward J. Mullen is on target when he writes that by the mid-seventies, the "Black Aesthetic paradigm had become a dominant theoretical model for such critics as Martha Cobb, Antonio Olliz Boyd, and Ian Smart."[3]

Although Black Aestheticism represented an important element in her theoretical formulations, Cobb was hardly a derivative thinker. Her views on race and literature were also shaped by her family background, her academic training in historically black institutions, and her immersion in a black literary, historic, and philosophic tradition. This black intellectual tradition was initiated by nineteenth-century thinkers and activists such as David Walker and Martin Delaney, but it was fully developed in the first half of the twentieth century by such theorists as W. E. B. Du Bois, Jean Price-Mars, Alain Locke, Léopold Sédar Senghor, Adalberto Ortiz, and others.

It was through her family that she was first exposed to the works of such writers. Born in 1917, Martha Kendrick grew up in an educated and racially conscious family of professionals and civil rights activists who valued African-American history and culture. According to her daughter Ann Cobb, Martha's parents, Ruby Moise Kendrick and Swan Marshall Kendrick, migrated from Greenville, Mississippi, to Washington, D. C., in 1916. After her husband's death in 1923, Ruby Kendrick, with three children to support, founded a news service, worked in public relations for the National Association of Colored Women, and became a librarian at Howard University. Located near the campus, the Kendricks' house on Sixth Street became a place where books by black writers—many of whom taught at Howard—were read and discussed. After graduating from Washington's Dunbar High School, one of the country's premier secondary schools, Martha Kendrick attended Howard University, where the faculty included such noted scholars as Charles H. Wesley, Mordecai W. Johnson, E. Franklin Frazier, James A. Porter, and Benjamin E. Mays. These black intellectual giants played a considerable role in the formation of her ideas and ideology. Two professors in her department, Valaurez B. Spratlin and Ben Frederick Carruthers, stimulated her interest in language teaching and scholarly research. Chair of the Department of Romance Languages from 1931 to 1961, Spratlin was one of the early pioneers of Afro-Hispanic literary history. His book-length study *Juan Latino, Slave and Humanist,* published in 1938 while Kendrick was a student, introduced her to the life and work of a sixteenth-century African slave who became a prominent Spanish scholar. Similarly, Carruthers's research on an Afro-Cuban poet, which culminated in his 1941 doctoral dissertation, *The Life, Work and Death of Plácido,* introduced the young scholar to literature by hispanophone blacks in the Americas.

While at Howard, Kendrick availed herself of other resources in the nation's capitol; she worked as a typist for Mary McLeod Bethune, through whom she met prominent social and political leaders. In 1938, she was awarded a bachelor's degree summa cum laude in French with minors in Spanish and English. On entering Howard's graduate school, she received a Lucy Moten Fellowship to spend a year in Paris studying at the Sorbonne, from which she received a certificat d'etude in 1939. On the trip abroad, she began a journal (unpublished), in which she recorded some of her experiences: for example, meeting Paul Robeson and William Saroyan on the ship to France, being urged by Saroyan to visit Gertrude Stein, and serving as an extra in the French film *Le Corsair*.[4] Upon acceptance of her thesis, "The American Negro as Seen by Contemporary French Writers," based on her research in Paris, Kendrick was awarded the M.A. degree in Romance languages in 1941. According to James Davis, her thesis was one of the first in her department to treat the representation of blacks in European literature.[5]

In 1940, while completing her graduate requirements, Martha Kendrick began teaching English, French, and Spanish at Baltimore's Dunbar High School, a position that she held for three years. This appointment initiated a thirty-year career in secondary school teaching, a career that was interrupted for five years by marriage to Charles Cobb and the births of their four children. Her work in the public schools of Baltimore, Maryland, Springfield, Massachusetts, and White Plains, New York, as well as her experiences as a teacher of English to Spanish-speaking adults in Washington, D. C., had an impact on Martha Cobb's teaching and scholarship at the university level. During her fourteen years on Howard's faculty, from 1969 to 1983, she was involved in curriculum development, creation of classroom materials, and in-service training for language teachers. Her advocacy of multiculturalism is evident in both her teaching and publication. In articles such as "Multi-Ethnic Materials in Second Language Classrooms" (1972) and in two chapters of a teachers' textbook (1973), Cobb urges the inclusion of literature by Latino, Afro-Hispanic, African-American, and Native-American writers. Another pedagogical essay is "A Role for Spanish in the Humanities Program" (1971). To counter the omission or misrepresentation of blacks, she proposes that humanities teachers expose students to the works of Moorish poet Antar, Afro-Spanish scholar Juan Latino, and Cuban poets Plácido and Nicolás Guillén. This article also gives a self-portrait of an engaged teacher at work, when Cobb writes: "I have written and passed out personality profiles, anecdotes, eyewitness reports, [and] biographical profiles . . . written in simple Spanish" (303–304).

The same year in which she published this article, Martha Cobb made innovative additions to the curriculum of her department. Although Mercer Cook had taught francophone literature through the 1960s, courses such as "The Negro in Spanish Literature" had been infrequently offered after the retirement of Valaurez B. Spratlin in 1961. Recognizing the importance of such courses at a historically black institution, Cobb developed, in 1971, an undergraduate course, "Introduction to Afro-Hispanic Literature," as an option for non-majors in fulfilling the language requirement. A few years later, she offered two graduate seminars: "African Themes in Hispanic Literature" and "Afro-Caribbean Poetry in Spanish." Through the initiative of Cobb and others, Howard became one of the first universities in the country to offer both graduate and undergraduate courses in Afro-Hispanic literature taught from an Africancentric theoretical perspective. When scholars such as Stanley Cyrus, Ian Smart, Annette Dunzo, and Miriam DeCosta joined the department in the 1970s, the faculty expanded course offerings in the field, developed a concentration in Afro-Hispanic literature, organized seminars and conferences, invited African-descended writers such as Adalberto Ortiz of Ecuador and Manuel Zapata Olivella of Colombia to lecture, and instituted a doctoral program with a concentration in Afro-Hispanic literature. When she was elected chair of the department in 1976,[6] Cobb took a leadership role in strengthening the M.A. and Ph.D. programs in francophone and Afro-Hispanic literature by recruiting graduate students, hiring faculty in those areas, and developing new course offerings. (Her work was so effective that one of the Spanish professors suggested, humorously, that she develop a program in *blanquitud* to counter all the courses in *negritud*.) In an article entitled "The *Afro Hispanic Review*," published in 1989, Ian Smart writes: "To its credit Howard University was one of the first [to offer courses in Afro-Hispanic literature] and is still the only one to translate this commitment into a coherent system of course offerings from the first year to the Ph.D. degree."[7] (Unfortunately, Howard has since eliminated the doctorate in this field.)

Although Cobb had helped initiate the Afro-Hispanic program in the early 1970s, she soon realized that a doctorate was essential for her progress as a scholar, university professor, and prospective administrator. Therefore, in 1972 she began the doctoral program in comparative literature at Catholic University, where she was trained in Formalist criticism. Although her studies focused on the philological approach of Erich Auerbach and Ernst Robert Curtius, as well as the text-centered perspectives of New Critics René Wellek and Austin Warren, Cobb's scholarship was African-centered. This is evident in her dissertation, *A Comparative Study—The Black Experience in the Poetry of Nicolás Guillén, Jacques Roumain, and Langston Hughes.* She completed the doctorate in only two years, and rose rapidly through the academic ranks. She was promoted to assistant professor in 1974, an associate the following year, and, after only three years as associate, attained the rank of full professor in 1978. Although she took a two-year leave to earn the doctorate, Cobb continued to publish articles, book reviews, translations of Haitian poetry, and literary profiles. Between 1973 and 1975, she wrote three biographical sketches: "Martín Morúa Delgado, Black Profile in Spanish America," "José del Carmen Díaz, A Slave Poet in Latin America / Un poeta esclavo en América Latina," and "Plácido, The Poet-Hero, 1809–1844." All of them were published in the *Negro History Bulletin.*

Although her work appeared in mainstream journals such as *Hispania* and the *TESOL Quarterly,* most of Cobb's articles and essays were published in the journals of black organizations and associations—an indication of her intended audience and of her commitment to African-American cultural institutions. She published three articles and a translation in *Black World,* the international and interdisciplinary journal whose founding editor was Hoyt Fuller, one of the primary architects of the Black Aesthetic movement. In addition to the profiles in the *Bulletin,* an essay of hers appeared in the *Negro History Journal;* both publications were products of the Association for the Study of Negro Life and History, founded by Carter G. Woodson in 1915. Two of her most important articles were published in the *College Language Association Journal,* edited by Therman B. O'Daniel between 1957 and 1978. Martha Cobb was also an early supporter of the *Afro-Hispanic Review,* which was founded in 1982 under the editorship of two of her colleagues, Stanley Cyrus and Ian Smart Howard. The *Review,* which contains articles of literary criticism as well as the creative works of African, Caribbean, and Latin-American writers, has become one of the leading journals in the field under editors Marvin A. Lewis and Edward J. Mullen at the University of Missouri-Columbia. Cobb served as one of the journal's first associates and published a seminal article of comparative literature in the September 1982 issue.[8]

In the early 1970s, Martha Cobb published essays that would help lay the foundation for critical discourse on Afro-Hispanic and black comparative literature. Forty years earlier, when she was a student at Howard, a group of pioneering scholars, including Valaurez B. Spratlin, John F. Matheus, and Carter G. Woodson, published in the *Journal of Negro History* groundbreaking essays on the black theme in Hispanic literature. Appearing in the 1930s, their essays are significant in documenting the historical and literary representation of Africans in Spain and the Americas. Their studies, however, are descriptive rather than analytical, and their essays often deal with the black-as-object in the works of European writers such as Miguel de Cervantes, Lope de Vega, and Francisco de Quevedo. Furthermore, these pioneers did not attempt to develop a coherent theoretical framework for interpreting literature. Other scholars, such as Ben F. Carruthers, Irene Diggs, and Howard H. Jason, continued this first-stage archaeological project, but it was not until the 1970s that Martha Cobb, Richard Jackson, Lemuel Johnson, and others—all products of the intellectual and ideological revolution of the 1960s—would develop theories and methodologies for analyzing Afro-Hispanic literary texts.

Cobb's theoretical formulations synthesize several theories, ideologies, and critical practices. Trained in Formalist, New Critical, and comparativist methods, she practiced close reading of texts, but she also studied literature within a social and historical context. In an analysis of several nineteenth-century Cuban novels, for example, she suggests that historical fiction can serve to deconstruct myths and to liberate the oppressed. Her words echo those of Frantz Fanon:

> Any significant comment on human survival has always depended
> on a people who are conscious of their history and thus able to
> evaluate their present position in terms of the past. From such an
> awareness come strategies for pressing on toward liberation.[9]

She concludes that the study of Cuban novels should dispel the myth that
"black people were 'treated better' by Spanish slavemasters."[10] In her politically
engaged interpretive practice, Cobb applied a racial aesthetic to the study of
black-diasporic literature. (And here I use the term "racial aesthetic," which
has a long history and a broad meaning,[11] in lieu of "Black Aesthetic," which
connotes the specific theory and movement of the 1960s.) She applied to this
body of literature a racial aesthetic that incorporates elements of Du Boisian
Pan-Africanism,[12] the Neo-Africanism of G. R. Coulthard,[13] the Africanist perspective of Janheinz Jahn, and the cultural nationalism of the Black
Aestheticians. Cobb's support of Pan-Africanism, particularly its emphasis
on ethnic unity and collective consciousness, was reinforced by her research
and travel. She conducted research in Cuba, the Dominican Republic, and
Puerto Rico; she studied at the University of Madrid and the InterAmerican
University at Saltillo, Mexico; and she traveled to Ghana, Kenya, Uganda,
Zambia, and Tanzania. In 1974, after attending a Pan-African conference in
Dar-es-Salaam, Tanzania, for example, she published an article, "Unity and
Liberation: The Sixth Pan-African Congress," in the *CRJ* (Commission for
Racial Justice) *Reporter* It is also significant that *Harlem, Haiti, and Havana*
opens with a portrait of Du Bois, followed by this first sentence: "In the year
1919 author and scholar W. E. B. Du Bois called a meeting in Paris of black
people, a Pan-African Congress . . . (3)."[14] Cobb subscribed to the racial aesthetic of theorists such as Du Bois and Alain Locke; she believed, as did Du
Bois, that African Americans must establish their own criteria for artistic and
intellectual excellence, and she advocated, as did Locke, cultural pluralism
and the use of vernacularisms in artistic creation.

   Like other scholars who contested the hegemonic theories and practices
of Western history, literature, and the social sciences, Martha Cobb began to
shape a theory and praxis for interpreting literature. Two of her early essays
trace the evolution of Afro-Hispanic literature from Africa to Spain and
then to the Americas; they demonstrate that the Afro-Hispanic literary tradition—both scribal and oral—originated in Africa. (Ian Smart and Josephat
Kubayanda would continue and sharpen this line of investigation.) In 1972,
she published "Afro-Arabs, Blackamoors and Blacks: An Inquiry into Race
Concepts Through Spanish Literature,"[15] in which she examines black African—particularly Islamic—influences on Spanish history and literature, and
she analyzes the shift in racial attitudes that occurred following the Moorish
expulsion from Spain in 1492. Her objective is clear when she writes: "It is

this awareness [of the significance of Africa in Hispanic culture] that will serve
to clear away the old myths, stereotypes, and misinformation that have pursued
Black men into the 1900s" (*Blacks* 24). According to Cobb, the engaged critic
must not only deconstruct racist attitudes but must also define terms and develop concepts for evaluating African-diasporic culture. A study of race concepts,
she writes, can serve as a tool in defining that heritage, and she ends the essay
with a challenge to scholars to engage in research and education in this emerging field of inquiry. She continues to map literary history in "Africa in Latin
America." The lead article in the August 1972 issue of *Black World*, this essay
examines the work of early Afro-Cuban poets, describes the literary treatment
of black historical figures, and analyzes literary archetypes such as the warrior
and the *cimarrón*. In this literary historiography, she underscores the common
identity of blacks in the Diaspora, writing that "despite differences of language
and life-style there is a pattern in the African confrontation with reality" (6)—a
theme that is repeated throughout her work.

The key text in the conceptualization of Cobb's racial aesthetic is an essay
published in the *CLA Journal* that deserves careful analysis by literary critics.[16] In this article, she does more than define terms such as "Afro-Hispanic,"
"black," "advocate literature," and "*literatura negrista*." She also establishes criteria for evaluating literature, insisting that blacks must create their own aesthetic
and must examine literature from a holistic point of view. After a two-page
introduction, she presents four subtopics: (1) conception, which refers to the
artist's vision, voice, or point of view; (2) structure, the writer's use of language
and organization of material into linear, cyclical, and impressionistic patterns;
(3) theme, particularly identity, liberation, and humanity; and (4) style, "a technique for representing what black people see, feel, and think" (158). Although
Cobb discussed many of these concepts in earlier works such as *Harlem, Haiti,
and Havana*, this is the fullest and most succinct expression of her view. In the
conclusion, she acknowledges her purpose:

> "The interpretive frame which I have outlined moves us necessarily
> toward conclusions about what precisely constitutes the Afro-
> Hispanic aesthetic and, in the comparative approach, what defines
> a black aesthetic." (158)

Her statement indicates that the interpretive frame outlined in this essay is also appropriate for the comparative analysis of texts. Trained as a comparativist, Cobb—along with Lemuel Johnson—helped shape the direction
of subsequent cross-cultural studies of black literature. She created a critical
model that could be used by scholars such as Josephat Kubayanda, Dellita
Martin-Ogunsola, and Richard Jackson in their studies of African, African-
American, and Afro-Hispanic literature. According to James Davis, "Cobb's

seminal comparative study which treats three writers of the African Diaspora ... provides a framework for Richard Jackson's *Black Writers and Latin America: Cross Cultural Affinities.*"[17]

The text to which Davis refers, *Harlem, Haiti, and Havana,* is particularly relevant this year, which marks the one-hundredth anniversary of the births of both Nicolás Guillén, the National Poet of Cuba, and Langston Hughes, the Poet Laureate of the Negro People.[18] Unfortunately, Cobb's award-winning book is out of print, and the demise of Donald Herdeck's Three Continents Press, one of the few in the United States that published literature by and about black Caribbean writers in the 1970s, means that a reprint would be difficult. In *The Devil, the Gargoyle, and the Buffoon,* published in 1971, Lemuel Johnson also analyzes the poetry of Hughes and Guillén, as well as that of Aimé Césaire, but he does not emphasize the cross-cultural connections between the writers. Instead, he treats their work in separate, discrete chapters. Although Johnson, like Cobb, recognizes African retentions and continuities in the Americas, his objective—to demonstrate and contest negative black stereotypes in Western literature—is quite different. In the Henderson mode, Cobb accentuates the positive by underscoring the "*continuity* and *wholeness*" of the black poetic tradition" (*Harlem* 7). She examines the thematic and structural continuities in the poetry of Guillén, Hughes, and Roumain, but she also follows Henderson's lead by focusing on black speech (oral, vernacular forms) and black music (blues, jazz, the *son,* the drum) as poetic references.

Besides *Harlem, Haiti and Havana,* Cobb's most significant comparative studies include three articles: "Concepts of Blackness in Guillén, Roumain and Hughes" (1974), "The Slave Narrative and the Black Literary Tradition" (1982), and "Ortiz, Glissant and Ellison: Fictional Patterns in Black Literature"(1982). In the first essay, based on her dissertation, she examines thematic parallels in the texts of three Neo-African writers whom she characterizes as "poets of transition" because in the 1930s they abandoned Eurocentric models to develop innovative themes, techniques, and languages that emerged from African oral culture. She concludes that these writers "furnished the instruments for defining a Black aesthetic in the Americas which is independent of other literatures."[19] In her critical practice, Cobb searches for the common images, themes, forms, and fictive devices that connect literary texts of the African Diaspora. The other two essays—the last that she would publish— examine the thematic and structural patterns evident in the works of African, Caribbean, and North American writers from Olaudah Equiano to Frederick Douglass, and from Esteban Montejo to Julién Raimond.

Martha Kendrick Cobb produced a significant body of scholarly work, which helped to shape the contours of Afro-Hispanic literature as a discrete and significant academic discipline; she helped to trace its origins in Africa and its expansion into the Americas; to define and to redefine the terms that characterize this material; to develop criteria for evaluating the literary works of diasporic writers; and to construct an interpretive frame that is still valuable to scholars. Those of us who walk, however tentatively, in her footsteps realize that we owe her an enormous debt.

Notes

1. The Black Aestheticians of the 1960s and early '70s advocated a folk aesthetic, use of vernacular language, development of new values and literary forms, an Africancentric mythology and symbolism, black-defined terminology, synthesis of ethics and aesthetics, and cultivation of black cultural traditions".

2. Later critics of the Black Aesthetic movement, such as Robert B. Stepto and Henry Louis Gates, Jr., as well as Houston A. Baker (who, ironically, began his academic career as a proponent of the Black Arts and Black Aesthetic movements), highlighted its weaknesses. Advocating a more theoretically sophisticated interpretation of literature, these critics pointed out that the black aesthetic was too romantic, idealistic, political, extraliterary, and male-centered. The more objective studies of Carolyn Fowler and Sandra Adell, however, acknowledge both the strengths and weaknesses of black-specific theories of writing. Although Cobb must have been aware of this theoretical debate in African-American literary criticism at the end of the 1970s, she does not address it in her work.

3. Edward J. Mullen, *Afro-Cuban Literature: Critical Junctures* (Westport, Conn.: Greenwood Press, 1998) 35.

4. Information about Martha Cobb's family and personal life came from interviews with her daughter and oldest offspring, Ann Cobb, a professor of English and world literature at Coppin State College.

5. James J. Davis, "An Interpretative History of the Study of Romance Languages at Howard University: 1967–1993," unpublished manuscript, 8 Dec. 2001.

6. James J. Davis, chair of the Department of Romance Languages at Howard, notes that Martha is "the only graduate to chair the department."

7. Ian Isadore Smart, "The *Afro-Hispanic Review*," *Philosophy of Literature in Latin America*, ed. Jorge J. E. Gracia and Mireya Camurati (Albany: State University of New York Press, 1989) 200.

8. Her essay on Ortiz, Glissant, and Ellison is among the twenty-two articles reprinted in the Special 20th Year Anniversary Issue of the *Afro-Hispanic Review* (Spring–Fall 2002). These include "representative selections" that are "judged to be original, insightful, in-depth, and well written/organized."

9. Martha K. Cobb, "Bibliographical Essay: An Appraisal of Latin American Slavery Through Literature," *Journal of Negro History* 58 (Oct. 1973): 460.

10. Cobb, "Bibliographical" 460.

11. When Cobb writes about a black aesthetic (in lower-case letters), it is clear that she is referring to a long, historical tradition of interpretation. She notes: "Only then will the black aesthetic—*evolving for three hundred years in the Americas . . .* " (*Harlem, Haiti, and Havana: A Comparative Critical Study of Langston Hughes, Jacques Roumain, and Nicolás Guillén* [Washington, D.C.: Three Continents Press, 1979] 144, emphasis added. Hereafter cited parenthetically in the text and notes).

12. A student of Pan-Africanism, Cobb writes: "Black studies, then, embraces the concept of a cultural Pan-Africanism which earlier scholars, writers, and those concerned with social action—W. E. B. Du Bois, Carter G. Woodson, Marcus Garvey, to name a few, had also envisioned" (*Harlem* 7).

13. She views the concept of Neo-Africanism as an important tool in a black-specific theory of literary production. She writes: "For Hughes, Roumain, and Guillén, Neo-Africanism offers an approach to the study of their works which takes into account the totality of a black literature" (*Harlem* 4).

14. Ann Cobb pointed out that her mother gave financial support to the Center for Black African Education, a Pan-African organization located on 14th Street in Washington, D.C., across from the Drum and Spear Bookstore, which was founded by a group of former SNNC members that included Martha's son, Charlie Cobb.

15. See Martha K. Cobb, "Afro-Arabs, Blackamoors, and Blacks: An Inquiry into Race Concepts Through Spanish Literature," *Black World* Feb. 1972: 32–40, rpt. *Blacks in Hispanic Literature: Critical Essays*, ed. Miriam DeCosta (Port Washington, N.Y.: Kennikat Press, 1977) 20–27. Hereafter cited parenthetically in the text.

16. See Martha K. Cobb, "Redefining the Definitions in Afro-Hispanic Literature," *CLA Journal* 23 (Dec. 1979): 147–159. Hereafter cited parenthetically in the text.

17. James J. Davis, "Crossing a Cultural Divide," *Black Issues in Higher Education* 18 Feb. 1999: 53. Ironically, the same year—1979—in which Cobb published *Harlem, Haiti, and Havana*, which advocated an Africancentric critical framework for analyzing literature, a group of African Americanists produced a collection of essays, *Afro-American Literature: The Reconstruction of Instruction*, which attacked black-specific theories of reading and writing, and proposed, instead, a Eurocentric theoretical framework that ignored the social and political foundations of the African-American literary tradition. Undaunted by this new direction, scholars such as Martha Cobb, Richard Jackson, Ian Smart, Josephat Kubayanda, and others continued to stress the African roots of black hispanophone literature.

18. Curiously, Melvin Dixon published an essay in Dexter Fisher and Robert B. Stepto's anti-Afrocentric *Reconstruction of Instruction*, which described Negritude as "the most resounding literary achievement on an international scale in the 20th century" (Melvin Dixon, "Rivers Remembering Their Source: Comparative Studies in Black Literary History—Langston Hughes, Jacques Roumain, and Négritude," *Afro-American Literature*, ed. Dexter Fisher and Robert B. Stepto [New York: MLA, 1979] 25). Although published in 1979, Dixon's compelling essay makes no reference to Cobb's seminal work. Dixon notes that cross-cultural comparative criticism frees "Afro-American literature from the cultural prison that automatically relegates it to minority, secondary, and thus inferior status" (42).

19. Martha K. Cobb, "Concepts of Blackness in the Poetry of Nicolás Guillén, Jacques Roumain, and Langston Hughes," *CLA Journal* 18 (Dec. 1974): 271.

A Selected Bibliography

Adell, Sandra. *Double-Consciousness / Double Bind: Theoretical Issues in Twentieth-Century Black Literature*. Urbana: University of Illinois Press, 1994.

Baker, Houston A. *The Journey Back: Issues in Black Literature and Criticism*. Chicago: University Chicago Press, 1980.

Carruthers, Ben Frederick. *The Life, Work and Death of Plácido.* Diss. University of Illinois, 1941.

Cobb, Ann, to Miriam DeCosta-Willis. 2 Dec. 2001, 8 Dec. 2001, and 13 Dec. 2001.

Cobb, Martha K. "Afro-Arabs, Blackamoors, and Blacks: An Inquiry into Race Concepts Through Spanish Literature." *Black World* Feb. 1972: 32–40. (Rpt. *Blacks in Hispanic Literature: Critical Essays.* Ed. Miriam DeCosta. Port Washington, N. Y.: Kennikat Press, 1977. 20–27.

———. "Africa in Latin America." *Black World* Aug. 1972: 4–19.

———. "Bibliographical Essay: An Appraisal of Latin American Slavery Through Literature." *Journal of Negro History* 58 (Oct. 1973): 460–469.

———. "Concepts of Blackness in the Poetry of Nicolás Guillén, Jacques Roumain, and Langston Hughes." *CLA Journal* 18 (Dec. 1974): 262–272.

———. *Harlem, Haiti, and Havana: A Comparative Critical Study of Langston Hughes, Jacques Roumain, and Nicolás Guillén.* Washington, D. C.: Three Continents Press, 1979.

———. "José del Carmen Díaz, A Slave Poet in Latin America / Un poeta esclavo en América Latina." *Negro History Bulletin* 37 (Jan. 1974).

———. "Martín Morúa Delgado, Black Profile in Spanish America." *Negro History Bulletin* 36 (Jan. 1973): 12.

———. "Ortiz, Glissant, and Ellison: Fictional Patterns in Black Literature." *Afro-Hispanic Review* 1 (Sept. 1982): 5–9.

———. "Plácido, The Poet-Hero, 1809–1844." *Negro History Bulletin* 38 (April/May 1975): 374–375.

———. "Redefining the Definitions in Afro-Hispanic Literature." *CLA Journal* 23 (Dec. 1979): 147–159.

———. "The Slave Narrative and the Black Literary Tradition." *The Art of Slave Narrative: Original Essays in Criticism and Theory.* Ed. John Sekora and Darwin T. Turner. Macomb: Western Illinois University Press, 1982. 36–44.

Davis, James J. "Crossing a Cultural Divide." *Black Issues in Higher Education* 18 Feb. 1999: 53.

———. "An Interpretive History of the Study of Romance Languages at Howard University: 1967–1993." Unpublished manuscript 8 Dec. 2001.

Dixon, Melvin. "Rivers Remembering Their Source: Comparative Studies in Black Literary History—Langston Hughes, Jacques Roumain, and Négritude." *Afro-American Literature.* Ed. Dexter Fisher and Robert Stepto. New York: MLA, 1979.

Fisher, Dexter, and Robert B. Stepto, eds. *Afro-American Literature: The Reconstruction of Instruction.* New York: MLA, 1979.

Fowler, Carolyn. "By Way of Preface: Balancing on the Brink." *Black Arts and Black Aesthetics: A Bibliography.* Atlanta: Author, 1976.

Fuller, Hoyt W. "Towards a Black Aesthetic." *Black Expression.* Ed. Addison Gayle, Jr. New York: Weybright and Talley, 1969.

Henderson, Stephen. *Understanding the New Black Poetry.* New York: William Morrow, 1973.

Matheus, John F. "African Footprints in Hispanic-American Literature." *Journal of Negro History* 23 (July 1938): 265–289.

Mullen, Edward J. *Afro-Cuban Literature: Critical Junctures.* Westport, Conn.: Greenwood Press, 1998.

Neal, Larry. "The Black Arts Movement." *Black Literature in America.* Ed. Raman K. Singh and Peter Fellowes. New York: Thomas Y. Crowell, 1970.

Smart, Ian Isadore. "The *Afro-Hispanic Review*." *Philosophy and Literature in Latin America.* Ed. Jorge J. E. Gracia and Mireya Camurati. Albany: State University of New York Press, 1989. 194–200.

Spratlin, Valaurez B. *Juan Latino, Slave and Humanist.* New York: Spinner, 1938.

———. "The Negro in Spanish Literature." *Journal of Negro History* 19 (Jan. 1934): 62–71.

Woodson, Carter G. "Attitudes of the Iberian Peninsula." *Journal of Negro History* 20 (April 1935): 213.

RICHARD F. PATTESON

Oscar Hijuelos: "Eternal Homesickness" and the Music of Memory

In his richly implicative study of Caribbean culture, *The Repeating Island*, Antonio Benítez-Rojo charts the region's poetics in almost geographical terms as a dialectic between chaos and insistent pattern: "[W]ithin its historiographic turbulence and its ethnological and linguistic clamor, within its generalized instability of vertigo and hurricane, one can sense the features of an island that 'repeats' itself, unfolding and bifurcating until it reaches all the seas and lands of the earth" (3). He goes on to characterize the "original" island, the "island at the center," as a location "impossible to reach" (4). The "search that the novel of the Caribbean undertakes" becomes for Benítez-Rojo a voyage toward a conjectural point of origin "fashioned by desire" and "in continuous displacement" (187). This twin notion of a hypothetical autochthonous island—existing at best only in the imagination—and a novel that persists in seeking it, is particularly germane to exiled or emigré Caribbean writers, whose work often resonates with echoes of an "actual" island home that has been transposed by time, distance, or politics to an imagined space.

Oscar Hijuelos's best-known novel, *The Mambo Kings Play Songs of Love*, enacts a process in which remembering and imagining such an island (in this case a Cuba increasingly receding into myth) become an essential element in the composition of an evolving, present-day, and very American reality. Alejo Carpentier has more than once alluded to the influence of Proust on

CRITIQUE: Studies in Contemporary Fiction, Volume 44, Number 1 (Fall 2002): pp. 38–48. Copyright © 2002 Heldref Publications and the Helen Dwight Reid Educational Foundation.

Cuban literature, as Sally Harvey points out in her study of Carpentier's own debt to the French novelist: "*En Cuba se leyó a Proust posiblemente antes que en cualquier otro país del Continente*" (8). Discussing Carpentier's and Proust's treatments of the relationship of past to present, she quotes and comments on an often cited description of the jungle in *Los pasos perdidos:* "*Entonces, el coloso, nunca salido de la prehistoria* [. . .] *acababa por yacer sobre el humus milenario de la selva* [. . .]."[1] In Harvey's reading of this excerpted passage, "[T]he giant trees [. . .] because of their longevity, bear the growth of previous ages in their trunks, so that their past literally forms part of their living present. When after centuries, they finally fall to the ground, they continue to form part of the living reality of the jungle as they are incorporated into its humus" (20). Surely this can be seen as a metaphor for the relationship of past to present in Hijuelos's novel also. The past (however reshaped by the imagination) is inextricable from the present in *The Mambo Kings* and gives the work much of its resonance. Perhaps a fine distinction can be drawn between Proust and Hijuelos because, far from attempting, like *A la recherche du temps perdu,* to summon up a "vast structure of recollection" (*Swann's Way* 51) to create an aesthetically based, atemporal reality, *The Mambo Kings Play Songs of Love,* its pervasive nostalgia notwithstanding, employs an aesthetic engagement with the past to enrich a present reality that continues to change.

Much of the novel's form and significance are encapsulated in a single sentence: "He was the man plagued with memory, the way his brother Cesar Castillo would be twenty-five years later, the man with the delusion that the composition of a song about María would bring her back" (44). Cesar is a Cuban who has come to New York in 1949 with his younger brother Nestor and formed a band called the Mambo Kings. Mambo, a style of music (and dance) originating in Cuba as a synthesis of African and European elements, became popular in the United States during the forties and fifties. In the novel the Castillo brothers are part of a musical milieu that included such actual performers as the Mambo Aces, Machito, Desi Arnaz, and Tito Rodríguez. They achieve a moderate degree of success, at one point even appearing, at the invitation of Arnaz, on an episode of the television program *I Love Lucy*. All the while, however, Nestor is haunted by an aching love for María, a girl who deserted him back in Cuba. He marries another woman and becomes the father of two children, but he remains tormented by an "eternal homesickness" (94) that includes his seemingly inexplicable yearning for María but also embraces other concepts associated with his Caribbean origins. All of these things—María, Cuba, his mother, his childhood, his home—Nestor attempts to "bring back" through the artistry of his music; and the source of his creative energy (as in Proust) is ultimately his ineradicable sense of loss. As Michael Seidel observes, analyzing Marcel's "agony of separation from his mother" near the beginning of *Swann's Way,* "It is almost as if the imagination requires the impediments of time or distance to activate it" (6). The second half of *The Mambo Kings* in a sense replays the first. After Nestor's death in an automobile accident, Cesar's recollections of his life turn increasingly into an improvisational medley of longing—with the lost Nestor now replacing the lost María. Two brief episodes narrated by Nestor's son Eugenio frame the narrative—a prologue recounting an instance of watching his uncle and his dead father on *I Love Lucy* and an epilogue describing a visit to the "real" Desi Arnaz after Cesar's death in 1980. These scenes, particularly the latter one, put the novel's discordant and frequently distressing memories into perspective, placing them within Eugenio's imagination and placing Eugenio himself squarely in an American present that would be meaningless without his family's island past.

The prologue to *The Mambo Kings* might just as accurately be called an overture, because it anticipates the dominant themes in Hijuelos's orchestration of memories. In the first paragraph, Eugenio recalls a Saturday afternoon "years and years ago" hearing their neighbor, Mrs. Shannon, shouting out her window that his uncle Cesar was on television again: "When I heard the opening strains of the *I Love Lucy* show I got excited because I knew she was referring to an item of eternity" (3). Seeing his uncle and father playing their greatest song, "Beautiful María of My Soul," takes Eugenio into a realm where the past can coexist with the present. "For me," he says, "my father's gentle rapping on Ricky Ricardo's door has always been a call from the beyond" (3).[2] The episode, including the crucial element of Nestor's singing his song, acts as a catalyst on Eugenio's imagination and memory, not unlike the effect of the madeleine *in A la recherche:*

> The first time I saw a rerun of this, I could remember other things about him—his lifting me up, his smell of cologne, his patting my head [. . .] and so many other moments happening in my thoughts simultaneously that it was like watching something momentous, say the Resurrection, as if Christ had stepped out of his sepulcher [. . .] because my father was newly alive and could take off his hat and sit down on the couch in Ricky's living room [. . .]. (4)

Eugenio also acknowledges that the Mambo Kings' music "packed clubs, dance halls, and theaters," introducing many Americans to the world "beyond death, beyond pain, beyond all stillness" (3) so closely linked, through the music itself, to Cuba. It is therefore appropriate (though he does not realize how much so until his epiphany in the novel's epilogue) that Eugenio's own most intense experience of music's power to bring the past into the present occurs through the medium of an iconic American comedy.

Riffs of recollection structure *The Mambo Kings,* and the "sad business of memory" (193)—Cesar's, Nestor's, and Eugenio's—generates its entire plot. But Cesar and Nestor initially display different stances toward the past. As a young man Cesar prefers "to look forward and never back [...]." Occasionally he misses the daughter he left behind in Cuba and regrets "that things didn't work out with his former wife," but once in America, he sets out to live in the present and plan for the future. Moments of melancholy that occur when he thinks about his wife and daughter are fixed by "a drink, a woman, a cha-cha-cha [...]" (44–45). Only after Nestor's death does Cesar become, as his brother had always been, "plagued with memory" (44). It is almost as if Nestor has borne for both of them the burden of attempting to reconnect with the past, so that his death leaves Cesar alone with the task of yearning after, in Proust's words, "the forgotten strains of happiness" (*Swann's Way* 375). For the entire span of the novel, with the exception of the prologue and epilogue, Cesar sits in his room in the Hotel Splendor in 1980, an old man very near death, and recalls his past while listening to old Mambo Kings records—most especially "Beautiful María of My Soul."

From the moment he leaves Cuba the past obsesses Nestor, but that sense of absence in his life also quickens his creativity and provides him with his subject matter. He composes song after song "written to take the listeners back to the plazas of small towns in Cuba, to Havana, to past moments of courtship and love, passion, and a way of life that was fading from existence" (39). His specialty soon becomes "songs about torment beyond all sorrow" (40); in the greatest of these, "Beautiful María," he attempts to "write a song communicating such pure love and desire that María, far away, would magically reinstate him into the center of her heart" (42). Cesar repeatedly advises his brother to forget about that woman and get on with his life, but Nestor is drawn back to that brief romance by a force greater than reason: "He relived their life over again so often that he sometimes had the sensation of being buried by the past, as if the details of this shattered love (and the other sadnesses of his life) had been turned into stone, weeds, and dirt and thrown over him" (42).

Although Nestor's love for María is the focal point of his melancholy, the source of it is deeper and more comprehensive. Most important, his lovesickness is linked to "the other sadnesses of his life" through his mother, whose name is also María. It is only after he tells his mother about María that his romance seems real, and he all but fuses the two in his imagination: "*Mamá,* I wanted María the way I wanted you when I was a baby [...]" (43). In one remarkable scene, Nestor is making love to his faithful wife Delores, but when he closes his eyes instead of her face he sees that of María. Guilt-stricken, he opens his eyes and looks at Delores, but when he closes them again he once more feels "the worst sadness" about his lost love: "And yet, when he saw María, he pictured her in a room, and in that room a doorway through which could be seen the sickbed of his youth and himself, unable to move, calling out, '*Mamá!*'" (90). The structure of this tableau is telling: the reality of Delores is submerged by the memory of María, and that in turn is submerged by the deeper memory of his mother. A few pages later Nestor recalls thinking that the "peaceful sleep in his mother's arms was the sleep he missed" and "wishing that he had never left Las Piñas or the loving grip of his mother" (95). The association of the mother not only with Cuba and the past, but also with a state of ineffable bliss, also echoes through Cesar's memories. When he visits his family in Cuba for the last time, "His mother's affection was so strong that for one brief moment he had an insight into love: pure unity. […] Because for a few moments he felt released from this pain, which had withered the coil at the bottom of his spine; felt as if his mother was an open field of wildflowers through which he could run" (209).

Passages like these (in addition to providing *The Mambo Kings* with several of its more obvious Proustian flourishes) lead ever closer to a still more primordial source for Nestor's longing. Reflecting on the difficulties of finding such release so far away from the island home of his childhood, Cesar recalls his strategies for alleviating anguish, depression, or homesickness: visiting expatriate *santeras* and going to confession in the Catholic church. In this extended passage the comfort provided by the Castillos's mother is closely linked to that offered by *santeras*, "his goddess Caridad, or charity," and "the goddess Mayari, for whom [they] were intermediaries," as well as by "the Holy Mother" (115). The cluster of references to María Castillo, Mayari, and the Virgin Mary is not incidental. Like the patron saint of Cuba, the *Virgen de la Caridad del Cobre* (Cesar's "goddess Caridad"), the mother in *The Mambo Kings* is a syncretic icon. Benítez-Rojo argues that the *Virgen*, because of her multiple origins in Amerindian, European, and West African belief systems, should be read in terms of "wandering signifiers" (13) and not just as a symbol of Cuba itself. Devotion to the Virgin of Charity should be construed "as a meta-archipelagic text" in addition to "a Cuban cult" (16), but for Hijuelos the syncretism of the mother icon—possibly his version of the *Virgen de la Caridad*—always seems to lead back to Cuba. In both a closely personal and a broader cultural sense, she is the ultimate point of origin and the very embodiment of that primal island toward which Nestor's music and memory hearken.

Nestor never fully understands (though he vaguely intuits) that this past can exist in the present only as an imaginative construct. It is left to the dominant narrative voice of the novel, speaking through but also over Nestor, to make that apparent: "He would send his mother in Cuba tender letters written in his simple script, speaking about his love for her and the family; heartsick letters nostalgic for the security of the home he had—or thought he had—in Cuba" (114). Nestor subconsciously edits out the unpleasant parts, creating a past that is more comforting than the "real" one—a childhood he

can continue to mourn as he does his lost María. Characters in other Hijuelos's novels often perform a similar transaction. Mercedes Santinio in *Our
House in the Last World*, for instance, "would try to find shelter in her old
dreams of Cuba, remembering only the good and rejecting the bad" (46), and
in *The Fourteen Sisters of Emilio Montez O'Brien* there is this:

> Years later, when remembering that night, his mind fogged by
> drink, he would not only have shared a tender kiss with Antonella
> but believe that she, too, had fallen in love with him. In that
> invention of memory, when he left the house she went walking
> with him toward the church, and there [. . .] she rested on the
> ground and he covered her with kisses. (257)

Cesar constructs the same kind of shelter even more explicitly when he
meets Desi Arnaz in New York. The two chat for a while, discover that they
came from the same province in Cuba, and finally collaborate on a fictional
version of their youth: "And then in the way that Cubans get really friendly,
Arnaz and Cesar reinvented their pasts so that, in fact, they had probably
been good friends" (127). Later the same evening, Desi and his wife accom-
pany the Castillo brothers to their apartment on La Salle Street for a late
Cuban dinner, and an enduring relationship takes root. Here a "reinvented"
past, one shaped into a kind of art by the imagination, not only engages with
the present but exhibits a capacity to change it.

Although narrative, like Cesar and Desi's storytelling on the night they
meet, is the art form that structures the past in *The Mambo Kings*, the characters themselves confront and shape the past primarily through music. The
novel's epigraph, taken from the liner notes to the brothers' most successful
album, describes the process plainly:

> [. . .] with a flick of your wrist on your phonograph switch, the
> fiction of the rolling sea and a dance date on a Havana patio or in
> a smart supper club will become reality. Certainly, if you cannot
> spare the time to go to Havana or want to revive the memories of
> a previous trip, this music will make it all possible. [. . .] (v)

And when Cesar listens to one of the Mambo Kings' own records, it is "as if
he's a kid again running through the center of Las Piñas at carnival and the
porches of the houses are lit with huge lanterns and the balconies garlanded
with ribbons and tapers and flowers, and past so many musicians, musicians everywhere [. . .]" (25). Throughout the novel, music, particularly
mambo music, and most particularly "Beautiful María of My Soul," distills
an "extratemporal essence" (Proust, *Letters* 227) of the past and brings it

into the present. For both brothers the effect is rather like that of the little phrase from the Vinteuil sonata in *Swann's Way.* When Swann hears it, "all his memories of the days when Odette had been in love with him" awaken "the forgotten strains of happiness" (375).[3] In Hijuelos's novel, of course, it is the protagonists themselves who compose and play the music, "fashioning by desire" (to paraphrase Benítez-Rojo) a form of the past that can be experienced within the living present.

Cesar Castillo, sitting in the Hotel Splendor and waiting to die, is anything but the supremely self-aware Marcel of *A la recherche,* and his mental faculties are considerably impaired by alcohol. Yet as he keeps returning to the turntable, spinning platter after platter of Mambo Kings' music, he recognizes the power of his art to bring the past back, even if only through the artful "invention of memory":

> Sometimes when the music got faster, he would feel like a kid running up and down the steep and beautiful stairways of Santiago de Cuba. [. . .] The music set him leaning drowsily under the shade of a bottle-palm tree in Holguin. Late in the night he returned to a street in Santiago he had not thought about for years [. . .]. (382–383)

He remembers his marriage, his daughter, his many love affairs. He recalls how he gave up performing after Nestor's death but went back to it when Castro came to power to earn money to get his family out of Cuba. His memory chronicles his years of work as a building superintendent, his unsuccessful attempt to run his own nightclub, and his abiding affection for Nestor's children, Eugenio and Leticia. But the main events of his later life, filled in circuitously by Cesar's impromptu, miscellaneous recollections, seem almost like interludes between his agonizing moments of grief for Nestor, such as the time he awakes from a nap and hears the *I Love Lucy* theme coming through the walls of the apartment building: "And when he opened his eyes he found himself standing beside Nestor, poor, nervous Nestor, as they were preparing to leave the stage wings to make their appearance on the show" (312). During his final days, Cesar finds himself drawn inexorably toward the inarticulable, perhaps unattainable, source of fulfillment and repose that beckoned to his heartsick brother. As if to make one more attempt to reach that unreachable island, his last act before he dies is to write out, in his own hand, the lyrics to Nestor's ballad, "Beautiful María of My Soul."

If "Beautiful María" is a semiotic link to the Cuban past, the theme from *I Love Lucy,* the novel's other signature song, heralds a syncretic American future. The show itself presented America with a romanticized model of life in the 1950s. Throughout *The Mambo Kings* this Hollywood version of wedded bliss and ethnic assimilation is counterpointed with the harsher realities of the Castillo brothers' lives. Cesar's failed marriage contrasts especially sharply with Lucy and Ricky's happy one. "I love Luisa," he recalls having once said of his ex-wife, "with all my heart" (52), echoing both the title and the satin heart emblem of the television program. Reality definitively trumps fantasy in the epilogue, when Eugenio visits Desi Arnaz at his home in 1981. Lucy is conspicuously missing; she and Desi, unlike their happy fictional personae, have been divorced for many years. The show also, as we have seen, provides a way for Eugenio and Cesar to "resurrect" Nestor and the past life he embodies for them. But perhaps the most striking and important effect relating to *I Love Lucy* has to do with the narrative's *gestalt:* a dynamic of cultural convergence in which Cuban characters play other Cuban characters on an American television comedy and the television show itself, along with its "real" creators and stars, is incorporated into a novel by a Cuban American writer. As for Nestor's song, the distillation of all his longing for a mythic island home "in continuous displacement," it too plays its part in the construction of a culturally syncretic, present-day reality. Absorbed into the vast songbook of America, "Beautiful María of My Soul" is turned into Muzak by the Castillos's old pianist Miguel Montoya and comes "out over supermarket, airport, bus-terminal loudspeakers everywhere [. . .]" (340).

Eugenio's visit to Desi Arnaz in the novel's brief coda replays the strains of music and memory, but in a new key. For a long time he hesitates to respond to Arnaz's invitation, issued after Cesar's death. Eugenio has inherited his father's "moods of prolonged anguish and discontent" (365), and he fears that Arnaz's "kindness would turn into air, like so many other things in this life" (399). Eugenio has grown up to be a decent, if moody, young man, but he has never reconciled himself with the forced exile from his own past that his father's early death precipitated, and he has never really felt at home in his own skin. When he finally arrives at the Arnaz estate, however, he finds the hospitality genuine and the house filled with reminders of the past. As he approaches the front entrance half expecting "to hear the *I Love Lucy* theme" (400), he notices instead the singing of birds, the splashing of running water, and the rustling of trees. Arnaz later explains, "'I chose this climate here because it reminds me of Cuba'" (402). A small patio-garden is even modeled after one of his "favorite little plazas in Santiago" (402). Inside the house are such memorabilia as a framed map of Cuba, a portrait of Arnaz's former wife, Lucille Ball, and photographs of many family and friends, including a familiar one of Desi with Nestor and Cesar Castillo. Arnaz, reminiscing about the Castillos, "started to sing 'Beautiful María of My Soul,' and although he couldn't remember all the words, he filled in the missing phrases with humming" (401). The nostalgic ambience leads Arnaz to say, "You know what was beautiful, boy? When I was little and my mother would hold me in her arms"

(403). That line, touching one of the narrative's major chords, makes an immediate, intensely emotional impression on Eugenio. Here, at the end of an exquisitely realistic novel, *real* modulates quickly into *maravilloso*.[4]

Desi Arnaz leaves the room for a few minutes; and Eugenio, thinking about his father and uncle's appearance on *I Love Lucy*, finds himself not visualizing the episode, but actually in it. There before him are Lucy, Ricky, Nestor, and Cesar. Eugenio tells Nestor how glad he is to see him, and his father replies, "It is the same for me, son. It will always be the same." This exchange, the reassuring word "always," and the embrace that follows are what Eugenio has been waiting for to bring the lost past back into his life, if only through the power of his imagination: "And I couldn't help myself. I walked over and sat on the couch and wrapped my arms around my father. Expected to find air, but hit on solid flesh. And his neck was warm. His expression pained and timid, like a hick off the boat. He was alive!" (404). Feeling himself "falling through an endless space" that is his father's heart—not his "flesh and blood" heart but one "filled with light and music"—Eugenio is "pulled back into a world of pure affection, before torment, before loss, before awareness" (404). He is drawn toward a state of repose very close to those near mythic, lost times and places that his father's music has always evoked.

The concluding sequence brings a kind of closure to Eugenio's struggle to reconnect himself to his father and all that Nestor represents. Sitting in the Tropicana, he watches and listens as the Castillo brothers perform "Beautiful María of My Soul," but that vision yields to another, in which Eugenio sees his late uncle's heart swell "to the size of the satin heart on the *I Love Lucy* show" and float over the rooftops of their old neighborhood on La Salle Street. A confirmation ceremony in a local church shifts dreamlike to a funeral, and when the organist starts to play, mambo music comes out. There is "a full-blown mambo orchestra straight out of 1952 playing a languid bolero," and yet the sound is scratchy, like an old record. When the coffin is carried outside the church "another satin heart escapes" (406–407), and the two hearts, Cesar's and Nestor's, disappear together into the sky. Eugenio's epiphany, fusing once again the fictive *I Love Lucy* with the reality of lived experience, has allowed him at last to internalize his family's Cuban past, through music and memory and bring it into his own American present. According to Proust's Marcel, "the countries for which we yearn occupy, at any given moment, a far larger place in our actual life than the country in which we happen to be." (5) *The Mambo Kings Play Songs of Love* records the difficult struggle to achieve a synthesis between those disparate countries and times. The country for which Eugenio yearns, Benítez-Rojo's "island at the center," is an imagined but not at all an imaginary place, part of his consciousness and his life, and now part of the country in which he happens to be. Perhaps it is not too fanciful to suggest that for Eugenio Castillo, first-generation American, the "forgotten strains of happiness" might well have metamorphosed into the *I Love Lucy* theme, always to be accompanied in his imagination by the vision of Ricky Ricardo, Cuban immigrant, opening the door to that New York apartment, in episode after episode, and confidently announcing, "Lucy . . . I'm home."

NOTES

1. "Then the colossus, never disturbed since prehistory [. . .] ended by lying down upon the ancient humus of the forest. [. . .]" See Alejo Carpentier, *Obras completas* (México, D.F.: Siglo Veintiuno Editores, 1985) 2:296.

2. Hijuelos weaves his narrative skillfully into an actual episode of the *I Love Lucy,* in which Ricky Ricardo's country cousins come to New York, show up at the Ricardos' apartment, and appear in Ricky's nightclub act at the Tropicana. Hijuelos in effect re-imagines those characters as the protagonists of his novel.

3. "[T]ous ses souvenirs du temps où Odette était éprise de lui [. . .] les refrains oubliés du bonheur." See *Du Coté de chez Swann* 412–413.

4. "Lo real maravilloso se encuentra a cada paso en las vidas de hombres que inscribieron fechas en la historia del Continente y dejaron apellidos aún llevados [. . .]." See Carpentier, Introduction to *El reino de este mundo* (Santiago, Chile: Editorial Universitaria, 1971) 14.

5. In the original, "les pays que nous désirons tiennent à chaque moment beaucoup plus de place dans notre vie véritable, que le pays où nous nons trouvons effectivement." See *Du Coté de chez Swann* 465.

WORKS CITED

Benítez-Rojo, Antonio. *The Repeating Island: The Caribbean and the Postmodern Perspective.* Trans. James Maraniss. Durham: Duke University Press, 1992.

Harvey, Sally. *Carpentier's Proustian Fiction: The Influence of Marcel Proust on Alejo Carpentier.* London: Tamesis, 1994.

Hijuelos, Oscar. *The Fourteen Sisters of Emilio Montez O'Brien.* New York: Penguin, 1993.

———. *The Mambo Kings Play Songs of Love.* New York: HarperPerennial, 1992.

———. *Our House in the Last World.* New York: Persea, 1983.

Proust, Marcel. *Du Coté de chez Swann.* Paris: Gallimard, 1954.

———. *Letters.* Trans. Mina Curtiss. New York: Vintage, 1966.

———. *Swann's Way.* Trans. C. K. Scott Moncrieff and Terence Kilmartin. New York: Vintage, 1982.

Seidel, Michael. *Exile and the Narrative imagination.* New Haven: Yale University Press, 1986.

B. MARIE CHRISTIAN

Many Ways to Remember:
Layered Time in Mora's House of Houses

That Pat Mora arranges her memoir *House of Houses* according to a Western secular calendar seems apparent at first browse. At first reading, however, this orderly notion of a "representative year" breaks down, for the book begins not with January or even with a preface or introduction, but with a title chapter. Immediately, therefore, the essentiality of the Western calendar comes into question. The title chapter establishes that Mora will shed the restrictions of time and logic: her house is a dream house in which the dead walk alongside the living, the past is simultaneous with the present, and the future is so certain that she can name grandchildren yet to be conceived.

Why, then, should Mora impose a calendar at all? An answer is suggested in past comments by Mora herself. During an interview conducted by Elisabeth Mermann-Jozwiak and Nancy Sullivan, Mora reiterates her fascination with concepts of space and geography as they help define a person's psychological landscape, a zone she refers to as "one's internal rooms, issues of the psyche" or "the world of dreams, mental space" (145). In *House of Houses,* she interjects time into the definition of this region. In response to her own query, "How much does our body know that we know not?" (2), she declares that the inner body, the house of self, knows all because the psyche remembers all. "Through generations," she writes, "sun, wind, rain, hands, voices, and dreams create and alter this place pregnant with possibilities in a landscape

MELUS, Volume 30, Number 1 (Spring 2005): pp. 135–148. Copyright © 2005 MELUS.

as familiar to me as my body" (4). Fluid and accepting, the inner space carries one's knowledge as well as one's still unsettled questions. Within it, the people, stories, fears, joys, doubts, and certainties of many lives rise bidden and unbidden to surround, interpret, and absorb a new experience. This "house" is the repository for all that creates a sense of heritage, belonging, and identity. Mora further concludes that people both influence and are influenced by the psychological construct in which they are raised. The house of self is a living, reciprocating entity impervious to time, a grouping that "nest[s] like bodies inside one another" (3).

The notions that time is concentric rather than linear and that all of our past is simultaneously available to us are reiterated throughout *House of Houses* by the foregrounding of landscape and generations. Insisting that we internalize our pasts, Mora writes, "the landscape imprints itself; and when we can't see the world that is home . . . we yearn to see the shapes and vistas that live in our interior" (25). Viewing her family as a "house" in her imagination, she describes a home of concentric design. Orchards surround this home, which itself presents a smooth adobe wall to the outside but allows guests to penetrate increasingly more intimate zones until they reach the very heart of the family. In this house, the rooms open onto a covered porch, which in turn opens onto a garden, which in turn surrounds the family life source, a central fountain. The internal sphere is a separate world of flowing water, living greenery, shifting shade, and timeless intimacy: a personal space, the womb of the family.

Investigating such a space presents a significant writing challenge. Mora's readers, receptive as they may be, live outside her body house and must be invited in before they can learn its geography. Even as they learn to accept the cumulative presence of people and influences in her inner world, they need to know which characters and events preceded the others. Mora must consolidate her extended family even while she preserves the family's numerous personalities; their ethnic, social, religious, and political diversity; their sometimes polarized generations; their gender issues; and their levels of information and misinformation. She has to demonstrate that the inner space allows living and dead to exist simultaneously, for the line between corporeality and spirituality is hazy there. She must prove that past, present, and future are seamless because the present encompasses the past, and the future is expected to offer new information on present and past alike. She must convince the reader that these layers of experience are identifiable but permeable, so information may seep to the foreground when needed. The layers must be seen to both mark time and defy time; they must be contradictory in themselves so they may in turn embrace contradictions.

The superimposed calendars of *House of Houses* provide a framework for this literary venture by offering three-dimensional structure upon which

Mora may hang the details of her complex self. The twelve-month Western calendar becomes the primary organizational tool; but from the very start, she reveals that it, too, is a layered construct. Parallel and equally powerful with it are several other calendars: the Christian and Mesoamerindian liturgical calendars, the moon-measured months as counted before Western contact, and the task-identified year of the gardener. By invoking multiple calendars, she echoes human ways of knowing. One is the recursive habit of the mind that sends it over and over the chronological facts, looking for patterns, links, causes and effects. She caters to this approach when she reports the family's official history according to the Western calendar, for these facts derive from legal records. Likewise, she provides a family tree in which generations are discernible even when specific dates are unavailable.

A second way of knowing is the intuitive awareness that comes from internalizing natural and social rhythms. Human sensitivity to light patterns, for example, might inform a family of the approaching solstice whether they have a calendar or not; or a glance at public decorations may reveal the coming or passing of a holiday. When Mora tells family stories, she invokes this kind of time, a flexible time more concerned with the accumulation of family wisdom than with factual accuracy. She further stretches the standard chronology of calendar months through references to spring-summer-winter-fall, to moon-related Amerindian seasons, and to the weather-responsive cycles of planting and harvesting.

By layering these perceptions of a "year," Mora emphasizes the diverse heritage of her family and her inner self. She also imitates the fluid layering of memory and the sense of continuity that have kept her own family and their wider culture alive despite a shifting political frontier, the ongoing marginalization of border peoples, and the economic colonization of Mexico. One significant element of that wider culture is the Catholicism brought by the Spanish and adapted over the centuries by the peoples of the Americas.[1] Through her calendar-based memoir, Mora discovers how deeply the religious events embedded in her culture have continued to influence her perceptions. The very title of the book, repeated as the title of the first chapter, plays upon Christ's assertion that the Father's house encompasses many dwellings (John 14:2). By extension, Mora suggests, her house is also commingled; that is, she and her heritage are similarly diverse and receptive.

Mora furthers the religious parallel by beginning the book with the poetic prelude "House of Houses" rather than the chapter labeled "January." On the Catholic liturgical calendar, the year begins with the season of Advent, a changeable period that commences four Sundays before Christmas Day and ends on Christmas Eve. Its length varies because Christmas falls on a different day of the week each year. During Advent, according to the logic of Catholic pedagogy, the faithful will re-view the promises of the Old Testament and pre-view the stories of Christ's life and teaching that will fill the coming year. This repetition will give the people an opportunity to understand Christ's message a little better each year. Mora follows this logic on a personal and family level as she prepares herself to renew her knowledge of family habits and teachings in the coming chapters, each of which will condense generations of related wisdom and history into one floating season. The literal time of this chapter is the hiatus between Christmas and New Year's Day: the Christmas tree has fulfilled its holiday function but is still fresh enough to place outside as a perch for birds, and the family enjoys the slippered ease that follows the Christmas Day rush. Christian Advent is over.

In figurative terms, however, the chapter consistently invokes the symbols of Advent. Just as the Bible stories of Advent recall the House of David that engendered Christ, she recalls the houses of Mora and Delgado that joined to create her. In this past-yet-present house, she writes, "time loses its power and past-present braid as they do within each of us, in *our* interior" (4). Anticipating the coming year, she refers to a Mexican folk practice of guessing the year's weather by analyzing the first twenty-four days of January. She thereby reinforces the overall structure of the book in two ways: she proposes that calendrical time is only one way of predicting change, and she reaffirms that the best information comes from juxtaposed systems. Furthermore, she suggests that the examination of alternate cycles and conflicting beliefs may help her understand the folds of her inner landscape.

In this chapter, Mora begins to braid the voices and events of multiple pasts into individual, representative seasons, using an anti-chronological, recursive, multivocal style that underscores her tolerance of differences and her willingness to reinterpret time. Against the organization of the Western calendar, she places the more fluid and unpredictable time familiar to women and gardeners, who are closely involved in the variable timeframes of reproduction and maturation: the unpredictable length of a pregnancy, the span of one's childbearing years, the years in a generation, or the duration of the journey from childhood to maturity. The gardening year, a time reference favored by Mora and her female relatives, requires patience and trust. The day to plant and the day to harvest will come, but not by schedule. Rather, gardeners remain open to subtle hints from the soil and air. They accept that the speed and success of plant growth will depend upon uncontrollable natural elements. The filling and waning moon will exert its magic pull, but not on the same days as in the year past or the year to come. The seasons will create an average by never being average. Knowing these things, the family women, living and dead, gather to plan their spring garden, confident that "[t]he world's flora nourish, inspire, intoxicate. . . . [They are] like our subconscious, fertile and full of promise" (8). The spirit women, the memory women who have penetrated Mora's subconscious, are no less present in the conversation than she is. Their presence emphasizes nurture and continuity, hope for the future, the usefulness of the past remembered.

As the memoir progresses, Mora will delineate the family within a loose weave of time, nature, growth, and religion. One significant strand of the net will be Aunt Lobo's missal, her personal copy of the prayers and the yearly cycle of readings for Catholic Mass. From its pages, holy cards and family pictures alike will tumble, for Lobo believes that the family and its special moments are just as important as holy days, saints, and scripture. The women of the family, most of whom are present as spirits, examine this missal in the liturgical ambiance of a scented candle as they drink tea brewed in a "sacramental act" (11). They begin reconstructing their past on the orderly plan of a twelve-month Western calendar; but they soon superimpose the flexible time of family generations as well as the rotating, astronomy-influenced calendars of the Catholic Church and the pre-Conquest religions of Mexico.

These liturgical seasons, whether linked to successful crop production or the production of a book of seasonal readings, do not always begin on the same calendar date. The fixed celebrations of numerous religions fall on slightly different dates or days of the week each year. In the Catholic calendar, which reveals itself to be a powerful force as *House of Houses* unfolds, celebrations follow the lead of Easter, which falls upon the first Sunday after the first full moon after the vernal equinox. When Mora recites the Catholic Church seasons, "Advent, Christmas, Epiphany, Ordinary Time, Lent, Easter, Pentecost," she notes they are "rhythmic as the seasons" (12).

Significantly, she also refers to the *Popol Vuh*, the oldest recorded origin stories of the Quiché Maya; and she consistently invokes the moon seasons as named by other indigenous groups: Snow, Awakening, Sprouting Grass, Full Flower, Full Rose, Full Thunder, Big Harvest, Full Long Nights. Her layering of time imitates the complex cyclical calendars of the Aztec and Maya civilizations, calendars that allowed the priests to predict how a single day might be influenced by its simultaneous representation on several ongoing, superimposed cycles. Mora and her family have absorbed this layered perception of time along with their Catholic and secular calendars.[2] She would shrug them off no more than she would drop her first language. To ignore any such influence would be *el olvido:* the sin of forgetting roots and thereby sacrificing wisdom.

The Catholic liturgical calendar and the shared Chicano Catholic experience are prominent in *House of Houses,* and they affect the telling and comprehension of favorite family stories. Indeed, Mora worries that she has robbed her own children of their heritage by not raising them in the ways of the Catholic Church. An outwardly small incident pierces her cultural conscience: her children cannot grasp a family story about genuflection, the Catholic practice of demonstrating respect, humility, and servitude by touching the right knee to the floor during worship, before entering a church pew, or after leaving the pew. Mora's sister recalls her own ingrained impulse to genuflect: one day she forgot where she was and touched her knee to the floor before entering a row at the movie theater. To the adults who grew up with the practice, it is an evocative story, an inside joke; but for Mora's children, it requires explanation, and even then it seems quaint and a bit ridiculous. The gap in her children's background troubles Mora because she understands the importance of children wanting to remember and retell family stories. A story they do not value will be lost to their children, subtracted into the great silence of *el olvido*. As if to stave off that loss, Mora textures every page of her memoir with details of Chicano Catholic life, whether she is speaking of family celebrations, petitions to the saints, escape from Pancho Villa's forces, or survival during the Great Depression.

Mora likewise records customs borrowed from non-Catholic or even non-Christian sources. From her family spirits, she learns that adaptation is a matter of addition rather than reduction. What is added to the culture may very well strengthen it by increasing the available responses to daily challenges. Mora seems to relish such additions to her language, her religion, and her folk art. She records that *adobe*, the familiar Mexican name for the very material of her house, came from the Spanish colonizers, who in turn had long before mimicked the Arabic word for brick. She refers often to the ubiquitous rosary, a Catholic prayer string that originated in twelfth-century Europe and has similarities to Muslim prayer beads. She continues to enjoy popular folk customs that originated far away, such as the art of cutting decorative patterns in tissue paper, a practice adopted from the Chinese. Ultimately, Mora declares that "cultural purity is a myth" (96); and she devotes much of the memoir to proving the point. Layers of language and culture become as permeable as layers of time.

As *House of Houses* moves beyond its prelude and into the twelve months of the year, the layers of time and culture appear and recede seamlessly. The first thematic interval runs roughly from January through April. Mora renders the months in their familiar personalities—Chilly January, Crazy February, Windy March, and Rainy April—and each gets its own chapter; but the content flows through them thematically, with emotionally linked events overlapping the months. The remembered events seem chosen not for their chronological accuracy but for their aesthetic fit with the personality of the month or the general season. Mora privileges cycles over fixed dates through her references to the moveable feasts of the Catholic Church calendar, the steadily changing moon, and the progress of the family garden.

The Church feasts begin with the arrival of the Three Kings, celebrated on January 6 no matter where the date falls in the week, and concludes with the death and resurrection of Christ, celebrated on a weekend determined by the vernal equinox. Just as the Church condenses the life of Christ into the months between the start of winter and the arrival of spring, she compresses her family history, presenting an overview of the Mora and Delgado lives from the great-great-grandparents down to her own children. Aunt Lobo insists on beginning with an overview, naming the Spanish regions where the Delgados originated and then reciting the generations begotten on Mexican soil, the places they dwelt, the work they performed, and the politics that displaced them to the U.S. Mora continues the genealogy of deaths and burials and births that made them belong to the new land. By the end of February, awakening spring flowers lead Mora to muse on the gardening year, another cycle with nonspecific dates:

> We probably dig some of ourselves into all that we pursue, but there's something eerie or maybe appealing—all the Catholic dust-to-dust stuff—about digging ourselves into earth, loosening the soil and burying some of our essence, our breath, as we turn the earth, even while we're alive becoming part of the compost. (67–68)

Like the Church calendar, like the turning Earth, she has been readying herself for the seeds of stories and the subtle but momentous period of gestation. The moon is the Snow Moon, high and chilly and revealing.

This "dust-to-dust" period of self-examination becomes most devastating around March, a month that always finds the Catholic Church in its penitential season of Lent. Accenting the religious practice of self-denial during Lent, Mora calls this the "penance and purification" time and the uncomfortable "'I Won't' season: I Won't Eat Candy, I Won't Chew Gum . . . I Won't Taste Pleasure, I Won't, I Won't" (69). Outside, the garden is still cold. The vernal equinox approaches, but too slowly. During this dark time of year, the period of the Snow Moon and March wind, the family stories are sorrowful. Aunt Lobo tells of Pancho Villa's attacks and the difficulties faced by the displaced Moras and Delgados as they started their lives over in Texas. The events are consistent with the liturgical year and its devastating descent toward Christ's passion and death, the bitterness that must precede renewal.

March must become April, however, and the Awakening Moon must succeed the Snow Moon. Mora contemplates renewal in the form of the spiritual rain of Easter and the physical rain of spring. Fittingly, she tells of her father Raúl, who holds deathbed conversations with the Virgin of Guadalupe and his dead ancestors. The family is gratified rather than shaken by such visits because their personal Catholicism embraces a pre-Christian conviction that the dead remain accessible to the living. As Mora says later, her father believed that the family dead "have no use for cemeteries, staying underground. They drift through the rooms like incense, like a prayer, a melody, a breath" (268). Comforted by this belief, Raúl and his family trust more in his spirits than they do in the final sacramental rites performed by the priest. The spirit visitors promise Raúl joyful relief after his years of mental and physical pain, but the Church rites remind him of a lifetime of error and threaten him with more punishment. In April, with its parallels of Easter, an Awakening Moon, young animals, and green shoots, the family chooses hope over despair.

Four days after Raúl dies, Mora finds him at her side in memory as she strolls their favorite market. Papá's continued existence is one of the miracles in this "month of miracles" (121). The other is the improving eyesight of Aunt Chole, who physically has been almost blind for years. Always capable of "seeing" by means of her unerring intuition, Aunt Chole has communicated equally well with birds, children, and spirits. She has forced people to read to her or describe what she can't see; and in return, she has told them what they don't see, don't notice, or don't remember. With other family elders, mostly women, she has spun out the family history, adding the detail, nuance, and depth of long memory. Still, she and the family rejoice in her better sight. Her physical improvement, like Raúl's sudden spiritual presence, is an expression of rebirth, of seeing once more and in a new way.

May to September provides a long season of growth. In the garden cycle, it necessitates "endless, endless watering" (156), a duty echoed in the ministry of Christ as related during Catholic Ordinary Time. Mora examines the cultural and racial biases practiced against the Moras, as well as some practiced by them. Such stories lead Mora to wonder if her own children "want to push away their names or skin or accent or family or weight or home or language with one hand while they long to clutch tight to the familiar with the other" (181). Suddenly she realizes how deeply European her family is, in both its religion and its names. She asks, "Where are the . . . non-Christian songs—chants for rain, corn-growing songs, sunrising songs? . . . What are the names of Indian women and men, part of this family, who sang the songs?" (156). They are lost to *el olvido*. The garden of memory withers without care.

In early autumn, the family lingers for gentler stories. The liturgical year dallies, too, delaying the contemplation of death and darkness until early November. During this golden interlude, Mora tells of Mamá Cleta's charming spirit party for Saint Rafael, Our Lady of Guadalupe, and all the rest of her favorite spirits. All of them attend, of course; such camaraderie persists between the house and its heavenly darlings. The Virgin even searches her pockets for seeds for the parrot. When Jesus shows up in the form of the Holy Child of Atocha, the Virgin gathers him onto her lap and fusses over his manners and the little shoes he has worn thin on "His errands of mercy" (231). Mora's tone is wistful as she recounts these friendly modifications of the austere Mary and Jesus of Catholicism. Such adaptations have long sustained her family.

Parties for the departed appear again in November, but then they have a more somber tone. In family Day of the Dead celebrations, the women entice the spirits back for a visit, even if they will come for only one night:

> We sprinkle sand from the Chihuahua desert on the floor to create a desert garden around a series of small altars to family who have died. . . . We scatter marigold petals, creating a path from the front gate, through the front courtyard, to the house and garden gates, down the worn tile of the *portal* [entrance hall] to the *altares* [altars] . . . (255)

This sensual invitation to rejoin the living includes the tang of crushed marigolds, the taste of sugar skulls and *pan de muerto,* the touch of familiar sand and tile, the noise of the gathered living, and the quiet flicker of dozens of candles. And the family spirits do gather. Later, she and her children both greet them and return them to their invisible realm by floating lighted candles on the Río Grande, one starlike flame for each person recalled.

Contemplating the family spirits amid the memories, folk tales, *mole,* and *pan dulce,* Mora wonders if the dead are sympathetic. According to her Aunt Lobo, who as an educated, celibate woman is as powerful as a priestess in the family, these spirits offer advice about adaptation, a skill which Aunt Lobo calls "the generational pattern for women and the dark-skinned and the poor" (22). Perhaps, Mora speculates, these spirits "rub the shoulders of those who cry for them"; perhaps they inform the living that "the universe is more than matter" (263). Giving her spirit relatives appropriate spirit gifts and bidding their lights good-bye on the Río Grande, she marks the end of her year. She is ready for another advent, another preparation to renew the cycle. She is wiser than before, and wise enough to know that she will learn still more if she listens again.

Having gone full cycle, *House of Houses* culminates with "December" and Advent. Again, the emphasis is on gathering the family, on sharing stories, on expanding the traditions, and on anticipating future generations. During their rituals, Grandma Lito reminds them, "The seasons should be respected and savored for what they bring, just as we savor the liturgical seasons, *el año liturgico,* like Advent, these four weeks of anticipation" (276). Comparing the season to the frozen garden, she asserts that "the family needs to hear and feel *algo alegre, algo de esperanza*" [something happy, something hopeful] (281).

Mora agrees. The memory year has renewed her belief in the importance of family solidarity. Furthermore, it has proven her earlier impression that, like the Holy Family of Catholic tradition, her family "is a holy body too, crazy, but holy" (43). Its blessings comfort her, dispelling her fear that she has lost her heritage through neglect. Although she has abandoned the practice of her religion, at Christmas she gravitates toward the planning, cutting, baking, and storytelling that precede the holiday. Another myth she dispels is the ability to eradicate one's heritage. Almost unconsciously, she continues to fill at least part of the role social scientist Ana María Díaz-Stevens attributes to the Latin American Catholic woman: helping the community prepare for liturgical and agricultural festivals. When she insists that her children help arrange the hodgepodge of figures the family has collected over the years for its manger scene, she is handing them the shapes, the textures, and the communal nature of their own heritage. When she involves them in family ritual, she gives them over to the older women of the family, who pass on the prayers and religious stories she herself has neglected.

In "December," as in the rest of *House of Houses,* Mora's recursive style allows her to revalue her family's space in Mexican and U.S. history, culture, and religion. The family story is one of years, moons, seasons, and births-deaths-rebirths. Information flows through generations of linked females just as the Río Grande flows through their history. The timeless river protected her family from Pancho Villa and severed them from Mexican nationality; but more than that, it provided the very substance of the family's adobe house. This house, in turn, is her metaphor for the place, the body, the spirituality, and the memory of her inner landscape. The family, too, is timeless. Its rhythms can parallel agricultural and liturgical calendars. Its members can celebrate together even if some no longer say the prayers when they are apart. They can rub elbows with deities and saints, can stroll beside their dead and receive guidance from them. The only failing is *el olvido.* If the family layers its past, its heritage, its landscape, its *memory,* it will build and maintain a house of comfort and belonging.

NOTES

1. Although the heavy influence of Catholicism in Latino spirituality is generally acknowledged, both Catholic theologians and specialists on Latino cultures recognize that the Catholicism of Latino peoples differs from the mainstream U.S. version of the religion. It draws upon two millennia of Mesoamerindian spiritual beliefs; from multiple centuries of official and popular versions practiced by the Spanish in the vast Americas; from centuries of the spiritism of Africa, Europe, and the Antillean Caribbean; from decades of Latin American liberation theology; and recently, from *mujerista* theology. This spirituality is "popular" or "folk" in the same way music, art, dance, and even psychology may be: that is, it holds comfort and value for that undefined group called "the common folk" or "the people."

2. Some current leaders of Catholic Church ministries for U.S. Hispanics acknowledge this persistence of Catholic identity even in the absence of Catholic practice. Davis finds this tenacity akin to the concept of *mestizo,* or mixed blood, and relates it to the "exuberant acceptance of ambiguity" that he identifies in U.S. Latina/o expression (112).

Works Cited

Davis, Kenneth G. "Still Gringo After All These Years." *Bridging Boundaries: The Pastoral Care of U.S. Hispanics.* Ed. Kenneth G. Davis, O. F. M. Conv., and Yolanda Tarango. Scranton PA: University of Scranton Press, 2000. 107–115.

Díaz-Stevens, Ana María. "Latinas and the Church." *Hispanic Catholic Culture in the U.S.: Issues and Concerns.* Ed. Jay P. Dolan and Allan Figueroa Deck, S.J. Notre Dame IN: University of Notre Dame Press, 1994. 240–277.

Mora, Pat. *House of Houses.* Boston: Beacon Press, 1997.

———. "Interview with Pat Mora." By Elisabeth Mermann-Jozwiak and Nancy Sullivan. *MELUS* 28.2 (2003): 139–150.

Further Reading about Latino Spirituality

Anzaldúa, Gloria. *Borderlands/La Frontera: The New Mestiza.* San Francisco: Aunt Lute Books, 1987.

Castillo, Ana. *Massacre of the Dreamers: Essays on Xicanisma.* New York: Plume, 1995.

———, ed. *Goddess of the Americas: Writings on the Virgin of Guadalupe.* New York: Riverhead, 1996.

Christian, Barbara Marie. *Folk Catholicism in the Works of Six U.S. Latina Writers.* Dissertation. ProQuest Information and Learning, 2000.

Davis, Kenneth G., O. F. M., Conv., and Yolanda Tarango. *Bridging Boundaries: The Pastoral Care of U.S. Hispanics.* Scranton PA: University of Scranton Press, 2000.

Dolan, Jay P., and Allan Figueroa Deck, S.J., eds. *Hispanic Catholic Culture in the U.S.: Issues and Concerns.* Notre Dame IN: University of Notre Dame Press, 1994.

Isasi-Díaz, Ada María, and Yolanda Tarango. *Hispanic Women: Prophetic Voice in the Church.* 1988. Minneapolis: Fortress Press, 1992.

FIONA MILLS

Living "In Between": The Identification of Afro-Latino/a Literature

I'd like to be able to deal with the whole American continent in my fiction—the whole Americas—and to write imaginatively of blacks anywhere/everywhere.

Gayl Jones[1]

Ethnicity is thus constantly being invented anew in contemporary America

Werner Sollors[2]

1. Introduction. Crossing Cultures, Crossing Boundaries

A few years back, I attended the College Language Association Conference during which I joined a roundtable discussion entitled "Teaching Afro-Hispanic Literature at Historically Black Colleges". While the participants in this discussion were all very knowledgeable about their subject matter and pedagogical issues in general, their dialogue centered solely on teaching Afro-Hispanic literature; namely texts written in Spanish that implicitly or explicitly depicted the experiences of blacks.[3] Although that was the title of the roundtable, and hence I should not have been disappointed by their conversation, something really puzzled me—namely, the absence of any consideration for Anglophone texts written by U.S.-based authors that presented cross-cultural exchanges between African Americans and Latino/as. When

Anglistik und Englischunterricht, Volume 66 (2005): pp. 33–55. Copyright © 2005 Universitätsverlag WINTER GmbH.

I broached this subject, no-one seemed to know what to say as they had given little if no consideration to the existence of what I termed 'Afro-Latino/a' literature. One professor was willing to concede the sociological usefulness of this term given the existence of persons who identify themselves as in between the traditionally disparate ethnoracial[4] categories of African American and Hispanic or Latino/a; for example, as 'Afro-Dominicano' or 'Afro-Caribbean'. When I pushed the subject matter a little farther, I was quickly dismissed as suggesting an insubstantial area of study. I mention this anecdote not as an attempt to criticize those panel members who were resistant to my inquiry; rather, this experience exemplifies the kind of palpable resistance I have encountered all too often while attempting to bring this area of research to light. This resistance, I believe, literally signifies the efforts of those within and without the academy to keep the disciplines of African American and Latino/a literature separate, whether consciously or unconsciously. It is within this context that my project has emerged: borne of a desire to transgress these traditional boundaries in an effort to open up spaces of cross-cultural exchange within the field of multi-ethnic American literary study.

Until recently, most scholars of African American and Latino/a literature have insisted on keeping African American and Latino/a literary traditions distinct. However, many authors, including Gayl Jones, Ntozake Shange, and Miguel Algarín, have resisted such separation and routinely lay claim to a more complex 'Afro-Latino/a' heritage[5]—one that is neither singularly African American nor Latino/a, but both. Several important literary theorists, including William Luis, Antonia Darder, and Rodolfo Torres, have similarly argued for the breakdown of false barriers between literary and cultural groups in order to better understand the complex relationships among ethnic groups within the United States. My study of the cross-cultural exchanges in Afro-Latino/a literature examines interactions between writers from African American, African, Latin American and American diasporic communities. The underlying concerns of these writers include a critique of U.S. foreign policy and interaction with their island communities (a kind of neo-colonialism), an emphasis on more fluid conceptions of identity, and fusion of African and Latin American peoples and heritages based on shared experiences of discrimination and displacement. A major unifying element of this literature is its emphasis on social change—these authors use their work to protest the oppression of persons of color in the Americas and issue calls for change. Specifically, they argue against oppressive racist, sexist, and classist American ideologies.

I am proposing a new way to read, understand, and interpret African American and Latino/a literature under the rubric of 'Afro-Latino/a Literature' through the examination of the complicated exchanges between these two literary traditions. Recent re-conceptualizations of diaspora have opened up a space in which an examination of the exchanges between African American and Latino/a literatures can occur. Within this diasporic context, various critics contend that ethnoracial identities are naturally fluid and shape-shifting. Thus, it is within the diaspora that new categories of identity emerge as a result of interracial political coalitions between previously disparate groups of people. The term 'Afro-Latino/a' privileges the hybrid nature of these texts and emphasizes the similarities in the ways in which authors from these two groups grapple with issues of nationality and ethnicity. These authors refigure the map of the Americas in order to tell a very different tale about the relationships between persons of color within the United States. Specifically, such authors reveal as yet unheard of histories about the relationships between African American and Latino/a peoples. They, in effect, broaden popular conceptions about these distinctive cultural groups. By using the term 'Afro-Latino/a' rather than 'African American' or 'Latino/a', one can better distinguish the location of such work as in-between traditionally defined African American and Latino/a categories of literature. Consequently, the foregrounding of such interchanges broadens our understanding of both of these categories of literature and the experiences of ethnic persons in the United States. My study, centered on twentieth-century authors of the United States, brings these connections to the foreground through its development of a new understanding and interpretation of African American and Latino/a literature under the classification of 'Afro-Latino/a'. This approach breaks down rigidly constructed borders between both traditions by emphasizing alliances between these American ethnic groups. Accordingly, my study is informed by a concept of culture that does not insist on the purity of tradition but instead emphasizes the similarity of experience, shared suffering, shared need, and shared political mission. Given that this particular categorization of literature has yet to be formally determined, part of the aim of this study is to define this nascent literary discipline and make a case for the importance of its incorporation into the study of American literature.

Both African American and Latino/a authors grapple with the task of establishing identity and claiming citizenship within the United States in their writing. These texts often focus on the hardship of attempting to forge identity in the face of oppression and injustice. This common effort links African American and Latino/a literature since authors from one particular cultural background invoke those from the other as rhetorical figures. For example, many Chicana and Latina authors make specific references to radical and political African American women writers, including Audre Lorde and Angela Davis, in their works. Writers such as Cherríe Moraga and Gloria Anzaldúa credit these writers as 'paving the way' for them as radical women writers of color. Additionally, U.S.-based Latino/a writers, including Piri Thomas, Rosario Morales and Victor Hernández Cruz, have increasingly laid claim to an African heritage in order to define themselves in opposition to Anglo-Americans. Similarly, African American writers, including Langston Hughes, Gayl Jones and Ntozake Shange, have declared ties to Latin America in their work. Both groups of writers collectively articulate a much more complex understanding of identity and citizenship within the United States than most critical and popular ideologies have allowed for. They argue, implicitly and explicitly, for the breakdown of barriers between these American ethnic groups. My project explores the basis for this argument and examines the attempts of both African American and Latino/a writers to forge successful alliances between these ostensibly disparate groups. Given the importance of such connections, my project ultimately argues for the recognition and establishment of Afro-Latino/a literature within the academy. Since the writers have explicitly politicized Afro-Latino/a literature, the teaching of that literature is inherently politicized. Consequently, if we teach African American and Latino/a literatures as two distinctly separate literary traditions, then our politics are interfering with those of the writers.

2. New Notions of Diaspora. Movement, Geography and the Creation of Transracial Identifications

Since the 1980s, new understandings of diaspora have begun to emerge— ones that move beyond established perceptions of the African diaspora to encompass the experiences of Latino/a and Afro-Latino/a peoples displaced from their island homelands and living abroad in the United States. New visions of diaspora that move beyond traditional conceptions of African diaspora include examinations of the diasporic island homelands of Puerto Ricans, Dominicans, and, in particular, Cubans. In their essay "Introduction. Latinos and Society. Culture, Politics, and Class" Latino/a critics Antonia Darder and Rodolfo D. Torres underscore the importance of reconceptualizations of diaspora to incorporate the experiences of Latino/a peoples with their assertion that "[w]hile paradigms founded on the notion of the diaspora have been quite abundant in the writings of African Americans, it is only recently that it has begun to emerge more consistently in the literature on Cubans and Puerto Ricans in the United States".[6] Their discussion of the importance of the concept of diaspora in regards to Latino/a peoples implicitly emphasizes the significance of geography and movement in the formation of inter-ethnoracial exchanges and identities: "the conditions faced by members of diaspora communities toss them into interactions with organizations which force them into constant negotiation of their identities and new ways of thinking about multiple identities".[7] These contentions relate back to Hall's arguments about the implicit fluidity inherent in identities formed within the diaspora. Darder and Torres acknowledge the influence of Hall's understanding of diasporic identity by stating that

[a] critical definition of 'ethnicity' is also of vital concern to diasporan scholars, particularly those who are rethinking notions of Puerto Rican, Cuban and Dominican identities here and in the homeland [. . .]. But the assumption that seems most promising to a radical politics of diaspora is the notion that ethnicity is "a mobile and unstable identity which contains many possibilities, including that of becoming a diaspora" (Toloyan, 1996: 27) [. . . W]e can draw from the work of Hall (1990) who argues that a critical notion of ethnicity is required in order to 'position' the discourse of racialized populations within particular histories related to the structure of class formations, regional origins, and cultural traditions [. . .]. As scholars attempt to move away from a language of 'race' and the common practice of negating the multiplicity of Latino identities, critically rethinking the category of ethnicity comes to the forefront as an important intellectual and political project.[8]

Darder and Torres connect the ways in which history, geography, and movement underscore the creation of ethnoracial identities within the diaspora. The instability inherent in identities formed in the diaspora allows for the formation of inter-ethnoracial alliances and the development of new types of cross-ethnoracial exchanges—hence, as they state, the category of ethnicity necessarily must be re-evaluated. Such understandings allow scholars to move beyond static notions of race to embrace more multiplicitous renderings of identity within and without traditional United States borders. The diaspora is also an important concept in understanding this new category of literature since it is within this space of cultural exchange and identity formation that interactions across customary ethnoracial and national borders often occur which, in turn, give rise to the development of new ethnoracial identities such as 'Afro-Latino/a'.

3. Nationhood, Imagined Communities, and Fictive Kinships.
Forging Cross-Cultural Connections

In relation to issues of diaspora and the formation of Afro-Latino/a identifications, questions of community, kinship and nationality remain central in the work of both African American and Latino/a writers. Working within Benedict Anderson's theory of 'imagined communities',[9] I contend that, as African American and Latino/a communities in the United States merge, there arises a new 'Afro-Latino/a' community based on shared ideological concepts and experiences rather than on shared nationality. In his book *Beyond Ethnicity. Consent and Descent in American Culture*, Sollors purports to draw upon "more recent conceptualizations of kinship and ethnicity [. . .] and look[s] at the ways in which symbolic ethnicity and a sense of natural kinship that weld

Americans into one people were *created*".[10] In my assertion of the formation
of inter-ethnic alliances between African American and Latino/a persons,
I am building upon Sollors's allusion to the creation of a 'symbolic kinship'.
Although the writers I am working with all acknowledge the existence of
cultural traits and traditions unique to each ethnoracial community, they
also insist upon the creation of inter-ethnic alliances, such as I am terming
'Afro-Latino/a', on the basis of shared experiences of oppression, a working-
class ideology, emphasis on speaking from and for 'the people', i.e., those
average, regular folks on the streets, a desire to offer cultural alternatives to
assimilation, and to express anger and outrage at the existence of oppressive ideologies.[11] My examination of the collective work of various authors
of African American and Latino/a ethnoracial backgrounds that addresses
such topics and is marked by this aesthetic supports my contention of the
existence of an identifiable body of Afro-Latino/a literature.

Theories of fictive kinship are particularly useful in supporting my decision to link together African American and Latino/a communities via their
respective literatures in which these writers espouse similar political ideologies
and shared experiences of racial and gender oppression. In his essay "Racenicity. The Relationship between Racism and Ethnicity" critic Pepi Leistyna
discusses the various applications of the term 'fictive kinship'. He states that

> Signithia Fordham uses the term 'fictive kinship' to describe
> the collective identity that develops among racially subordinated
> groups who are mistreated and segregated in society. She argues
> that this kinship is based on more than just skin color in that
> it also implies "the particular mindset, or world view, of those
> persons . . ." (Fordham 56). George A. DeVos refers to this
> phenomenon as 'ethnic consolidation'.[12]

Working within these definitions of fictive kinship, I contend that many
African American and Latino/a writers forge fictive communities of resistance based on their 'oppositional identities'[13] created in response to their
marginalized status within the U.S. and the subordination that has been
forced upon them by dominant Anglo-American society. Notably, this fictive kinship is most often expressed by Latino/a writers who identify with
African American writers and activists and cite specific influences in their
work. Sollors also acknowledges the formation of fictive communities and
summarizes the ways in which American ethnoracial groups have created
symbolic kinships via their use of the language of consent and descent:

> The intricate ways persist in which a sense of kinship has been
> created by such elements as boundary-constructing antithesis,

biblically derived constructions of chosen peoplehood, mixed rhetoric of melting pots, naturalization of love as a ligament, curses and blessings by adoptive ancestors, symbolic tensions of parent and spouse figures, regionalist ethics, and generational thinking. The language of consent and descent has been flexibly adapted to the most diverse kinds of ends and has amazingly helped to create a sense of Americanness among the heterogenous inhabitants of this country.[14]

As he suggests, ethnoracial groups in the United States have often re-configured their ethnic and racial status through the creation of inter-ethnic and inter-racial alliances based on various linguistic modes of consent in order to gain greater access to political and socio-economic resources. Sollors takes the purpose of these inter-ethnoracial alliances one step further with his assertion that such coalitions allow persons from various ethnic and racial backgrounds access to an American identity through their interaction with older, more established ethnic American communities. His argument is particularly relevant in regard to the ways in which some Latino/as, in particular Evelio Grillo and Piri Thomas, have integrated into African American communities as a means of acquir-ing acceptance and success in larger Anglo-American society.[15]

4. The Politics of Resistance in the Formation of Afro-Latino/a Literature. The Civil Rights Movements, Historical Context, and Time Frames

The 1960s and 1970s are particularly important time periods in which to begin my examination of Afro-Latino/a literature. It was during this era that both African American and Latino/a literatures began to gain promi-nence within the academy. There also existed a close connection between the Black Arts and Black Power Movements of the 1960s and the Chicano Rights Movement of the 1970s. In some sense, it could be argued that the Black Arts and Black Power Movements set the stage for the later Chi-cano Rights Movement. Additionally, similar to the rise in publication and popularity of African American female writers, there has been a gradual emergence of Chicana authors, although on a much smaller scale, since the 1970s and, in the last decade or so, they have become increasingly popular. Due, in part, to the influence of womanist African American female writ-ers, including Alice Walker, Audre Lorde, and Gayl Jones, Latina authors, such as Gloria Anzaldúa and Cherríe Moraga, likewise have incorporated strong feminist characters in their work who counter sexism within both Latino and Anglo societies. This leads to my final reason for locating this study within a relatively contemporary time frame, that is, the emergence of an identifiable Afro-Latino/a literature since the late 1970s.[16] Accordingly, my interest in exploring connections between African American and Latina writers under the rubric of 'Afro-Latino/a literature' necessitates that I limit my study to the last three decades.

Historical Connections

Although I am limiting this study to a contemporary time frame, there exist many historical alliances between numerous African American writers and Latino/a literature and culture and vice versa. Perhaps one of the earliest expressed connections between African American and Latino/a writers was that of African American author Martin Delaney's professed admiration for the Cuban poet Placído, who also appeared in his nineteenth-century novel *Blake, or the Huts of America. A Tale of the Mississippi Valley, the Southern United States and Cuba.* The figure of Arthur A. Schomburg (Arturo A. Schomburg), founder of the famed Schomburg Center for Research in Black Culture, also demonstrates significant links between African American and Latino/a communities. Although Schomburg has long been admired and revered for his pioneering research as a world-renowned owner and purveyor of one of the world's largest collections of African American books, prints and artifacts, as well as a prominent supporter and promoter of African American artists during the Harlem Renaissance, little has been written about his Latino/a heritage or his labor on behalf of working-class Puerto Rican communities within the United States.[17] Initially, Schomburg, born in Puerto Rico as the son of a mestizo German father and a freed black mother, was involved in political movements throughout the Caribbean, including Puerto Rico, Haiti and Cuba.[18] Once he had moved to the U.S., he quickly involved himself in advancing the plight of Puerto Rican and Cuban working-class communities in New York City. However, after visiting New Orleans and coming into contact with the African American community there, Schomburg shifted his allegiance to the black community and went on to make the aforementioned contributions to the research and preservation of African American culture.[19] As demonstrated, Schomburg readily made the transition from labor activism in the Latino/a community to cultural activism in the African American community, which suggests that he saw a logical connection between these two kinds of work. Schomburg's shift of allegiance demonstrates the overlapping concerns of both African American and Latino/a communities in response to socio-economic circumstances in the United States. Both of these communities have engaged in the use of minority culture as forms of political resistance. The case of Arturo/Arthur Schomburg and his move from Latino/a labor activism to African American cultural activism is especially relevant to this study because it exemplifies the symbolic and historical appeal of African

American culture to those involved in minority activism in the United States. Schomburg's actions underscore the inherently political nature of the term 'Afro-Latino/a' through their demonstration of the power of an African American political identification. Additionally, an examination of the trajectory of Schomburg's political and cultural work reveals the Latino/a community's historic efforts to draw upon this force. The purpose of my 'uncovering' of Schomburg's Latino/a heritage and his work on behalf of that community, within the U.S. and the Caribbean, is not to lessen his contributions to the African American community, as might be feared by some African Americanist scholars, but to demonstrate alliances between these two communities. Such an act of recovery broadens our understanding of Schomburg's work and depicts him in a more complex light. Although some critics may decry such work as undercutting the purity of Schomburg's status as a preeminent figure in African American literature and culture, I would argue that it is imperative to understand aspects of Schomburg's heritage and affiliations in order to fully appreciate his work.

James Weldon Johnson, another early scholar and writer in the field of African American literature, also explicated significant links between Latin American and African American writers in his seminal work *The Book of Negro Poetry*. In the preface to this work, Johnson discusses the overlaps between various Negro and Latin American 'colored' poets. He focuses particular attention on Latin American writers of African descent such as the Brazilian poet Machado de Assís and the Cuban poet Plácido and places them on a par with the great African American poet Paul Laurence Dunbar. Significantly, Johnson proclaims that Latin American poets of African descent are superior to Negro writers in the United States because they do not have to contend with the racism and oppression rampant in U.S. society and "can voice the national spirit without any reservations".[20] He also makes the prescient prediction that the first world-renowned Negro poet will be Latin American.[21] As these remarks suggest, Johnson affirmed connections between Latin American and African American writers and implicitly advocated forging links between these two groups in the future. Unfortunately, his remarks went unheeded as the consideration and validation of such connections is just now slowly beginning.

As previously mentioned, although it is hard to find definitive texts within the field of African American writers that proclaim themselves to be creating 'Afro-Latino/a' literature, numerous African American authors have professed affiliations with the Latino/a community and expressed such connections in their work. Some of these writers also were and/or are politically involved with the Latino/a community. Perhaps one of the best-known cases is the relationship between Langston Hughes and Cuban poet Nicolás Guillén in the 1940s. These authors were enamored of one another's work and visited each other on several occasions. There are also documented ties between Marcus Garvey and Claude McKay, Afro-Caribbean writers and activists, and larger Caribbean and Latino/a countries.[22] Amiri Baraka is another African American author who has not only been politically involved in the Latino/a community, primarily in his hometown of Newark, New Jersey and elsewhere, but has acknowledged that Latino/a writers and activists have impacted the development of his writing[23] and has been very involved in Miguel Algarín's Nuyorican Poets Café. Other African American writers demonstrate ties to the Latino/a community in their work, including Wanda Coleman, Rita Dove, Zora Neale Hurston, Sonia Sanchez, Ntozake Shange, and Jay Wright. Artists such as Hurston, Hughes, and Sanchez have spent time in Latin American countries and Mexico and have linked their struggles against oppression as African Americans to that of Latino/as. For example, Lorde not only spent time in Mexico (about which she writes in her 1982 biomythography *Zami. A New Spelling of My Name*), but also wrote a short unpublished prose piece, entitled "La Llorona", that centers on a legendary mythic figure (La Llorona) from the Chicano/a community that appears in the work of many Latina writers, including Sandra Cisneros, Ana Castilla, and Yvonne Yarbro-Bejerano. Sonia Sanchez, like Lorde, also has visited various Latin American countries, including Cuba and Central America, and has incorporated the concerns and culture of the Latino/a community in her work. Notably, she acknowledges the influence of Latin American poets Pablo Neruda and Nicolás Guillén on her work. Sanchez has also spoken openly about her interest in the relief of racial and political oppression on an international level, and this commitment is reflected in poems such as "M.I.A.", in which she makes references to the 'disappeared' villagers of El Salvador's repressive government. Poet Rita Dove has also demonstrated a similar commitment to representing the struggles of oppressed people of Latin American descent in her poem "Parsley", written about the murder of hundreds of Haitians who could not correctly pronounce the Spanish word for 'parsley' by Rafael Trujillo, the infamous dictator of the Dominican Republic. Still other African American writers, such as Ntozake Shange and Barbara Smith, have collaborated with Latina authors—most notably in works such as anthologies from the Women of Color Press and the Kitchen Table Press, including the well-known volume *This Bridge Called My Back. Writing by Radical Women of Color*.[24]

The Influence of the Civil Rights Movement

As many critics contend, the 1960s and 1970s were watershed time periods for the establishment of cross-cultural connections between African Americans and Latino/as. In particular, the Black Power Movement of the 1960s and 1970s was especially important in regard to its establishment of race as a means around which political movements could be articulated that later influenced the trajectory of Latino/a nationalism. Just as the Black Power Movement made 'black' a political term, the later Latino/a Civil Rights Movement of the 1970s used 'brown' as a term around which to rally in the struggle to attain political equality and socio-economic resources. Significantly, the decision of Latino/as to use race-based terms instead of ethnic ones denotes the impact of African American models of political resistance upon Latino/a scholarship and activism. Critics Darder and Torres contend that Latino/as shifted from using the term 'ethnicity' to using the term 'race' in the 1960s in an attempt to follow the use of the 'race paradigm' employed by scholars to "address the conditions of African Americans".[25] This switch distanced Latino/as from theories of ethnicity used to understand European ethnic groups and crystallized their identification as 'the brown race'. Such identification "provided a discursively powerful category of struggle and resistance upon which to build in-group identity and cross-group solidarity with African Americans".[26] In her essay "The Fiction of 'Diversity without Oppression'. Race, Ethnicity, Identity, and Power" Margaret L. Andersen concurs by contending that

> [n]ew understandings of ethnicity first surfaced in the aftermath of the Black Power movement of the 1970s. The emergence of Black nationalism in the United States during this period also inspired other similar movements, such as La Raza and the mobilization of Asian American movements with a focus on pan-Asian identity.[27]

Accordingly, Andersen broadens the influence of the Black Power Movement to include its impact on the formation of other political groups around specifically ethnoracial identifications. Critic Acosta-Belén similarly locates the development of a specifically Puerto Rican ethnoracial identity in the United States within the context of the Civil Rights Struggles of the 1960s and 1970s during which time other ethnoracial groups emerged:

> [T]he affirmation of a Puerto Rican identity in the United States, a process similar to that undergone by other ethnoracial minorities such as the Chicano, African-American, and Native American communities, is part of the broader process of multicultural revitalization among ethnic groups in many parts of the world, which had its most sparkling moments during the 1960s and 1970s.[28]

The end product of this multicultural revitalization has led to a critique of the myth of the American 'melting pot' theory. Instead, this has led to the "affirmation of a U.S. society in which diversity, differentiation, and multiethnic interaction constitute its true cultural nucleus".[29] As these critics suggest, the Civil Rights Movement profoundly impacted the shape of Latino/a political struggles. Interestingly, the similarities between the black and Latino/a struggles for civil rights were not always positive as both groups, at times, exhibited negative practices in regard to women in their respective communities. In their essay "Merging Borders. The Remapping of America", critics Acosta-Belén and Carlos E. Santiago discuss the exclusion of Chicanas and Latinas within the Latino/a Civil Rights movement.[30] They compare the efforts of Latina women to enter the political arena to the struggles of African American women within the Black Power and Black Arts Movements who encountered similar sexism. The attempts of these women to combat overwhelming sexism within their respective communities of ethnoracial origin further underscore the significance of this time period in forging links between African Americans and Latino/as.

Afro-Hispanic Literature

The 1960s and 1970s are also particularly relevant time frames when examining the emergence of Afro-Latino/a literature since it was during this period that critical studies of Afro-Hispanic literature first began to be published. Critic Vera M. Kutzinksi carefully delineates the emergence of Afro-Hispanic literature from the early twentieth century up to the 1980s in her essay "Afro-Hispanic American Literature", in which she analyzes some major Afro-Hispanic writers including Nicolás Guillén, Nancy Morejón, and Carlos Guillermo Wilson (Cubena). According to Kutzinski, literary exchanges between African American and Latin American writers and scholars were frequent during the 1960s and 1970s, stemming from political interaction in the Black Power and Civil Rights Movements and the rise in popularity of the Latin American novel. Moreover, several well-known Afro-Hispanic journals, including "Cuadernos Afro-Americanos (Caracas, 1975), Negritud (Bogotá, 1977), Studies in Afro-Hispanic Literature (Purchase, New York, 1977), and the Afro-Hispanic Review (Washington, D.C., 1982, now located in Columbia, Missouri)", were established in the United States at this time as well.[31] During this time period, several Latin American presses reissued classic Afro-Hispanic novels including Juyungo by Adalberto Ortiz. Numerous texts examining the black presence in and black poetry by Hispanic writers were also published.[32] Kutzinski argues for the recognition of an Afro-Hispanic literary canon and contends that Afro-Hispanic writers such as Adalberto Ortiz, Manuel Zapata Olivella, and Placído must appear alongside celebrated ostensibly white authors such as Gabriel García Márquez. The ethnoracial essentialism of the 1960s Black Power Movement also shaped the development of the Afro-Hispanic canon in that the racial identity of authors and the "project[ion of] a unified cultural identity, a kinship based on a shared 'black experience'" were its main concerns.[33]

Several other well-known critics have explored Afro-Hispanic poetry and literature as well as the depiction of blacks in Latin American literature including Richard Jackson in his 1998 book *Black Writers and Latin America. Cross-Cultural Affinities,* Miriam DeCosta Willis in her 1977 collection of essays *Blacks in Hispanic Literature. Critical Essays,* Marvin A. Lewis with his anthology *Afro-Hispanic Poetry 1940–1980. From Slavery to "Negritud" in South American Verse,* and Rosemary Geisdorfer Feal in her essay "Afrohispanic Poets and the 'Policy of the Identity'", to name a few.[34] Thorough as these works may be, their aims differ significantly from my project in that they focus almost exclusively on Spanish-speaking authors and fail to include Anglophone U.S. authors in their examination of Afro-Hispanic literature.[35] Their singular examination of texts written in Spanish necessitates their use of the term 'Afro-Hispanic', thereby emphasizing the Spanish language and Latin American nationality of such authors, in comparison to my use of the term 'Afro-Latino/a' in order to emphasize my project's focus on Anglophone texts written by U.S.-based authors. Consequently, as of yet, little scholarship has been conducted in this emerging field of study. Scholars have considered the Africanist presence in Brazilian, Caribbean, and South American literature as evidenced by studies exploring Afro-Hispanic poetry or examinations of blacks in Brazilian and Latin American literature. However, limited research has focused on either the Latin American presence in African American literature or the Africanist presence in Anglophone Latino/a authors. It is within this tangible gap in literary criticism that my project is situated.

5. Afro-Latino/a Alliances and the Creation of a Resistant Political Ideology

In regards to the terms under which I am bringing together African American and Latino/a literature, I am basing this alliance on shared experiences of oppression, discrimination, under-employment, overrepresentation in the American prison system, similar experiences of displacement from their cultural homelands, shared experiences of poverty, and lower standard of living as non-white peoples in the United States. In short, I link African American and Latino/a literatures on the basis of their similar creations of a literature that resists dominant Anglo-American ideologies that discriminate against persons of color. As far as explicating cross-cultural connections between these two groups beyond the mere fact that they are non-white peoples living in the U.S., I defer to critics Acosta-Belén and Santiago's description of links between non-white peoples in the U.S. They contend that "we find diverse populations bound by a shared legacy of colonialism, racism, displacement, and dispersion".[36] Acosta-Belén makes a similar statement in another essay, "Beyond Island Boundaries. Ethnicity, Gender, and Cultural Revitalization in Nuyorican Literature", in which she professes to "underscore [. . .] the 'anti-Establishment' character of this literature and its commitment to denouncing inequality and injustice in U.S. society and as a consciousness-raising tool for promoting social change among the writers' respective communities".[37] Acosta-Belén and Santiago emphasize the politically radical component underlying Latino/a literature based on the desire of these authors to counter destructive ideologies in mainstream Anglo-American society. I contend that contemporary African American literature is also marked by a similarly radical political aesthetic in its depictions of the struggles of black Americans within an oppressive United States.

Female Authors and the Creation
of a Specifically Afra-Latina Literary Aesthetic

At times, women within both African American and Latino/a communities have expressed a greater willingness to address issues of racism, sexism, and classism in their writings in comparison to the male writers in those same communities. Female writers have also been more willing to espouse the formation of cross-cultural alliances between these two ethnoracial groups based on their collective efforts to identify and denounce oppressive Anglo-American ideologies. Several critics have acknowledged the politicism underlying Latina texts. For example, Darder and Torres assert that "Edna Acosta-Belén (1992) documents in her work the emergence of a literary cultural discourse among Latina writers that moved beyond national origins and more inclusively addressed issues of class position, sexual orientations, and racialized relations".[38] Furthermore, they refer to the groundbreaking anthology *This Bridge Called My Back. Writings by Radical Women of Color* that demonstrated that "Latina, African American, Asian, and Native American women were not only collectively challenging the language, style, and discourse of the patriarchy, they were actively involved in counter-hegemonic activities that would open up political spaces where their particular issues and struggles would never again remain silent." [39] As Darder and Torres contend, the willingness of female authors from myriad ethnoracial backgrounds to openly acknowledge and criticize ideological ills within and without their respective cultures of origin effectively put an end to the silence that had previously surrounded such issues. They, in effect, paved the way for future politically radical texts to be written. An important distinction to note, though, is that my analysis here is specific to women writers from African American and Latina communities and not just about women of color writers in general. However, at times, my project does build upon previous critical examinations of women of color writers in general. It is about women of color uniting in general, and it is also about the unique unification of women from African American and Latina communities. In a sense, my examination of alliances between African American and Latina female authors is the same yet different than that which has been done before.

The foregrounding of a mixed American ethnoracial heritage is at the root of a radical political ideology espoused by many women writers of both African American and Latina descent. They argue for women of color to unite across racial and ethnic borders in order to eradicate racial and sexual oppression. Although these writers insist upon the unification of women of color, they also advocate the simultaneous maintenance of ethnoracial distinctions. The purpose is *not* to privilege one ethnoracial group over the other, but, instead, to embrace all groups in the struggle for equality as women and, more specifically, as women of color. Such an alliance between women of color is complex for, in the coming together, there must also be deep-seated respect for unique ethnoracial attributes of each woman. This is most specifically not a project of assimilation, as is often the case with multicultural endeavors. Although these writers call for cross-ethnoracial alliances to be forged, they do not advocate the privileging of one specific ethnoracial group over the other. Instead, they propose the recognition of shared similarities, including legacies of racial and gendered oppression, a female-based spirituality grounded in an African heritage, a privileging of an inclusive, communal perspective that opposes traditional Western systems of rationality, and an oppositional stance towards Anglo-American capitalism and imperialism. Activism is also an integral aspect of an Afra-Latina perspective. It is grounded in the belief that women of color must collectively unite in order to combat pervasive racism and sexism that threatens to destroy them. Within this perspective is a fervent call for women of color to unite across traditional ethnoracial divides in order to effect social change within and without the United States. African American and Latina women are urged to bond across shared stories of struggle in order to access a collectively greater power. Through the recognition of these similar experiences and beliefs, African American and Latina women of color can join together and form a stronger collective base of power from which they can work to oppose destructive racist and sexist ideologies. Consequently, these articulations are central to the creation of an Afra-Latina political ideology in that the texts, themselves, are calls to action—they demand that their readers acknowledge the racial and sexual oppression experienced by women of color. The articulation and subsequent recognition of such oppression is essential to its eradication.[40]

The alignment between African American and Latina women, which I am identifying as a specifically Afra-Latina political perspective, is grounded in a borderlands ideology as explicated by Anzaldúa's theory of a '*mestiza* consciousness'. According to Anzaldúa, this new mestiza consciousness, *una conciencia de mujer,* is "a consciousness of the Borderlands".[41] This consciousness is marked most specifically by its embrace of a cultural 'in-betweenness'. Anzaldúa contends that this includes an oppositional stance towards Western rationality in favor of "divergent thinking, characterized by movement away from set patterns and goals and toward a more whole perspective, one that *includes* rather than excludes".[42] As such, this consciousness privileges inclusivity, as can be seen in the writings of the authors examined in this chapter as they embrace both African and Latino/a heritages in their work. Bridges must be built, in the words of the editors of the seminal text *This Bridge Called My Back. Writings by Radical Women of Color,* in order to make this world a better place for women, in general, and for women of color, in particular. The future belongs to those who are willing to embrace a more complex, hybrid identity, according to Anzaldúa, who contends that "the future depends on the breaking down of paradigms, it depends on the straddling of two or more cultures".[43] Embracing an 'Afra-Latina' perspective, one that privileges both African American and Latino/a cultures, exemplifies Anzaldúa's charge that, in the future, one must be willing to embrace a multiplicity of cultures.[44] Significantly, Anzaldúa maintains that in order for Chicana/o peoples to move forward, they must "know our Indian lineage, our afro-*mestizaje,* our history of resistance".[45] This 'afro-*mestizaje*' of which Anzaldúa speaks is similar in theory to an Afra-Latina ideology due to its recognition of a hybrid ethnoracial category that encompasses African, Indian, and Latino/a cultures. For Anzaldúa, this borderlands ideology, although feminist at its core, is all-encompassing, and she proclaims that, in order to overcome prejudice that oppresses and divides, "we can no longer [. . .] disown the white parts, the male parts, the pathological parts, the queer parts, the vulnerable parts".[46] Instead, all components of a person, be they Mexican, Chicano/a, Anglo, African, queer, male, female, etc., must be embraced in order to achieve a healing wholeness in opposition to divisive racial and sexual oppression. According to Anzaldúa this way is "the *mestiza* way, the Chicano way, the woman way".[47] Building upon Anzaldúa's mestiza/borderlands theory, I argue that women writers of African American and Latina descent call for alliances across ethnoracial divides in an embrace of an ideology that can be specifically identified as Afra-Latina.

6. Conclusion. Living 'In Between'

Afro-Latino/a literature is emerging as an extremely relevant field of study when examining texts written by African American and Latino/a authors. To date, the term 'Afro-Latino/a' possesses marginal status and has not yet gained a wide audience. However, given the similarities in themes, political concerns and writing styles among writers of African American and Latino/a literature, this categorization proves to be very useful. Notably, when discussing both African American and Latino/a literature, critics and scholars often point to the cross-cultural components of both fields given their diasporic roots. Accordingly, the examination of similar concerns and characteristics shared by these literatures is not a new thing. The willingness of various Latino/a authors to use the term 'Afro-Latino/a' to describe their work testifies to this fact. Curiously enough, though, the category of Afro-Latino/a literature has yet to gain sufficient currency within the field of American literature. In my initial exploration of this term, I found that numerous Latino/a authors, including Rosario Morales, Victor Hernández Cruz, Sandra María Estevez, Tato Laviera, Piri Thomas, and Cecilia Rodriguez Milanés, repeatedly emphasized their African origins and/or readily acknowledged their incorporation of African mythology and culture in their writing. On the contrary, African American writers less readily acknowledge and/or deliberately incorporate Latino/a mythology or culture in their work. Perhaps due to the disjuncture in regard to the willingness of these two groups to acknowledge common cultural values and heritage as well as shared political concerns and themes, the category of Afro-Latino/a literature has yet to be fully established and stands as a field ripe for literary exploration and study.

In addition to work that centers on a non-fictional examination of the connections between African American and Latino/a communities, many Latino/a writers incorporate African mythology and culture in their work. This is best exemplified in the work of numerous Latino/a poets, including Morales, Laviera, Hernández Cruz, and Estevez. Significantly, several of these writers, including Laviera, Hernández Cruz, and Estevez, refer to their poetry as either 'Afro-Latin' or 'Afro-Caribbean'. The work of Cruz, for example, focuses on a wide range of multicultural and multiracial themes. Notably, one of his most anthologized poems, "African Things", is a tribute to the African spirits of his maternal ancestors. Although he is Puerto Rican, in this poem, he claims that being Puerto Rican "is all about the Indios & you better believe it the African things". The poem ends with him invoking his "black & shiny grandmother" to tell him about his African roots.[48] Poet and playwright Estevez foregrounds her Puerto Rican/African/ Caribbean heritage in a similar vein. This is exemplified in her poem "From Fanon" in which she describes the enslavement of non-white peoples in the diaspora by "europeans thru power and fear". She laments that "as slaves we lost identity / assimilating our master's shadows".[49] As such, she unites the struggles of all enslaved peoples, most notably those of African descent. In her poem "It Is Raining Today", Estevez acknowledges the multiplicitous ethnoracial backgrounds of Puerto Ricans with her reference to their "Taino, Arawak, Caribe, Ife, Congo, Angola, Mesa/Mandinko, Dahome, Amer, African" ancestors.[50] Lastly, in her work *Getting Home Alive*, writer Morales includes a poem entitled "Africa" in which she asserts Africa as the source of her cultural roots. With the statement "Though my roots reach into the soil of two Americas, / Africa waters my tree" she insists that, although she is a Puerto Rican born in the United States (the 'two Americas'), Africa is the ultimate source of her cultural heritage.[51]

I use the term 'Afro-Latino/a' to underscore the in-betweenness of this category of ethnoracial identification in that it equally privileges 'African American' and 'Latino/a' cultures. This term is also intentionally broad in that I use it to refer to persons of myriad ethnoracial backgrounds including African American, Latino/a, Chicano/a, Afro-Caribbean, etc., to name a few. This term also refers to both male and female authors—hence, my decision to use 'Afro-Latino/a' instead of the masculinist term 'Afro-Latino'. The deliberate inclusiveness of the term Afro-Latino/a implicitly emphasizes the inherent fluidity of ethnoracial identities. In keeping with my disavowal of racial essentialism, this term also underscores the fact that borders are constantly in flux. Try as we might, we simply cannot keep rigid borders between cultural groups. Individual cultures eventually merge to form new ones, such as I am espousing in this study, in various contact zones—for example, in the multicultural neighborhoods of New York City and Los Angeles. The term, thus, represents this type of inter-ethnoracial amalgamation and engenders more complex examinations of ethnoracial identity that take into consideration the multiple ways in which people self-identify across seemingly fixed borders of race, ethnicity, class, and nationality.

In conclusion, I contend that the categories 'African American literature' and 'Latino/a literature' obscure the interchanges between these two literary traditions and fail to accurately describe authors whose work reflects an interest in both of these cultures. Moreover, as previously demonstrated, the category of 'Afro-Latino/a' is a most valuable tool when assessing connections and overlaps between African American and Latino/a literature. The literary examples I have analyzed in this study are but a few of the innumerable links between these two communities. Critics and scholars have just begun to recognize and explore this area. The field is wide open. However, given the disjuncture between some African American and Latino/a writers and scholars in regard to their willingness to acknowledge and embrace shared cultural roots and literary traditions, critical exploration in this field will surely be accompanied by some resistance. One of the ultimate outcomes of this project is to internationalize the African American literary canon and recognize authors who cross traditional literary and cultural borders.

Another significant goal of my study is the project of recovering and/or revealing heretofore untold or ignored stories, since inherent in these texts is the revelation of previously obscured histories of political alliances and connections between African American and Latino/a peoples. Consequently, these authors tell new tales about the Americas. Although the recognition of these connections is a relatively recent phenomenon, in reality, alliances between these two ethnoracial groups have existed for centuries both in the United States and on a much larger global scale (including the Caribbean, Mexico, Latin America, and Africa). Many of these writers reference these historical connections in an attempt to bring them to light in the present and to solidify such alliances for the future. In a sense, they are going back to the past in order to secure the future. In the end, examining texts from an Afro-Latino/a perspective propels scholarly debates about issues of nationality and ethnicity beyond conventional black-white dichotomies in order to render a more comprehensive understanding of the complex histories of African American and Latino/a persons in the United States.

Notes

1. See Rowell.

2. See Sollors (1986:14).

3. Not surprisingly, their discussion kept returning to the work of Richard Jackson—a noted scholar of Afro-Hispanic literature. For example, see Jackson (1998).

4. In regard to my decision to use the term 'ethnoracial' in this article, I am borrowing this term from Latina critic Edna Acosta-Belén as articulated in her essay "Beyond Island Boundaries. Ethnicity, Gender, and Cultural Revitalization in Nuyorican Literature". I prefer to use 'ethnoracial' for its amalgamation of the terms 'ethnicity' and 'race' into one word, thereby symbolizing the inter-connectedness of these terms instead of conventional tendencies to separate the two. See Acosta-Belén (1992: 980). I am also drawing upon the distinctions between these two terms as articulated by Margaret L. Andersen in "The Fiction of 'Diversity Without Oppression'. Race, Ethnicity, Identity, and Power" (1999). Thus, although I personally prefer to use the term 'ethnicity', I have chosen to use the collapsed term 'ethnoracial' because I feel it best references the complicated experiences of both African American and Latino/a persons since both groups have been labeled as 'races', yet they are now often referred to as 'ethnic groups'. Additionally, each group has used each label at one time or another in their struggle for political and socioeconomic equality. However, when referring to cross-cultural connections between African American and Latino/a peoples, I prefer to use the term 'ethnicity' to describe such a group. The term 'ethnicity' makes most sense here because it allows for such connections not on the basis of shared physical characteristics, as the term 'race' does, but on the basis of common experiences of oppression and colonialism and a shared consciousness. Furthermore, ethnicity scholar Werner Sollors similarly addresses the discrepancies between the terms 'race' and 'ethnicity' and contends that 'race' and 'ethnicity' are not separable terms but, in the end, 'ethnicity' takes precedence as 'race' is, according to Sollors, but 'one aspect of ethnicity'. See also Sollors (1986: 39).

5. To date, the term 'Afro-Latino/a' possesses marginal status and has not yet gained a wide audience. However, given the similarities in themes, political concerns and writing styles among writers of African American and Latino/a literature, this categorization proves to be very useful.

6. Darder & Torres (1998:17).

7. *Ibid.*

8. *Ibid.*, 9–10.

9. For a thorough explication of the creation of imagined communities see Anderson (1991).

10. Sollors (1986: 11, emphasis in the original).

11. Significantly, Edna Acosta-Belén describes Nuyorican literature in a similar vein, contending that it emerged out of the Civil Rights Struggles of the 1960s and 1970s and notes the "'anti-Establishment' character of this literature and its commitment to denouncing inequality and injustice in U.S. society and as a consciousness-raising tool for promoting social change among the writers' respective communities" (1992: 980).

12. Leistyna (1998:154).

13. Leistyna goes on to discuss the existence of 'oppositional identities' in accordance with scholar John Ogbu. He states that "John Ogbu makes reference to 'oppositional identities' and 'survival strategies', which he describes as instrumental, expressive, and epistemological responses to cope with subordination and exploitation [. . .]. Both Ogbu (1987) and Fordham (1988) observe that generations pass down this fictive kinship—norms, values, and competencies, and that racially subordinated children thus learn different survival strategies and markers of solidarity from their parents or caregivers and peers." (*Ibid.*)

14. Sollors, (1986: 245).

15. In making the transition to U.S. life (after immigration), many Latino/as initially make contact with the African American community (in particular due to the geographic concentration of ethnic groups within similar locations, i.e. New York City, Los Angeles, Chicago, etc.). According to Werner Sollors, this group often serves as a means of acculturating new immigrants to the American way of life (1986: 17).

16. For a thorough description and delineation of the emergence of this literary category see Kutzinski (1996: 164–194) and DeCosta (1977).

17. In fact, although I have read some of Schomburg's work and have studied about him in several classes on African American literature, it was not until I began researching Afro-Latino/a literature that I learned of Schomburg's Latino/a heritage. Schomburg was born in Puerto Rico and later moved to the United States. His father was German and his mother was of African descent from St. Thomas.

18. For a brief autobiographical overview of Schomburg that underscores his Puerto Rican heritage see Knight (1995).

19. Augenbraum & Fernández Olmos (1997: 159–160).

20. Johnson (1922: 40). It is important to note that Johnson's contention that Latin American poets of African descent were not subjected to the same kinds of racism that African American poets were forced to endure is somewhat naïve and ill-founded. However, Johnson's assertions are in keeping with the common depiction of Latin American and Hispanic countries, such as Cuba and Brazil, as idyllic racial paradises.

21. *Ibid.*

22. Garvey tried unsuccessfully to involve persons of African heritage in Haiti and Cuba to join his 'Back to Africa' movement during the 1930s.

23. See his collection of essays: Baraka (1998).

24. Anzaldúa & Moraga, 1983.

25. Darder & Torres (1998: 9).

26. *Ibid.*

27. Andersen (1999: 9). Here Andersen is referring to Yen Le Espiritu (1992).

28. Acosta-Belén (1992: 986).

29. *Ibid.*

30. They include a brief historical overview of their involvement in various radical movements. See Acosta-Belén & Santiago (1998: 11–14).

31. Kutzinski (1996: 164).

32. *Ibid.*, 164–165.

33. *Ibid.*, 166–167.

34. For other examples of Afro-Hispanic literature see Adams (1998), Birmingham-Pokorny (1993), Birmingham-Pokorny (1994), LaCapra (1991), Miller (1991), Ortiz (1982).

35. Jackson (1998) is the exception to this rule as he includes a brief close reading of U.S. authors Gayl Jones, Audre Lorde, Ntozke Shange, Paula Marshall and Toni Cade Bambara in his discussion.

36. Acosta-Belén & Santiago (1998: 29).

37. Acosta-Belén (1992: 980).

38. Darder & Torres (1998: 13).

39. *Ibid.*, 13-14.

40. I am indebted to Dr. Thomas Fahy for his input in helping me better articulate the theoretical framework for this section.

41. Anzaldúa (1999:99).

42. *Ibid.*, 101 (my emphasis).

43. *Ibid.*, 102.

44. Significantly, Anzaldúa identifies the 'queer' as the person best equipped to cross borders (1999: 106–107).

45. *Ibid.*, 108.

46. *Ibid.*, 110.

47. *Ibid.*, 110.

48. Turner (1991: 30).

49. *Ibid.*, 182.

50. *Ibid.*, 188.

51. Levins Morales & Morales (1986: 55).

Works Cited

Acosta-Belén, Edna: "Beyond Island Boundaries. Ethnicity, Gender, and Cultural Revitalization in Nuyorican Literature", *Callaloo* 15, no. 4, 1992, 979–998.

Acosta-Belén, Edna & Carlos E. Santiago: "Merging Borders. The Remapping of America".—In Antonia Darder & Rodolfo D. Torres (Eds.): *The Latino Studies Reader. Culture, Economy and Society*, Malden, 1998, pp. 29–42.

Adams, Clementine R.: *Common Threads. Themes in Afro-Hispanic Women's Literature*, Miami, 1998.

Andersen, Margaret L.: "The Fiction of 'Diversity without Oppression'. Race, Ethnicity, Identity, and Power".—In Mary L. Kenyatta & Robert H. Tai (Eds.): *Critical Ethnicity. Countering the Waves of Identity Politics*, New York, 1999, pp. 6–12.

Anderson, Benedict: *Imagined Communities. Reflections on the Origins and Spread of Nationalism*, revised edition, New York, 1991.

Anzaldúa, Gloria, & Cherríe Moraga (Eds.): *This Bridge Called My Back. Writings by Radical Women of Color*, second edition, New York, 1983.

Anzaldúa, Gloria: *Borderlands/La Frontera. The New Mestiza*, San Francisco, 1999 [first edition 1987].

Augenbraum, Harold & Margarite Fernández Olmos (Eds.): *The Latino Reader. An American Literary Tradition from 1542 to the Present,* Boston, 1997.

Baraka, Amiri: *Hom. Social Essays,* New York, 1998.

Birmingham-Pokorny, Elba D.: *Denouncement and Reaffirmation of the Afro-Hispanic Identity in Carlos Guillermo Wilson's Works. A Collection of Criticism,* Miami, 1993.

————. *An English Anthology of Afro-Hispanic Writers of the Twentieth Century,* Miami, 1994.

Darder, Antonia, & Rodolfo D. Torres (Eds.): "Introduction. Latinos and Society. Culture, Politics, and Class".—In A.D. & D.R.T. (Eds.): *Latinos and Society. Culture, Politics, and Class,* Malden, 1998, pp. 3–26.

DeCosta, Miriam (Ed.): *Blacks in Hispanic Literature. Critical Essays,* Port Washington, 1977.

Dove, Rita: *Museum. Poems,* Pittsburgh, 1983.

Espiritu, Yen Le: *Asian American Panethnicity. Bridging Institutions and Identities,* Philadelphia, 1992.

Jackson, Richard L.: *Black Writers and Latin America. Cross-Cultural Affinities,* Washington, 1998.

Johnson, James Weldon: *The Book of American Negro Poetry,* New York, 1922.

Knight, Robert: "Arthur 'Afroboriqueño' Schomburg", *Civil Rights Journal* website, 1995, http://www.wbaifree.org/earthwatch/schombrg.html (accessed 17 February 2003).

Kutzinski, Vera M.: "Afro-Hispanic American Literature".—In Roberto Gonález Echevarría & Enrique Pupo-Walker (Eds.): *The Cambridge History of Latin American Literature,* vol. II, Cambridge, 1996, pp. 164–194.

LaCapra, Dominick: *The Bounds of Race. Perspectives on Hegemony and Resistance,* Ithaca, 1991.

Leistyna, Pepi: "Racenicity. The Relationship between Racism and Ethnicity".—In Mary L. Kenyatta & Robert H. Tai (Eds.): *Critical Ethnicity. Countering the Waves of Identity Politics,* New York, 1999, pp. 133–171.

Levins Morales, Aurora & Rosario Morales: *Getting Home Alive,* Ithaca, 1986.

Miller, Ingrid Watson: *Afro-Hispanic Literature. An Anthology of Hispanic Writers of African Ancestry,* Miami, 1991.

Ortiz, Adalberto: *Juyungo. A Classic Afro-Hispanic Novel,* Washington, 1982.

Rowell, Charles: "An Interview with Gayl Jones", *Callaloo* 5, 1982, 32–53.

Sanchez, Sonia: *Homegirls & Handgrenades,* New York, 1984.

Sollors, Werner: *Beyond Ethnicity. Consent and Descent in American Culture,* New York, 1986.

Turner, Faythe (Ed.): *Puerto Rican Writers at Home in the U.S.A.,* Seattle, 1991.

West, Cornel: *Prophetic Reflections. Notes on Race and Power in America. Beyond Eurocentrism and Multiculturalism,* vol. II, Monroe, 1993.

JASON FRYDMAN

Violence, Masculinity, and Upward Mobility in the Dominican Diaspora: Junot Díaz, the Media, and Drown

An interviewer asked Junot Díaz whether it matters "to you at all where they shelve your book in the library or in the bookstore, meaning in what section, whether it's called writers of color, recent fiction, Latino writers, or anything else?" Díaz responded: "I've been fortunate enough to be considered literary fiction. They're so happy to claim me as literature because it makes them all look better. They don't want to relegate me to areas of ethnic studies."[1] Books by minority authors are often seized upon to project a certain image of multicultural America. In this instance, Díaz claims that he has been welcomed into the literary mainstream as a gambit to make "the mainstream, the publishers, everybody" look better.[2] With Díaz on their team, "they" can deflect accusations of being exclusionary, of being uninterested in the plight of Dominican immigrants and its implicit critique of the U.S. status quo. The question remains, however, whether such a celebratory popular and critical reception manages to preserve the challenging moral and artistic vision of the author of immigrant or minority literature. My analysis of Díaz's text calls for an attention to the disjuncture between what the author and his reviewers insist is the book's key site of violence and tension, namely the intersection of English and Spanish, and the alternative sites that *Drown* itself forces upon the reader.

Columbia Journal of American Studies, Volume 8 (Spring 2007): pp. 270–281. Copyright © 2007 Columbia Journal of American Studies.

Published in 1996, *Drown* brought critical and popular acclaim to Junot Díaz. The geography of this short story collection ranges from the capital and countryside of the Dominican Republic to New York City and its New Jersey periphery. The book loosely organizes itself around the consciousness of Yunior, from his childhood in a poor neighborhood of Santo Domingo through to an adolescence of underachievement and petty crime in north-central Jersey.

With its epigraph from a poem of Gustavo Pérez Firmat, *Drown* announces the problematic role of English in telling these stories: "The fact that I / am writing to you / in English / already falsifies what I / wanted to tell you. / My subject: how to explain to you that I / don't belong to English / though I belong nowhere else." The reader may recognize, then, her imminent encounter with a double-falsification. Not only will she be reading fictional narratives, but falsified fictional narratives, narratives diverted from what the author "wanted to tell you" (as if she ever had transparent access to what the author wanted to tell her). Nor does the reader have the comfort of treating this book like a translation from another language: "I don't belong to English / though I belong nowhere else." Instead, the reader is asked to imagine an unsettled linguistic space, an uneasy co-habitation with the English language.

Drown demands a double linguistic consciousness. Unmarked, unglossed Spanish words and phrases are common throughout the book. On the one hand, Díaz attributes this feature of the book to his place in a literary tradition: "I learned to write not from old Dominican texts, but from Cristina García, Sandra Cisneros, Oscar Hijuelos."[3] Latino literary texts by these authors frequently reflect the bilingual world they write from; *Drown* follows the model of its literary forbears and inscribes itself into this tradition. However, Díaz claims that there is another motive at work, as well:

> When I learned English in the States, this was a violent enterprise. And by forcing Spanish back onto English, forcing it to deal with the language it tried to exterminate in me, I've tried to represent a mirror-image of that violence on the page. Call it my revenge on English.[4]

Díaz seems heavily invested in the violence of his code-switching. Violence is a theme that recurs in his interviews and appears to have been decisive for his career and journalists covering it. Bill Buford, author of *Among the Thugs*, a first-hand account of life among English soccer hooligans, tapped Junot Díaz for the *New Yorker* and gets an acknowledgement in the final pages of *Drown*. Ed Morales reports that while playing phone tag with Díaz for a *Village Voice* piece, Díaz left "a joke message about needing to be bailed out of the slammer: 'Yo, Ed, they got me man. You gotta get me outta here!'"[5] Richard Eder begins his *Los Angeles Times* review of *Drown:* "The empire always strikes back," and proceeds to discuss Cromwell's subjugation of Ireland, the French colonization of Algeria, and the African slave trade before locating Díaz in the violent history of U.S. imperial encounters with Mexico, Puerto Rico, and the Dominican Republic.[6]

All things considered, perhaps violence does represent the most apt rubric for discussing the state of multicultural America. Díaz, for example, speaks of his militant campus activism at Rutgers University in support of expanding the Latino studies curriculum. At the Cornell MFA program, when people would ask him if he was a writer, he would respond, "No, I'm a Dominican writer."[7] From Díaz's perspective, immigrant and/or minority identity formation in the United States, like language acquisition, is a violent process:

> You come to the United States and the United States begins immediately, systematically, to erase you in every way, to suppress those things which it considers not digestible. You spend a lot of time being colonized. Then, if you've got the opportunity and the breathing space and the guidance, you immediately—when you realize it—begin to decolonize yourself. And in that process, you relearn names for yourself that you had forgotten.[8]

Richard Eder, among others, reiterates this outlook on the violent state of U.S. diversity; Díaz, he writes:

> depict[s] his fellow Dominicans in their struggling transit between island poverty and a laborious, denaturing effort to make their way here. . . . Our society has become so stratified, so internally isolated by class, color, culture, language and crime, or the fear of it, that today the only news from across the barriers comes from younger Latino, Asian and black novelists and street poets.[9]

Díaz and Eder's statements may accurately reflect a "systematically" "denaturing" U.S. society, but strangely, they do not accurately reflect the world of *Drown.*

Drown does not rehearse the conventional immigrant narrative of assimilation and its attendant anxieties. The boundaries of the Dominican community in the U.S. appear more fluid than, say, the Brooklyn Jewish ghetto of *Call It Sleep* or the Chicago Lithuanian community of *The Jungle.* Of course, *Drown* does depict thoroughly Dominican spaces:

> Everything in Washington Heights is Dominican. You can't go a block without passing a Quisqueya Bakery or a Quisqueya

Supermercado or a Hotel Quisqueya. If I were to park the truck and get out nobody would take me for a deliveryman; I could be the guy who's on the street corner selling Dominican flags. I could be on my way home to my girl. Everybody's on the streets and the merengue's falling out of windows like TVs.[10]

In the world of *Drown*, though, people are not confined to their particular national, ethnic or racial spaces. The very title of "How to Date a Browngirl, Blackgirl, Whitegirl, or Halfie" makes clear the lived diversity represented in the book. "Edison, New Jersey" hilariously navigates New Jersey's class geography, from unpresuming working- and middle-class towns to the rich suburbs of northern New Jersey. The narrator is a pool table deliveryman and assembler. He remarks of his wealthy clientele:

Sometimes the customer has to jet to the store for cat food or a newspaper while we're in the middle of a job. I'm sure you'll be all right, they say. They never sound too sure. Of course, I say. Just show us where the silver's at. The customers ha-ha and we ha-ha and then they agonize over leaving, linger by the front door, trying to memorize everything they own, as if they don't know where to find us, who we work for (122–123).

This passage suggests that we may not live so closed off from one another as Richard Eder would have us believe. There are still interactions, even if they are mediated by economic hierarchies and shot through with class resentment, tension and anxiety. So while "crime, or the fear of it" may erect all sorts of physical and psychological barriers, *Drown* suggests that as long as rich people still need their pool tables delivered and houses cleaned, individuals will witness and circulate "news from across the barriers."

The open-ness of class and race barriers in *Drown*, although by no means utopian, does offer a counterpoint to the outright violence with which Díaz colors his outlook on U.S. society in his interviews. The same could be said of the use of language in the book. As discussed above, Díaz repeatedly highlights the violence of the encounter between Spanish and English, both in his life and in his book. Nonetheless, in an essay about translation, he draws attention to another aspect of his use of language:

My English isn't very transparent. There's plenty of "urban" language, youth language, hiphop language, and a lot of "intellectual" language. To be able to juggle them all at once and get the valence of all of them as a translator is difficult. I found my interventions to be the most useful on the boundaries between all these areas.[11]

It's clear that Díaz considers this Bakhtinian play of multiple social languages central to the craft of his writing. Following his lead, we may align this heteroglossia with his self-location in numerous creative traditions:

> I have multiple traditions, like anyone else. I'm part of the mainstream of "American" literary tradition. I'm part of the Latino literary tradition. I'm a part of the African Diaspora literary tradition as well as the Dominican literary tradition. But there's also the oral tradition and the rhythmic tradition of the music I grew up with which deeply influence how I write a sentence and how my work sounds.[12]

The overlapping and intersecting of all these traditions in *Drown* certainly contributes to its voice, and perhaps to its celebrity too. It certainly makes it more interesting for literary critics. What's remarkable, though, is how easily (and frequently) Díaz inscribes himself in all these traditions without mention of friction or tension between them. It appears the only site of friction and tension that he identifies in his book is along the English-Spanish axis.

Well-versed readers of Latino literature, not to mention people who regularly ride public transportation in major metropolitan areas of the United States, may be surprised by the emphasis on the "English-Spanish tension and violence" purportedly so central to the book. For example, in a study of Puerto Rican-American language usage (i.e. code-switching or "Spanglish"), Juan Flores presents a different vision of the co-habitation of English and Spanish. He reports:

> Sentences that used both Spanish and English were found to be grammatical in both languages; switching occurs only where the structures of Spanish and English are congruent. We found that balanced bilinguals engaged in more intimate, intricate kinds of switching, while those with fluency in one language avoided syntactic risks by switching between sentences or switching only independent particles and exclamations. Rather than compensating for monolingual deficiency, code-switching often signals an expansion of communicative and expressive potential.[13]

Rather than violence and tension between English and Spanish, Flores describes balance, intimacy, intricacy and "an expansion of communicative and expressive potential." This is not to suggest that social fractures along linguistic lines in the United States are not marked by violence. Nor that Díaz would deny that code-switching enhances the "communicative and expressive" elements of his prose. Quite the opposite, *Drown* employs code-switching to expressively enhance its whole emotional range. This is why it is remarkable, and puzzling, that Díaz and others have so singularly focused on the violence of the English-Spanish relationship.

What if this unequivocal, repeated identification of the source of tension and violence in *Drown* were a sign of resistance, in the psycho-analytic sense? What if, more specifically, it constituted a form of displacement, diverting the reader's attention away from more perilous sites of tension and violence in the book, sites that Díaz or his reviewers may not be so comfortable discussing in print? As we discussed earlier, Díaz values how the book interweaves social languages and participates in numerous narrative traditions. Furthermore, the social landscape of *Drown* depicts all sorts of mixing of color and class. Perhaps it is somewhere in this context, treated so unproblematically outside the book, that we can locate what is problematic inside the book. If we are suspicious of locating and containing the violence and tension of the book in the neat opposition between Spanish and English, perhaps we should look to these messy sites of intermingling to discover where *Drown,* in spite of its author and reviewers, pinpoints the troubled experience of multicultural America.

In the story "Boyfriend," the young male narrator becomes interested in the life of his downstairs neighbor, "the two of us separated by a floor, wires and some pipes" (112). His neighbor (Girlfriend) is in the midst of a protracted break-up (with Boyfriend), and he himself is in the process of recovery from a break-up. The narrator has seen Boyfriend out before: "He was one of those dark-skinned, smooth-faced brothers that women kill for, and I knew for a fact, having seen his ass in action at the local spots, that he liked to get over on the white-girls" (114). This interracial play, though, does not surprise the narrator anymore:

> I used to think those were the barrio rules, Latinos and blacks in, whites out—a place we down cats weren't supposed to go. But love teaches you. Clears your head of any rules. Loretta's new boy was Italian. Worked on Wall Street. When she told me about him we were still going out. We were on the Promenade and she said to me, I like him. He's a hard worker.
>
> No amount of heart-leather could stop something like that from hurting (114).

On its face, it appears that the narrator does not suffer from the fact that Loretta's new boyfriend is Italian, i.e. white in the U.S. racial schema. Instead, it is her admiration for his hard work, as opposed to the narrator's own underachieving, that really stings. However, the response of the narrator's friends as they try to console him reveal a complicated relationship between race and economics: "It was easy for them to say, Forget her sellout ass. That's not the sort of woman you need. Look how light you are—no doubt she was already shopping for the lightest" (115). It is unclear whether the narrator's friends brand Loretta a sellout for dating a Wall Street broker, or for choosing someone lighter-skinned. Perhaps this ambivalence points to the fact that whiteness often implies, especially to the economically subordinate non-white, high economic status and a committed work-ethic.[14] Conversely, the economically subordinate non-white will often become abject about his/her own subordinate economic status and perceived inferiority.[15]

The retreat to a discourse of race (or pigment) loyalty and betrayal serves the purposes of consolation, though, not genuine indictment. In fact, the narrator's conscience refuses to condemn interracial dating if it involves some sort of upward mobility. The two working-class male characters of "Edison, New Jersey" never denigrate the recently arrived, 20 year-old Dominican maid for her relationship with Pruitt, her wealthy employer. Their dialogue suggests quite the opposite:

> [Wayne:] Pretty predictable. She's probably in love with the guy. You know how it is.
> [Narrator:] I sure do (139).

The two characters voice no suspicion of the young woman's possible mercenary motives. They empathize with her instead, recognizing that love often keeps people bound to situations they would do best to get out of. Despite his own desire for the young woman, the Dominican narrator refuses to accuse her of race betrayal. This refusal is consistent with the "Boyfriend" narrator's refusal to accuse his ex of race betrayal when she begins dating her Wall Street Italian. Once again, that she admires his "hard work" hurts the narrator more than anything else, touching as it does upon his abject attitude toward his own racial worth and economic status.

The narrators throughout the stories of *Drown* have a fraught relationship with the idea of financial success. "Fiesta, 1980" takes place after Yunior, his brother Rafa and their mother have joined their father in the United States. The family will be attending a party in Washington Heights to welcome a recently arrived Dominican uncle to the United States:

> None of us spoke until we were inside Papi's Volkswagen van. Brand-new, lime-green and bought to impress. Oh, we were impressed, but me, every time I was in that VW and Papi went above twenty miles an hour, I vomited. I'd never had trouble with cars before—that van was like my curse (27).

The VW van, emblem of Papi's financial success, and perhaps the family's imminent upward mobility, provokes a nascent neurotic condition in Yunior.

"Fiesta, 1980" aligns the lime-green VW van with another aspect of Papi's life-style, his cheating: "I met the Puerto Rican woman right after Papi had gotten the van. He was taking me on short trips, trying to cure me of my vomiting" (34–35). Papi saddles both his sons with the knowledge of his affair, even taking them over to eat dinner at the Puerto Rican woman's house. Yunior comments: "[W]e still acted like nothing was out of the ordinary. . . . The affair was like a hole in our living room floor, one we'd gotten so used to circumnavigating that we sometimes forgot it was there" (39–40). Yunior and his family waited five years in Santo Domingo for Papi to send for them, during which time, as recounted in the book's final story "Negocios," in addition to getting on firm financial footing, Papi started another family with another Dominican woman in the United States. Papi's efforts to make it in the U.S. seem to consistently intersect in the text with his betrayal of Yunior's mother.

Yunior's neurotic condition, his compulsive vomiting, then, seems to be entangled in this nexus of upward mobility and masculinity. The book's title story extends this entanglement. Set years after "Fiesta, 1980," Yunior, now a small-time drug dealer, and his mother, now separated from her husband, live in a small New Jersey apartment. The story begins with the announcement that his old friend Beto has come home from college. With his college education, Beto represents *Drown*'s only figure of upward mobility other than Yunior's father. The latter is marked by infidelity, the former by homosexuality.

Yunior's frustration, his lack of upward mobility, structures the neurotic circularity of the story "Drown." All of Yunior's activities in this story repeat themselves, compulsively: his three-mile run, his trips to the mall, his checking the windows to see if they are locked. Haunted by the compromised masculinities of his upwardly mobile models, Yunior remains stuck in a textually neurotic pattern of repetition. A perpetual adolescent, Yunior cannot find a way, in the words of Arnaldo Cruz-Malavé, "to gain authority, to emerge, as it were, into maturity and maleness."[16] Cruz-Malavé approaches this same predicament in three foundational Nuyorican texts: Piri Thomas's *Down These Mean Streets*, Miguel Piñero's *Short Eyes*, and *Nuyorican Poetry: an Anthology of Puerto Rican Words and Feelings*, all of which are admitted influences on Junot Díaz.[17] Cruz-Malavé writes:

> [H]omosexual practices [in these texts] occupy that zone of reversibility where the Nuyorican author's struggle to emerge from the spectral state of abjection to which he is subjected by "internal colonialism," by "the System," "the Man," always inevitably falls back on contested territory. In them, one could say, the "queen,"

the "faggot" are not so much the antithesis of their "macho" characters and poetic personae as that "proximate other" in whose likeness the latter see reflected the catastrophic condition of their own manhood.[18]

Yunior's "spectral state of abjection" lies in his lumpenproletariat status, outside the lines of social mobility, with apparent recourse only to drug-dealing and military service. Beto's homosexual practices (he once gave Yunior a handjob and another time a blowjob) "occupy that zone of reversibility" in which Yunior too could ascend the class hierarchy, but only by risking his own heterosexual masculinity.

Yunior, it seems, wants to navigate a passage "into maturity and maleness" that bypasses two "proximate others," the hyper-masculinized philandering father and the insufficiently masculinized homosexual (ex-)friend. Cruz-Malavé writes: "To validate masculinity with its ruin, to submit to sodomy, to 'bugger' in order to construct a male national identity, there is the paradoxical foundational project that Nuyorican texts set for themselves."[19] *Drown*, on the other hand, seems to want to construct an upwardly mobile Dominican male subject, not on the ruins of masculinity, but seemingly on a monogamous heterosexual masculinity. The book posits this project, but leaves it unfulfilled, compulsively repeating a frustrated, lumpen adolescence.

Like the foundational Nuyorican texts, Díaz and his reviewers denounce U.S. "internal colonialism"—evinced most clearly in the conflict between Spanish and English—as the constitutive site of violence and tension for the minority subject. However, our readings of *Drown* suggest that this extra-textual critique may simply attempt to displace the reader's analytic gaze. The stories in the book offer upward mobility to their Dominican male characters. Their underachievement is not attributed to "the System" or "the Man" but to a crisis of masculinity. Yunior refuses the upwardly mobile models of his adulterous and homosexual "proximate others," but fails to achieve an alternative.

Maybe that's why it is safe to celebrate minority fictions that are perceived to critique the oppressive socio-economic conditions in the United States. That critique, whether expressed in academic journals or in the mainstream press, frames and preserves the idea of minority identity as necessarily grounded in socio-economic subordination. Yet the stories of *Drown* suggest that it is not oppressive socio-economic conditions that constitute the direct obstacle to upward mobility for the diasporic Dominican male subject. Instead, it is that subject's own crisis of masculinity that seem to produce the neurotic conditions that interrupt his upwardly mobile trajectory.

Notes

1. Diógenes Céspedes and Silvio Torres-Saillant, "Fiction is the Poor Man's Cinema: An Interview with Junot Díaz," p. 905.

2. Ibid., p. 905.

3. Junot Díaz, "Language, Violence, and Resistance" (2002), p. 44.

4. Céspedes and Torres-Saillant, p. 902.

5. Ed Morales, "Junot What?" p. 63.

6. Richard Eder, "An Artist in Transit," p. 2.

7. Céspedes and Saillant, p. 896.

8. Ibid., p. 896.

9. Eder, p. 2.

10. Junot Díaz, *Drown* (1996), p. 137. Henceforth cited parenthetically.

11. Díaz 2002, p. 43.

12. Céspedes and Saillant, p. 904.

13. Juan Flores, "'La Carreta Made a U-Turn': Puerto Rican Language and Culture in the United States," p. 165.

14. Cf. Stuart Hall, *Policing the Crisis: Mugging, the State, and Law and Order,* Chapter 10.

15. In *Drown,* this sense of inferiority appears, for example, in "How to Date a Browngirl, Blackgirl, Whitegirl, or Halfie" when the narrator comments: "Run a hand through your hair like the whiteboys do even though the only thing that runs easily through your hair is Africa. She will look good. The white ones are the ones you want the most, aren't they, but usually the out-of-towners are black, blackgirls who grew up on ballet and Girl Scouts, who have three cars in their drive-ways" (145). Likewise, while hooking up with a white girl at another moment of this story, the narrator states: "Tell her that you love her hair, that you love her skin, her lips, because, in truth you love them more than you love your own" (147).

16. Arnaldo Cruz-Malavé, "'What a Tangled Web!': Masculinity, Abjection, and the Foundations of Puerto Rican Literature in the United States," p. 139.

17. Céspedes and Torres-Saillant, p. 900.

18. Cruz-Malavé, pp. 139–140.

19. Ibid., p. 140.

Works Cited

Balderston, Daniel and Marcy Schwartz (eds.). *Voice-Overs: Translation and Latin American Literature.* Albany: SUNY Press, 2002, pp. 42–44.

Céspedes, Diógenes and Silvio Torres-Saillant, "'Fiction is the Poor Man's Cinema': An Interview with Junot Díaz." *Callaloo* 23.3 (2000), pp. 892–907.

Cruz-Malavé, Arnaldo. "'What a Tangled Web!': Masculinity, Abjection, and the Foundations of Puerto Rican Literature in the United States." *Differences: a Journal of Feminist Cultural Studies* 8.1 (1996), pp. 132–151.

Díaz, Junor. *Drown.* New York: Riverhead Books, 1996.

———. "Language, Violence, and Resistance." In Balderston, Daniel and Marcy Schwartz (eds.), *Voice-Overs: Translation and Latin American Literature.* Albany: SUNY Press, 2002, pp. 42–44.

Eder, Richard. "An Artist in Transit." *The Los Angeles Times:* Sept. 1, 1996, p. 2.

Flores, Juan. "'La Carreta Made a U-Turn': Puerto Rican Language and Culture in the United States." In *Divided Borders: Essays on Puerto Rican Identity.* Houston: Arte Público Press, 1993, pp. 157–181.

Hall, Stuart, et. al. *Policing the Crisis: Mugging, the State, and Law and Order.* New York: Holmes & Meier, 1978.

Morales, Ed. "Junot What?" *The Village Voice:* Sept. 10, 1996, pp. 63–64.

NICOLÁS KANELLOS

Recovering and Re-constructing Early Twentieth-Century Hispanic Immigrant Print Culture in the U.S.

1. The Immigrant Press

Since the mid-nineteenth century, Hispanic immigrants in the US have written and published books and periodicals and sustained other forms of print culture to serve their enclaves in their native language, maintaining a connection with the homeland while helping the immigrants to adjust to a new society and culture here. Hispanic immigrant print culture shares many of the distinctions that Robert E. Park identified in *The Immigrant Press and Its Control* (1922): (1) the predominant use of the language of the homeland, in (2) serving a population united by that language, irrespective of national origin, and (3) the need to interpret events from their own peculiar racial or nationalist point of view, and furthering nationalism (9–13). According to Park, the immigrant press serves a population in transition from the land of origin to the US by providing news and interpretation to orient them and facilitate adjustment to the new society while maintaining the link with the old society. Underlying Park's distinctions and those of other students of immigration are the concepts of the American Dream and the Melting Pot: that the immigrants came to find a better life, implicitly a better culture, and that soon they or their descendants would become Americans and there would no longer be a need for this type of press. For Park, immigrant culture

American Literary History, Volume 19, Number 2 (Summer 2007): pp. 438–455. Copyright © 2007 American Literary History.

was a transitory phenomenon, one that would disappear as the group became assimilated into the melting pot of US society.

The attitude of *not* assimilating or melting, however, has characterized Hispanic immigrant culture and its use of the printing press from the nineteenth century to the present. The advice of Corpus Christi's *El Horizonte* (The Horizon, 1879–1880) to its Mexican readership was typical of many immigrant newspapers, novels, poetry, and other publications: Do not become citizens of the US because there is so much prejudice and persecution here that "we shall always be foreigners in the United States and they always consider us as such" ("permanceremos extrangeros en los Estados Unidos y como tal nos consideran siempre").[1]

To Park's observations I would add that the defense of the community was also important for the immigrant press. Hispanic newspapers, in particular, were sensitive to racism and abuse of immigrant rights. Almost all of the Hispanic immigrant newspapers announced their service in protection of the community in mastheads and/or in editorials, and some of them followed up on this commitment by leading campaigns to desegregate schools, movie houses, and other facilities or to construct their alternative institutions for the Hispanic community's use. Contrary to Park's prognosis for the ethnic identity of immigrants, the history of Hispanic groups in the US has shown an unmeltable ethnicity, and as immigration from Spanish-speaking countries has been almost a steady flow since the founding of the US to the present, there seems no end to the phenomenon at this juncture in history nor in the foreseeable future.

2. Important Immigrant Publishers*

While Hispanic immigrant newspapers had existed since the late 1820s,[2] it was not until much later, when larger Hispanic immigrant communities began to form, that more characteristic immigrant newspapers were founded to serve a burgeoning community of immigrants from northern Mexico and from throughout the Hispanic world who had been drawn to the San Francisco Bay Area during the Gold Rush and its collateral industrial and commercial development.[3] From the 1850s through the 1870s, in fact, San Francisco supported the largest number, longest running, and most financially successful Spanish-language newspapers in the US. Included among these during this period were two daily Spanish-language newspapers: *El Eco del Pacífico* (1856–?) and *El Tecolote* (1875–1879). The San Francisco Spanish-language press covered news of the homeland and generally assisted the immigrants in adjusting to the new environment. The newspapers reported on discrimination and persecution of Hispanic miners and generally saw the defense of the Hispanic *colonia*, or colony, to be a priority, denouncing abuse of the Hispanic immigrants, as well as of the natives.[4]

While San Francisco's Hispanic population was the state's largest in the nineteenth century, it was Los Angeles that received the largest number of Mexican immigrants with the massive exodus of economic refugees from the Revolution of 1910. It was thus Los Angeles in the twentieth century that, along with San Antonio and New York, supported some of the most important Spanish-language daily newspapers, periodicals, and publishing houses. Between 1910 and the Great Depression, approximately one million Mexican immigrants settled in the US;[5] Los Angeles and San Antonio were their most popular destinations. In these two cities, an entrepreneurial class of refugees came with the cultural and financial capital sufficient to establish businesses of all types to serve the rapidly growing Mexican enclaves; they constructed everything from tortilla factories to Hispanic theaters and movie houses,[6] and through their cultural leadership in mutual aid societies, churches, theaters, publishing houses, and periodicals, they were able to disseminate a nationalistic ideology that ensured the solidarity and insularity of their communities, or markets, if you will.

Hispanic immigrant print culture throughout the Southwest, Northeast, and the Chicago area was sustained principally by the Spanish-language newspapers and, secondarily, by publishing houses that were often associated with these newspapers. While many of these periodicals and publishing houses functioned as business enterprises, there were also numerous community-based periodicals published by various interest groups, such as clubs, mutual aid societies, and writers' associations, as well as labor unions, political organizations, and individuals. The more business-oriented publishing enterprises tended to be operated by educated business elites, while often the small weekly publications were written, designed, and operated without the profit motive by working-class organizations and individuals. Then, as now, the majority of the Latino community was made up of the working class.[7] While virtually all of the highly commercial publications to issue from the big-city Spanish-language presses targeted the immigrant community, the immigrant workers themselves were quite successful during the first half of the twentieth century in representing themselves in their own weekly and occasional publications.[8]

Among the most important big-city daily newspapers were *El Heraldo de México,* founded in Los Angeles in 1915 and called a "people's newspaper" (Chacón 48–50); the two Ignacio Lozano newspapers, San Antonio's *La Prensa* (1913) and Los Angeles's *La Opinión* (1926); and New York City's *La Prensa* (1913).[9] All four ostensibly catered to immigrant workers while serving the entrepreneurial class by promoting its business enterprises and purveying an ideology of an Hispanic culture in exile. All of them, at one time or another, led campaigns through editorials and even community action to protect immigrant rights, to protest discrimination, and to raise funds to assist in particular community crises.[10] While newspapers like *El Heraldo de México* and the Lozano newspapers promoted specifically Mexican nationalism, New York's *La Prensa* promoted pan-Hispanism to its more diverse Hispanic immigrant community. Nevertheless, all of these periodicals participated in an underlying, and at times not-so-subtle, message to preserve Hispanic identity and resist assimilation to Anglo-American culture.

In the Southwest, publishers, editorialists, columnists, novelists, poets, and playwrights were almost unanimous in developing and promoting the idea of a "México de afuera," or a Mexican colony existing outside of Mexico, in which it was the duty of the individual to maintain the Spanish language, keep the Catholic faith, and insulate the children from what community leaders perceived as the low moral standards practiced by Anglo-Americans. Basic to this belief system was the imminent return to Mexico, when the hostilities of the Revolution were over. Mexican national culture was to be preserved during what the intellectuals conceived of as an "exile" in the midst of iniquitous Anglo Protestants, whose culture was aggressively degrading even while discriminating against Hispanics. On the other hand, the expatriates believed that Mexico had been so transformed by the "bolchevique" hordes who had conducted and won the Revolution that the only true Mexican culture survived in exile, precisely in these *colonias*.[11] The ideology was most expressed and disseminated by cultural elites, many of whom were the political and religious refugees from the Mexican Revolution. They represented the most conservative segment of Mexican society in the homeland; in the US, their cultural and business entrepreneurship exerted leadership in all phases of life in the *colonia* and solidified a conservative substratum for Mexican American culture for decades to come. While these political refugees truly believed this ideology, they exerted themselves to promote it through publications to the economic refugees, i.e., the true immigrants whose descendants make up the largest portion of the Mexican American community today.

Among the most powerful of the political, business, and intellectual figures in the Mexican immigrant community was Ignacio E. Lozano, founder and operator of the Casa Editorial Lozano publishing house and of the two most powerful and well distributed daily newspapers, *La Prensa* and *La Opinión,* the latter founded in 1926 and still publishing today.[12] With the business training and experience that he received in Mexico, Lozano was able to contribute professionalism and business acumen to Hispanic journalism in the US, reflected in his hiring of well-trained journalists, starting at the top with his appointment to edit *La Prensa* of Teodoro Torres, known as the "Father of Mexican Journalism." The ideas of men like Torres and Lozano reached thousands not only in San Antonio but throughout the Southwest, Midwest, and northern Mexico through a vast distribution system that included newsstand sales, home delivery, and mail. In her day,

La Prensa was indeed influential. Lozano and many of his prominent writers and editorialists became leaders of the Mexican/ Mexican American communities. They shaped and cultivated their market for cultural products and print media as efficiently as others sold material goods and Mexican foods. The Mexican community truly benefited in that the entrepreneurs did provide needed goods, information, and services that were often denied by the larger society through official and open segregation. In addition, of course, the writers, artists, and intellectuals provided high as well as popular culture and entertainment in the native language of the Mexican community, which also was not offered by Anglo-American society: Spanish-language books and periodicals, silent films with Spanish-dialog frames, and Spanish-language drama and vaudeville, among other entertainment and popular art forms.

Various newspaper companies, in fact, operated publishing houses, as did both Lozano papers and *El Heraldo de México.* They also imported books and published reprint editions under their own imprints. The largest of these, Casa Editorial Lozano, advertised its books in the family's two newspapers to be sold via direct mail and in the Lozano bookstore in San Antonio. *El Heraldo de México* also operated a bookstore, in Los Angeles. In addition to the publishing houses owned by the large dailies, in the same cities and in smaller population centers there were many other newspapers publishing books as well.

Without a doubt, however, San Antonio became the publishing center for Hispanics in the Southwest, and housed more Spanish-language publishing houses than any other city in the US. During the 1920s and 1930s, San Antonio was home to the Casa Editorial Lozano, Viola Novelty Company, Whitt Publishing, Librería de Quiroga, Artes Gráficas, and various others.[13] They unanimously dedicated themselves to both publishing and importing books and printing catalogs for mail order. Lozano and Viola Novelty, which were connected to newspapers, also published book listings in their parent newspapers, *La Prensa, La Opinión* and the satirical *El Fandango*—quite often the authors of some of their books were drawn from their newspaper staffs. Those that were proprietors of bookstores, such as Lozano, Quiroga, and Librería Española, of course, had a ready sales outlet. In the San Antonio publishers' catalogs was everything from the practical, such as Ignacio E. Lozano's manual for (male) secretaries, *El perfecto secretario* (The Perfect Secretary, 1915), to autobiographies by exiled political and religious figures, to sentimental novels and books of poetry. Whitt Publishers issued religious plays appropriate for parish Christmas festivities, along with numerous other books of Mexican folklore and legendry. The Librería de Quiroga seems to have dedicated itself to supplying leisure reading for housewives, especially those of the middle class, with such sentimental fare as María del Pilar Sinués's novel *El amor de los amores* (The Love of Loves, n.d.), Rafael del Castillo's novel *Amor de madre* (A Mother's Love, n.d.), Joaquín Piña's novel *Rosa de amor* (Rose of Love, n.d.), Stowe's *La cabaña de Tom* (Uncle Tom's Cabin, 1853) and Antonio Plaza's poetry collection, *Album del corazón* (Album of the Heart, c. 1880). Catholic and Protestant publishing houses issued hundreds of religious books from their presses in San Antonio and El Paso; much of this fare established a culture of the Church in exile from Mexico.

This fare was in contrast to more working-class oriented literature that often was issued from these same presses.

3. The Labor Press

Both immigrant and native Hispanic workers have engaged in the founding and building of unions throughout their history as industrial and agricultural workers in the US. The fact that, since the nineteenth century, Hispanic workers have been imported on a large scale by industry makes their labor press mostly a phenomenon of immigrant life. Historically, the Hispanic labor unions and their periodicals were created by and for Latinos working in very specific industries—industries often associated with their native cultures or old-country backgrounds: cigar rollers, agricultural workers, cowboys, copper miners, and fruit harvesters. In more contemporary times, Hispanics have been leaders in organizing other trades and industries, such as the steel mills, the needle trades, hospitals, and manufacturing.[14]

One of the first, largest, and most significant industries to rely almost exclusively on Hispanic labor was the cigar manufacturing industry that had factories in Key West, Tampa, New York, and San Antonio, among other locations. In 1886, the first transfer of a whole industry from Latin America to the US began when Spanish and Cuban entrepreneurs acquired Florida swamp land near Tampa and built a cigar manufacturing town, Ybor City. By 1890, the population of Tampa and Ybor City was 5500, and that number tripled by 1900. The tobacco entrepreneurs hoped to attract a docile work force (unlike the labor union activists in Cuba), avoid US import tariffs, and get closer to their markets in the US. Also, the Cuban wars for independence were raging and continually disrupting business. The industry in Ybor City grew to ten factories by 1895, and it became the principal cigar-producing area in the US when smoking cigars was at its highest peak. By 1900, there were about 150 cigar factories in West Tampa and Ybor City, producing more than 111 million cigars annually (Henderson and Mormino 34).

Not only were the cigar company owners wrong about escaping the labor unrest that was endemic to the industry in Cuba, but the greater freedom of expression afforded on US soil also allowed the cigar workers to organize more openly and to publish their periodicals more extensively. The cigar workers formed the strongest unions of any Hispanic workers in the US,[15] and they struck in 1899, 1901, 1910, 1920, and 1931 (Henderson and Mormino 40–45).

Workers in the cigar crafts in Cuba and Puerto Rico had traditionally been more politicized because of the high level of informal education obtained through the institution of the *lector*, a person selected and paid by the workers to read to them throughout their laborious and boring work day rolling cigars.[16] The *lectores* would read extensively from world literature, as well as from national authors and, of course, newspapers and magazines.

The roots of the Cuban American labor press are to be found in Cuba in this tobacco workers' tradition.[17] Cuban tobacco workers in Tampa established their first labor newspaper, *La Federación* (The Federation), in 1899 as the official organ of their union. Before that, their interest in organizing and in anarchism had been addressed by their local newspapers, *El Esclavo* (The Slave) in 1894 and later in *La Voz del Esclavo* (The Voice of the Slave) in 1900 (Chabrán 157). Other important union newspapers from the Tampa area were: *Boletín Obrero* (Worker Bulletin, 1903–?), *El Federal* (The Federal, 1902–1903), *La Defensa* (The Defense, 1916–?), *El Internacional* (The International, 1904–?), and *Vocero de la Unión de Tabaqueros* (Voice of the Tobacco Workers' Unions, 1941–?). The unions and their newspapers, as well as individual working-class writers, published a steady stream of books and pamphlets to disseminate their ideas.

One of the most important of these writers was, in fact, a *lector* who had worked in Puerto Rico, Tampa, and New York, and who was an activist labor organizer. Celebrated today as an early Puerto Rican feminist (known to have been the first woman to wear men's clothes in public), Luisa Capetillo, in fact, published five books,[18] and wrote plays and numerous newspaper articles to convey to workers the details of her anarcho-syndicalism and free love ideologies. Her plays, published in her book *Influencia de las ideas modernas . . .* (The Influence of Modern Ideas . . . , 1916), were performed in union halls and, for the most part, took the form of truncated melodramas in which the female protagonists developed, through monologues and some action, their theses on the benefits of a return to nature, equality among the sexes, the evils of wage slavery, and the conflict between true love and money. In adapting and subverting the conventions of melodrama, Capetillo was also attacking the systems of social classes and gender roles.

At the end of the nineteenth century, New York received a large influx of Spanish working-class immigrants, just as it did other southern Europeans; they joined their fellow Spanish-speakers in Harlem, Fourteenth Street, and Brooklyn, and participated in raising working-class consciousness through such newspapers as *El Despertar* (The Awakening, 1891–1912), *Cultura Proletaria* (Proletarian Culture, 1910–1959) and *Brazo y Cerebro* (Arm and Brain, 1912), which were primarily anarchist periodicals (Chabrán 157). *Cultura Proletaria* became the longest lasting anarchist periodical published in Spanish in the US. Edited by the noted Spanish anarchist author Pedro

Esteves and published by Spanish workers, over the years the paper passed into the hands of Cubans and Puerto Ricans as the composition of the work force changed. Puerto Ricans early on established their own labor and radical press in such organs as *La Mísera* (The Miserable One, 1901), *Unión Obrera* (Worker Union, 1902), and, much later, *Vida Obrera* (Worker Life, 1930–1932).

4. Immigrant Writers

The most interesting story of working-class print culture emerging from the barrios of New York, Tampa, and the Southwest goes beyond the labor movement and the subscription to any specific ideology, such as the anarchism or socialism so studied and promoted by workers in the early twentieth century. Working-class immigrant writers and intellectuals developed their own newspapers and published books that represented their perspective on life in the US as individuals immersed in an epic displacement of peoples, relocated to the US Metropolis.[19] Often through the medium of weekly community newspapers or monthly magazines, but also in formally published books, these authors documented the experiences of Hispanic immigrants, often autobiographically, and often employing the vernacular dialects of their working-class readers. Much of the writing was infused with an orality that came from lived experience, anecdotes and jokes snatched from that experience, as well as from popular entertainments, including vaudeville performances.

One genre, closely associated with journalism, was the *crónica*, or chronicle, a short weekly column that often humorously and satirically commented on current topics and social customs in the local community. Rife with local color and inspired by the oral lore of the immigrants, it came to serve purposes in the US that went beyond its origins in England, Spain, and Spanish America.[20] From Los Angeles to New York, Hispanic moralists assumed pseudonyms in the tradition of the *crónicas*, such as "The Whip" (*Chicote*), "Samurai," and "Aztec" (*Az.T.K.*), and, from that masked perspective, became community moralists and commented in the first person as witnesses to the customs and behavior of the immigrant colony. It was the *cronista's* mission to promote Hispanic cultural identity and battle the influence of what he saw as Anglo-American immorality and Protestantism; his principal weapons were satire and humor, often directed at mocking the immigrants' supposed degradation of the Spanish language by mixing English words and concepts in their speech, their gawking awe at Yankee ingenuity and technology, and their penchant for deriding everything associated with the Old Country as backward. While cultural elites often penned these *crónicas* to promote such conservative ideologies as *el México de afuera*,[21] in the hands of such working-class writers as Jesús Colón and Alberto O'Farril of New York there was more ground-level representation of the working man, his struggles and aspirations. Using the pseudonym of Tiquis Miquis—one of three names the Puerto Rican Colón employed in his *crónicas*—Colón protested against the overcrowded and filthy conditions in tenements, the hordes of Latino con men ready to fleece greenhorn immigrants, as well as the uncultured and chaotic behavior of the transplants from the rural tropics.[22] With a humor tempered on the vaudeville stage, Cuban Alberto O'Farril created the persona of an unemployed mulatto *pícaro*,[23] who week after week narrated his struggles to find work during the Depression, at times through such marginal employment as passing out handbills, shoveling snow, or wearing a sandwich sign on the streets of Gotham; his downfall as a picaresque rogue was his laziness, his lack of understanding of English, and his ogling the American flappers. Both Colón and O'Farril, as well as the *cronistas* and novelists in the Southwest, chose the flapper as the embodiment of American womanhood, recently having won suffrage and entrance to the workplace and to public spheres still denied Hispanic women. Thus, while there were free—a freedom interpreted by Hispanic males as being synonymous with "loose"—they were portrayed stereotypically as aggressive blonde beauties. The writers were sexually attracted to the flapper, despite her representing a threat to Latino male power and prerogatives.[24] And the absolute worse flapper of them all was the Mexican or Latina who adapted American flapper ways. The epitome of this censure was penned in San Antonio's *El Heraldo Mexicano* newspaper in Quezigno Gazavic's (pseudonym of Ignacio G. Vásquez) weekly *crónica* "Tanasio y Ramona: Narración continuada en verso de las pintorescas aventuras de dos sujetos 'de Allá de Casa'" (Tanasio and Ramona: Continuous Narration in Verse about the Picturesque Adventures of Two Subjects Far from Home, 1928),[25] that narrated the suffering and misadventures of a poor country bumpkin whose wife abandons him to go North to the US and take up the life of a flapper; the poor greenhorn soon leaves his home town in order to follow in hopes of winning her back. Along the way, his conversations, letters, and interviews with the *cronista* Gazavic afford the reader a full-blossomed satire of immigrant life in the US while hammering home the message of remaining loyal to Mexican gender roles, culture, and, of course, the homeland.

The most syndicated and highly popular of the *cronistas* was journalist Julio G. Arce, who wrote under the pseudonym of Jorge Ulica. A Mexican political refugee who relocated to San Francisco in 1915, swearing never to return to the homeland, he soon purchased a newspaper. Amid news and advertising, Arce launched his weekly column, *Crónicas Diabólicas* (Diablolical Chronicles), in his own pages as a literary entertainment and soon attained a level of outreach and impact that no other Mexican writer ever achieved in the Southwest in the early twentieth century. As in the case of most of the other immigrant *cronistas*, it was Jorge Ulica's particular mission to correct the ways of the errant immigrant worker, often admonishing him to return to Mexico and not be exposed to the iniquitous influence of Yankee civilization. However, Ulica's most consistent censure was aimed at women, whom he saw as particularly open to acculturation and disloyalty to Mexican culture and nationality. His hilarious accounts of Mexican femininity included examples of women who went to the extreme of changing their Spanish names from Dolores Flores to "Pains Flowers," to giving up their Mexican cuisine for such American delicacies as hot dogs and liver and onions, and to outlandish attempts at whitening their skins. American men were depicted as having exchanged gender roles with their pants-wearing wives: cooking, cleaning house, walking three steps behind the wives on the streets while carrying their infant children and diaper bags. Ulica depicted Mexican American women as adapting the ways of flappers, forgetting their Spanish, and openly flirting with men in the workplace, including Ulica himself, who could not resist the advances, perfumes, and wiles of his flapper secretary, Miss Pink (Rosa), who at least symbolically had reduced him to an effeminate ("ajotado") subject of her scorn for his not making advances toward her. Ulica went on to indict the justice system and the entire American society for a structure which subjugated men to women and even condoned women committing homicide on their husbands—riffs by Ulica on headlines of the times. Ulica's particular perspective, however, was detached and elevated, maintaining his creator's upper-class and elite perspective, for Arce was a man of education and sufficient financial resources to have owned and operated newspapers both in Mexico and now the US.

Daniel Venegas, on the other hand, was a working-class writer who also satirized life in the immigrant communities, publishing his *crónicas* in his own "joco-serio" (comic-serious) weekly, *El Malcriado* (The Brat) and in his humorous novel of immigration, *Las aventuras de Don Chipote, o Cuando los pericos mamen* (The Adventures of Don Chipote or When Parrots Breast Feed, 1928). Venegas hand-set the type and fully illustrated all the stories and comic reportage for his *El Malcriado,* all of which he wrote himself, and, I suppose, he himself delivered for weekly sale at restaurants and boarding houses around Los Angeles. His novel, on the other hand, which seems to have emerged from the weekly *crónicas* he wrote for *El Malcriado,* was published by the all-important daily newspaper, *El Heraldo de México,* mentioned above. Truly a highpoint of working-class immigrant literature, *Don Chipote* sets out to satirize the struggles of another country bumpkin who, upon hearing how gold can literally be swept up from the streets of the US, leaves his poverty stricken family on their tenant farm to strike it rich up North. Along the way, he and his sidekick marvel wide-eyed at the advanced technology and other wonders of modern US life, not the least of which are the flappers. However, riches or even a modicum of a living are never within reach as railroads and other industries exploit them, rogues and ladies of the night try to fleece them, and they perennially suffer hunger pangs, discrimination, and abuse. Venegas goes well beyond the *crónica* format in writing what becomes not only a picaresque road novel but an explicit indictment of the governments of both the US and Mexico in their failure to create a decent life for their citizens and workers. Like so many an immigrant story, *Don Chipote* ends with the protagonist's return to the homeland, much disillusioned after his American misadventure. The epilogue clearly states, "Mexicans will become rich in the United States, when parrots breast feed"—that is, never.

Likewise, Conrado Espinosa's novel *El sol de Texas* (The Texas Sun, 1926) follows the destiny of two entire families who relocate to the US as economic refugees, and traces how the hopes and suffering of one family ultimately lead to a return home while the other family becomes so disillusioned and ruined that the surviving members are too ashamed and dispirited to return to the *patria*. The moral of this well-written but pessimistic narrative coincides with the burlesque moral enunciated at the end of *Don Chipote*. The most pessimistic outcome of such novels, however, is to be found in one of the earliest: Colombian Alirio Díaz Guerra's *Lucas Guevara* (1914), which terminates with the antihero committing suicide, after having been spiritually and economically annihilated by the heartless, infernal metropolis of New York. Ostensibly, all three novels were written to warn those in the homeland to never go North in search of a better life, but implicitly these novels entertain, albeit through biting satire, as well as allow Hispanic immigrants to reflect on their present economic and social circumstances. Where *Lucas Guevara* may have been aimed at a more educated reader, there is no doubt that *Don Chipote* had workers as ideal readers—even through reading aloud to workers during idle evenings (and there is ample textual evidence in *Don Chipote* that in fact certain workers did read to and draft letters for other workers in the labor camps and boarding houses).

Other immigrant novels emerged from the lives of their authors as workers in factories and heavy industries, such as Gustavo Alemán Bolaños's *La factoría* (1925), a detailed chronicle of the dehumanizing, boring, and dangerous work in a New York factory. Like many an immigrant who was unable to find work in the Metropolis commensurate with his experience and training, Salvadoran journalist Alemán Bolaños penned a subtle protest on the working conditions facing immigrants.[26] Similarly, Cuban Wenceslao Gálvez, also a *cronista* for the Tampa Hispanic newspapers, extended his first-person narrative, published as *Impresiones de un emigrado* (Impressions of an Émigré, 1897), to revealing the humiliation and marginalization of immigrant life as his protagonist struggles to make a living as a door-to-door salesman in the African-American ghetto, where his little English and his lack of knowledge of American culture and the Jim Crow South lead him to realize the futility of his marketing enterprise.

While so much of the lived experience of these writers created an immediacy and almost documentary chronicle of immigrant and working-class life,
the oral lore and journalism in the immigrant communities also provided much
ink for the pens of intellectuals, who created a more self-consciously literary
rendition of life in the US as seen by people displaced from the homeland by
politics and economic circumstance. From the early *crónicas* of José Martí and
Pachín Marín, in which they voice some of the same concerns about the cold,
dehumanizing, materialistic American Metropolis, to the voluminous novels of
immigration by such authors as Colombia's Alirio Díaz Guerra in his *Lucas Guevara*, Puerto Rico's J. I. de Diego Padró in his appropriately entitled *En Babia* (In
Babel, 1940), and *La Prensa* editor Teodoro Torres in his also appropriately titled
La patria perdida (The Homeland Lost, 1940?), the same binaries appear as in
the working-class novel: the constant comparison of life in the US with that of
the homeland; the inability to adapt to the new land and the inability to return
home in constant tension; admiration for the advances of American society conflicting with the perceived dehumanization, racism, and exploitation of the poor;
more progressive gender roles in the US threatening the integrity of the family
and Latino male-female relationships; and so forth. However, these narratives,
one and all, bring to bear the more elevated perspective of educated authors
who ground their narratives in a wide array of historical and literary allusions
and underpinnings, from biblical passages to the writings of philosophers. Their
rhetoric is not meant to be read aloud around a camp fire or in a saloon, but pon-
dered and meditated upon by individual educated readers, perhaps also displaced
under similar circumstances but desirous of continuing the life of elite culture
and breeding that they once sustained in the homeland, an elite self-concept that
may allow them to survive the poverty and/or humiliating blue-collar work that
has befallen them in the US as political or religious refugees. Whereas both Díaz
Guerra and Padró at least metaphorically reproduce the resolution of most novels of immigration, i.e., return to the homeland or die,[27] Teodoro Torres has his
narrator return to Mexico City, only to discover that he feels just as displaced in
the homeland; in a completely ingenious turn for these formulaic novels, Torres
has his protagonist return to his extensive farm outside Kansas City to create
a utopia for his family and his workers. He has thus resolved the binary of op-
posites: here versus there, the past versus the present, American versus Mexican
culture. By opting for neither and both, his utopia will combine the best of
both societies while being isolated from both of them, and this comes to be
symbolized in his son, adopted from Anglos but raised by Mexican parents.[28]
If I may be permitted a note of irony here, the authors who had so strenuously
advocated a return to the homeland, such as Arce, Díaz Guerra, and Venegas,
lived out their lives in the US as permanent residents. Torres, whose protagonist
returns to create his utopia in the US heartland, returned to Mexico to become
a famous editor and professor of journalism.

Today, there is an equally vibrant literature of Hispanic immigration that takes both oral and written form. The epic story of pulling up roots and resettling in the US while experiencing the continuing tug of the homeland and the need to preserve language and culture is still sung and finds voice in the ever-renewing *corrido, décima,* and *salsa* lyrics not only sung in dance-halls but packaged on CDs and in music videos. Both working class and elite immigrant authors continue to confront the Metropolis in their novels and first-person chronicles in Spanish, as in the works of Ramón Tianguis Pérez, Mario Bencastro, Alicia Alarcón, and others. And the language is key here, as is the lived experience of immigration. The works by Latino authors who came as children or were born and/or raised in the US and prefer to write in English do not fit my definition of immigrant literature. Preferring to write in English, cultivating the truly American genre of ethnic autobiography, and assuming a stance of an American-raised observer of the culture of Mexico, Cuba, the Dominican Republic, or Puerto Rico places such writers as Julia Alvarez, Sandra Cisneros, Junot Díaz, Cristina García, and so many others squarely in the tradition of American ethnic writing, but not that of the dis-placed Latin American author.

Notes

1. *El Horizonte* 24 March 1880: 1–2.

2. See *El Mercurio de Nueva York* (1829–1830) and *El Mensagero Semanal de Nueva York* (1828–1831).

3. Among these, I would include San Francisco's *Sud Americano* (1855), *El Eco del Pacífico* (1856), *La Voz de Méjico* (1862), and *El Nuevo Mundo* (1864).

4. Even Los Angeles's *El Clamor Público* (1855–1859), which was founded to protect the rights of the native Californios, became a defender of Hispanic immigrants, as did other native print efforts. See my article, "*El Clamor Público:* Resisting the American Empire." *California History* 84/2 (Winter 2006–2007) 10–19.

5. See Mario T. García, *Desert Immigrants: The Mexicans of El Paso, 1880–1920* (1981), 35–36, for a discussion of the statistics on Mexican immigration.

6. See my *A History of Hispanic Theater in the United States: Origins to 1940* (1990).

7. See my *Thirty Million Strong: Reclaiming the Hispanic Image in American Culture* (1998) for a review of the historical reasons for the predominance of working-class culture in Hispanic communities.

8. During the late 1920s and the 1930s, an autodidact writer like Jesús Colón had the option of publishing in a wide selection of worker-oriented newspapers; in fact he did publish his *crónicas* in *Boletín de la Liga Puertorriqueña e Hispana, Gráfico, Vida Alegre, El Curioso, Pueblos Hispanos,* and *Liberación.* See Jesús Colón, *Lo que el pueblo me dice. . . : crónicas de la colonia puertorriqueña en Nueva York* (2001), Edwin Karli Padilla Aponte, ed.

9. In the Northeast, the large daily and weekly Spanish-language newspapers flourished and also published books, as did small, ephemeral presses. In 1913, José

Campubrí founded *La Prensa* in New York City to serve the community of mostly
Spanish and Cuban immigrants in and around Manhattan's 14th Street (in 1962 it
merged with *El Diario de Nueva York*). One of the main reasons *La Prensa* survived
so long was that it was able to expand and adapt to the new Spanish-speaking
nationalities that immigrated to the city, especially the Puerto Ricans who migrated
from their island en masse during and after World War II and came to form the
largest Hispanic group in the city. In 1948, *El Diario de Nueva York* was founded
by Dominican immigrant Porfirio Domenici, specifically appealing to the Puerto
Rican community and giving *La Prensa* competition for this growing readership—
El Diario de Nueva York's slogan was "Champion of the Puerto Ricans." In 1962,
O. Roy Chalk, owner of *El Diario de Nueva York,* purchased *La Prensa* and merged
the two journals. In 1981, the Gannett newspaper corporation bought *El Diario–La
Prensa;* in 1989, it was sold to El Diario Associates, Inc., a corporation founded by
Peter Davidson, a former Morgan Stanley specialist in the newspaper industry. In
1990, the Times Mirror Corporation purchased a 50% interest in Los Angeles's *La
Opinión* (San Antonio's *La Prensa* had ceased to exist in 1963). In 1976, the *Miami
Herald* founded *El Miami Herald*—in 1987 it was transformed into the new and
improved *El Nuevo Herald*. Both the Spanish- and the English-language Miami
dailies are subsidiaries of the Knight–Ridder newspaper chain. Thus today, the
three major Hispanic dailies are owned and controlled by American (non-Hispanic)
multimedia corporations; how this has impacted their functioning in service of the
immigrants has not as yet been assessed. There are, however, other smaller dailies
publishing today in Chicago, Houston, San Antonio, and other cities.

10. Chacón found that, among the social roles played by *El Heraldo de
México*, the most important was the defense of the Mexican immigrant by
publishing editorials and devoting considerable space to combating discrimination,
mistreatment, and exploitation of immigrant labor. *El Heraldo de México* even went a
step further in 1919 by attempting to organize Mexican laborers into an association,
the Liga Protectiva Mexicana de California, in order to protect their rights and
further their interests (62).

11. See Bruce-Novoa, "*La Prensa* and the Chicano Community," *The Américas
Review* 17.3–17.4 (1989): 150–156.

12. Lozano, from a successful business family in northern Mexico, relocated
to San Antonio in 1908 in search of business opportunities; there he opened
a bookstore and gradually learned the newspaper business through on-the-job
experiences while working first for San Antonio's *El Noticiero* and later for *El
Imparcial de Texas* (Di Stefano, 99–103).

13. Many of the publishing houses and weekly newspapers did not, in fact,
survive through their publishing efforts alone; like Whitt Publishing and Artes
Gráficas, they also had an extensive job printing business.

14. See my chapter, "Labor," in my *Hispanic Firsts: 500 Years of Extraordinary
Achievement* (1997), 133–150.

15. See F. Arturo Rosales, *Dictionary of Latino Civil Rights History* (2006)
for details on the various Hispanic labor organizing efforts in the nineteenth and
twentieth centuries.

16. The importance of the *lector* institution was summarized by Ambrosio
Fornet: "The proletariat encountered in The Reading . . . the most democratic
and efficient means of acculturation that existed at the time. Oral transmission,
effected in their own work place during working hours, was the ideal mechanism for

satisfying the intellectual needs of a class that had emerged wanting books, but not having the resources, the time and in many cases the schooling to read them. The Reading was the first attempt at extending books to the masses for solely educational and recreational reasons. Among the privileged classes, the book had always been a sumptuous object and, ultimately, an instrument of domination or lucre; the proletariat converted it into an instrument of self-education, using it only to advance itself ideologically and culturally" (185–186).

17. *La Aurora,* the first workers' newspaper in Cuba, was founded by tobacco worker-poet Saturnino Martínez in 1865, and was highly identified with the *lector* tradition; in addition to publishing news of interest to workers, the newspaper pioneered schools for workers, encouraged workers to use libraries, and vigilantly protected the *lector* tradition from political repression (Fornet 138–140).

18. *Ensayos Libertarios* (1907); *La escuela moderna* (1911); *La humanidad en el futuro* (1910); *Influencia de la ideas modernas* (1916); *Mi opinión sobre las libertades, derechos y deberes de la mujer como compañera, madre y ser independiente* (1911). Also see, *Amor y anarquía: Los escritos de Luisa Capetillo* (1992), Julio Ramos, ed., and *A Nation of Women: An Early Feminist Speaks Out; Mi Opinión Sobre Las Libertades, Derechos y Deberes de la Mujer* (2005), Felix V. Matos Rodriguez, ed.

19. While workers' periodicals obviously served the immigrant working-class, Hispanic elites felt the need to reproduce the cultural refinement that was the product of their education and breeding in the homeland. Whether to remain connected to the cultural accomplishments of the greater international Hispanic community or to fill an intellectual void that existed in the foreign land, a number of high-quality periodicals were established in the Northeast and Southwest. Some of them, such as the New York monthlies *El Ateneo: Repertorio Ilustrado de Arte, Ciencia y Literartura* (The Athenaeum: Illustrated Repertoire of Arts, Science and Literature, 1874–1877) and *El Americano* (The American, 1892–?), retained the newspaper format but primarily published literature and commentary, along with illustrations. Others looked much like the cultural magazines being published at the turn of the century, such as *Harper's Magazine* and *Cosmopolitan.* What was most distinctive about them was that they placed the Hispanic immigrant community of the US on the international cultural map, for they drew their selections from essayists and writers of prose fiction and poetry from Spain and Spanish America as well as from the US. Despite their elitism, these magazines felt they had to protect language, culture, and Hispanic interests just as the working-class Hispanic newspapers did. For more information, see Nicolás Kanellos and Helvetia Martell, *Hispanic Periodicals in the United States, Origins to 1960: A Brief History and Comprehensive Bibliography* (2000), 64–73.

20. See Kanellos and Martell, 44–58, and Carlos Monsiváis, *A ustedes les consta: Antología de la crónica en México* (1980).

21. Julio G. Arce, for instance, who wrote under the pseudonym of Jorge Ulica. See Kanellos and Martell, 46–52.

22. See Edwin Karli Padilla Aponte's "Introduction" to Jesús Colón's *Lo que el pueblo me dice . . . : crónicas de la colonia puertorriqueña en Nueva York* (2001).

23. O'Farril, who considered himself a mulatto, was a playwright of and popular actor in Cuban farces, in which he donned blackface to play the stock negrito character.

24. For a detailed exploration of the *cronistas'* misogynist ramblings, see my article, *"Cronistas* and Satire in Early Twentieth-Century Hispanic Newspapers," *MELUS* 23.4 (1998): 3–25.

25. See Gabriela Baeza Ventura's University of Houston dissertation, *La imagen de la mujer en la crónica del "México de Fuera"* (2001).

26. Actually, according to the preface of his book, he lost his job as a journalist for New York's *La Prensa* because of political reasons or not coming to terms with the newspaper's commercial mission.

27. Lucas Guevara does commit suicide in the end, a death that can be understood as the death of Hispanic identity in the Metropolis, one akin to the death of Luis in René Marqués's play of Puerto Rican immigration to New York: *La Carreta* (The Oxcart, 1953).

28. Another novel which advocates an alternative solution is Guillermo Cotto-Thorner's *Trópico en Manhattan* (1951), which promotes Puerto Ricans staying in New York and transforming the city to reflect their culture.

*Side Note [T]he history of Hispanic groups in the US has shown an unmeltable ethnicity, and as immigration from Spanish-speaking countries has been almost a steady flow since the founding of the US to the present, there seems no end to the phenomenon at this juncture in history nor in the foreseeable future.

WORKS CITED

Arce, Julio G. *"Crónicas Diabólicas" de "Jorge Ulica."* Ed. Juan Rodríguez. San Diego: Maize Press, 1982.

Chabrán, Rafael. "Spaniards." *The Immigrant Labor Press in North America, 1840s–1970s.* Westport: Greenwood Press, 1987. 151–190.

Chacón, Ramón D. "The Chicano Immigrant Press in Los Angeles: The Case of 'El Heraldo de México,' 1916–1920." *Journalism History* 4.2 (1997): 48–50, 62–64.

Fornet, Ambrosio. *El libro en Cuba.* Havana: Editorial Letras Cubanas, 1994.

Henderson, Ann L., and Gary R.Mormino. *Spanish Pathways in Florida.* Sarasota: Pineapple Press, 1991.

Park, Robert E. *The Immigrant Press and Its Control.* Westport: Greenwood Press, 1970.

Stefano, Onofre di. "Venimos a Luchar: A Brief History of *La Prensa*'s Founding." *Aztlán* 16.1–2 (1985): 95–118.

Venegas, Daniel. *The Adventures of Don Chipote or When Parrots Breast Feed.* Trans. Ethriam Cash Brammer. Houston: Arte Público Press, 2002.

Chronology

1874   *Reminiscences of Dorotea Valdez*, recorded by Henry Cerruti.

1878   *Memoirs of Felipa Osuna de Marron*, recorded by Thomas Savage.

1881   *Aurora y Gervasio*, unpublished novel by Manuel Salazar.

1892   *Noches tenebrosas en el Condado de San Miguel / Spooky Nights in San Miguel County*, serialized narrative by Miguel C. De Baca.

1893   *Hijo de la Tempestad / Son of the Storm* and *Tras las Tormenta la Calma / After the Storm the Calm*, novellas by Eusebio Chacón.

1896   *Vicente Silva y sus cuarenta Bandidos / Vicente Silva and His Forty Bandits*, narrative by Miguel C. De Baca.

1916   *Las Primicias / First Fruits*, poems by Vicente Bernal.

1924   *Obras de Felipe Maximiliano Chacón, "El Cantor Neomexicano": Poesia y prose / The Works of Felipe Maximiliano Chacón, "The New Mexican Singer": Poetry and Prose*, by Felipe Maximiliano Chacón.

1935   *My Life on the Frontier, 1864–1882*, by Miguel Antonio Otero.

1940   *New Mexico Triptych*, short stories by Fray Angelico Chavez.

1941   *Shadows of the Past*, folklore narrative by Cleofas Martínez-Jaramillo.

1945	*Eleven Lady-Lyrics and Other Poems*, by Fray Angelico Chavez.
1948	*The Single Rose: Poems of Divine Love*, by Fray Angelico Chavez.
1954	*We Fed Them Cactus*, novel by Fabiola Cabeza de Baca.
1955	*Romance of a Little Village Girl*, autobiography by Cleofas Martínez-Jaramillo.
1956	*Spiks*, short stories by Pedro Juan Soto.
1957	*From an Altar Screen: Tales from New Mexico*, short stories by Fray Angelico Chavez.
1958	*With a Pistol in His Hand: A Border Ballad and Its Hero*, by Américo Paredes.
1959	*Pocho*, novel by José Antonio Villarreal. *Usmail*, novel by Pedro Juan Soto. *The Virgin of Port Lligat*, poems by Fray Angelico Chavez.
1962	*Autobiography of Jose Clemente Orozco*, translated by Robert C. Stephenson.
1969	*The Plum Plum Pickers*, novel by Raymond Barrio.
1970	*Chicano*, novel by Richard Vásquez.
1971	*"Y no se lo tragó la tierra" / "And the Earth Did Not Part,"* novel by Tomás Rivera. *Barrio Boy*, autobiography by Ernesto Galarza.
1972	*Bless Me, Ultima*, novel by Rudolfo A. Anaya. *The Autobiography of a Brown Buffalo*, novel by Oscar Zeta Acosta. *Schwammenauel Dam*, novel by Arturo Garcia.
1973	*Estampas Del Valle*, novel by Rolando Hinojosa. *Hot Land, Cold Season*, novel by Pedro Juan Soto. *The Revolt of the Cockroach People*, novel by Oscar Zeta Acosta. *Sabor a mi*, poems by Cecilia Vicuna. *Always and Other Poems*, by Tomás Rivera.
1974	*Two Ranges*, novel by Roberto C. Medina.
1975	*The Road To Tamazunchale*, novel by Ron Arias. *Puppet: A Chicano Novella*, by Margarita Cota-Cardenas.

Rain of Scorpions and Other Writings, by Estela Portillo Trambley.

1976   *Nambé—Year One*, autobiographical novel by Orlando Romero.
El Diablo en Texas, novel by Aristeo Brito.
Below the Summit, novel by Joseph Torres Metzgar.
The Castle, novel by Ron Arias.

1977   *Memories of the Alhambra* and *Inheritance of Strangers*, novels by Nash Candelaria.
Poems: Third Chicano Literary Prize and *Bloodroot*, poems by Alma Luz Villanueva.

1978   *Mother, May I?* poems by Alma Luz Villanueva.

1979   *Tortuga*, novel by Rudolfo A. Anaya.

1981   *Emplumada*, poems by Lora Dee Cervantes.

1982   *Hunger of Memory*, novel by Richard Rodriquez.
The Legend of La Llorona: A Short Novel, by Rudolfo A. Anaya.
Not By the Sword, novel by Nash Candelaria.

1983   *Our House in the Last World*, novel by Oscar Hijuelos.
Precario / Precarious, poems by Cecilia Vicuna.

1984   *Clemente Chacon: A Novel* by José Antonio Villarreal.
The Iguana Killer. Twelve Stories of the Heart, by Alberto Rios.
The Rain God: A Desert Tale, novel by Arturo Islas.

1985   *The Migrant Earth*, novel by Tomás Rivera.
Inheritance of Strangers, novel by Nash Candelaria.
The House on Mango Street, novel by Sandra Cisneros.
Partners In Crime and *Dear Rafe*, novels by Rolando Hinojosa.
Life Span, poems by Alma Luz Villanueva.
The Moths and Other Stories, short stories by Helena Maria Viramontes.
Rituals of Survival: A Woman's Portfolio, short stories by Nicholasa Mohr.

1986   *Trini*, novel by Estela Portillo Trambley.
A Chicano in China, travel journal by Rudolfo A. Anaya.
The Last of the Menu Girls, novel by Denise Chavez.

The Mixquiahuala Letters, novel by Ana Castillo.
Giving Up the Ghost: Teatro in Two Acts, by Cherrie Moraga.

1987   *Home Again*, novel by Jose Yglesias.

1988   *The Ultraviolet Sky*, novel by Alma Luz Villanueva.
Tortuga, novel by Rudolfo A. Anaya.
The Harvest: Short Stories, by Tomás Rivera.
The Day the Cisco Kid Shot John Wayne, novel by Nash
Candelaria.
The Brick People and *Death of an Anglo*, novels by Alejandro
Morales.

1989   *The Mambo Kings Play Songs of Love*, novel by Oscar
Hijuelos.
The Wedding, novel by Mary Helen Ponce.
The Line of the Sun, novel by Judith Ortiz Cofer.
Latin Jazz, novel by Virgil Suarez.
Five Against the Sea: A True Story of Courage and Survival,
biography by Ron Arias.

1990   *The Mambo Kings Play Songs of Love* wins 1990 Pulitzer
Prize.
Sapagonia: An Anti-Romance in 3/8 Meter, novel by Ana
Castillo.*La Wik'una*, poems by Cecilia Vicuna.
Migrant Souls, novel by Arturo Islas.
The Searchers: Collected Poetry, by Tomás Rivera.
A Summer Life, reminiscences by Gary Soto.
Fire and Rain, novel by Oswald Rivera.

1991   *From the Cables of Genocide: Poems of Love and Hunger*, by
Lorna Dee Cervantes.
The Rag Doll Plagues, novel by Alejandro Morales.
The Cutter, novel by Virgil Suarez.
The Doorman, novel by Reinaldo Arenas.
Leonor Park, novel by Nash Candelaria.

1992   *How the Garcia Girls Lost Their Accents*, novel by Julia
Alvarez.
Albuquerque, novel by Rudolfo A. Anaya.
Unraveling Words and the Weaving of Water, poems by Cecilia
Vicuna.
Mrs. Vargas and the Dead Naturalist, short stories by Kathleen
Alcala.
Dreaming In Cuban, novel by Christina Garcia.

The Hidden Law, novel by Michael Nava.
The Boy Without a Flag: Tales of the South Bronx, short stories
by Abraham Rodriguez, Jr.

1993   *Remembering to Say Mouth or Face,* short stories by Omar
        S. Castaneda, wins 1993 Nilon Award for Excellence in
        Minority Fiction.
        Hoyt Street: An Autobiography, by Mary Helen Ponce.

1994   *Loose Woman,* poems by Sandra Cisneros.
        Releasing Serpents, poems by Bernice Zamora.
        Weeping Woman / La Llorona and Other Stories, short stories
        by Alma Luz Villanueva.
        So Far From God, novel by Ana Castillo.

1995   *My Father Was a Toltec and Selected Poems,* by Ana Castillo.

1996   *El Milagro and Other Stories,* by Patricia Preciado Martin.
        Loverboys: Stories, by Ana Castillo.

1998   *Isis in the Heart,* love poem by Rudolfo A. Anaya.
        Ask a Policeman, novel by Rolondo Hinojosa.
        Uncivil Rights, and Other Stories, Cordelia Candelaria.

1999   *Peel My Love Like an Onion: A Novel,* by Ana Castillo.
        Shaman Winter, novel by Rudolfo A. Anaya.
        La Sombra Lejana, novel by Pedro Juan Soto.

2000   *Elegy on the Death of César Chávez,* Rudolfo A. Anaya.

2001   *I Ask the Impossible: Poems,* by Ana Castillo.

2002   *This Bridge We Call Home: Radical Visions for Transformation,*
        anthology by Gloria Anzaldúa and AnaLouise Keating.

2003   *Moving Target: A Memoir of Pursuit,* Ron Arias.

2004   *Narratives of Greater Mexico: Essays on Chicano Literary
        History, Genre, and Borders,* Hector Calderón.

2006   *Curse of the ChupaCabra,* novel by Rudolfo A. Anaya.
        We Happy Few, novel Rolondo Hinojosa.
        The Man Who Could Fly and Other Stories, Rudolfo A.
        Anaya.

2007   *The First Tortilla,* children's novel by Rudolfo A. Anaya,
        Amy Córdova, and Enrique E. Lamadrid.
        The Guardians: A Novel, Ana Castillo.

Contributors

HAROLD BLOOM is Sterling Professor of the Humanities at Yale University. He is the author of 30 books, including *Shelley's Mythmaking* (1959), *The Visionary Company* (1961), *Blake's Apocalypse* (1963), *Yeats* (1970), *A Map of Misreading* (1975), *Kabbalah and Criticism* (1975), *Agon: Toward a Theory of Revisionism* (1982), *The American Religion* (1992), *The Western Canon* (1994), and *Omens of Millennium: The Gnosis of Angels, Dreams, and Resurrection* (1996). *The Anxiety of Influence* (1973) sets forth Professor Bloom's provocative theory of the literary relationships between the great writers and their predecessors. His most recent books include *Shakespeare: The Invention of the Human* (1998), a 1998 National Book Award finalist, *How to Read and Why* (2000), *Genius: A Mosaic of One Hundred Exemplary Creative Minds* (2002), *Hamlet: Poem Unlimited* (2003), *Where Shall Wisdom Be Found?* (2004), and *Jesus and Yahweh: The Names Divine* (2005). In 1999, Professor Bloom received the prestigious American Academy of Arts and Letters Gold Medal for Criticism. He has also received the International Prize of Catalonia, the Alfonso Reyes Prize of Mexico, and the Hans Christian Andersen Bicentennial Prize of Denmark.

JUAN BRUCE-NOVOA is professor of Spanish and Portuguese at the University of California-Irvine. He has written extensively about Chicano/a fiction, poetry, and film. His novel *Only the Good Times* was published in 1995.

JEFFREY CASS is associate provost at Texas A & M International University. *Interrogating Orientalism: Theoretical Approaches and Pedagogical Practices,* co-edited with Diane Hoeveler, was published in 2006; *Romantic Border Crossings,* co-edited with Larry Peer, was published in 2008.

JULIANA DE ZAVALIA contributed to *Changing the Terms: Translating in the Post-Colonial Era* (2000).

SILVIA SPITTA is professor of Spanish and comparative literature at Dartmouth. Her *Between Two Waters: Narratives of Transculturation in Latin America* was published in 1995.

ANNE CONNOR is associate professor of Spanish at Southern Oregon University. Her 2005 dissertation was "Blurring the Constructs of Gender: Contemporary Latin American Women Authors of the Fantastic."

MIRIAM DECOSTA-WILLIS became the first African American to earn a Ph.D. at Johns Hopkins University in 1967. A full-time author, she edited *Daughters of the Diaspora: Afra-Hispanic Writers* (1998) and wrote *Notable Black Memphians* (2008).

RICHARD F. PATTESON is professor of English at Mississippi State University. His books include *A World Outside: The Fiction of Paul Bowles* (1987), and *Caribbean Passages: A Critical Perspective on New Fiction from the West Indies* (1998).

B. MARIE CHRISTIAN is a professor of English at the University of Alaska, Anchorage. Her *Belief in Dialogue* was published in 2005.

FIONA MILLS is editor of *After the Pain: Critical Essays on Gayl Jones* (2006).

JASON FRYDMAN is assistant professor of English at Brooklyn College.

NICOLÁS KANELLOS is the Brown Foundation Professor of Spanish at the University of Houston. His books include *Mexican American Theater: Legacy and Reality* (1987), *Biographical Dictionary of Hispanic Literature of the United States* (1989), *Hispanic-American Almanac* (1993), and *Thirty Million Strong: Reclaiming the Hispanic Image in American Culture* (1997).

Bibliography

Acosta, Oscar Zeta. *The Autobiography of a Brown Buffalo.* San Francisco: Straight Arrow Books, 1972.

———. *The Revolt of the Cockroach People.* New York: Bantam, 1974.

Acosta-Belen, Edna, ed. *The Puerto Rican Woman: Perspectives on Culture, History and Society.* New York: Praeger, 1986.

Alurista, Alberto. "Cultural Nationalism and Chicano Literature During the Decade of 1965–1975," *MELUS: The Journal of the Society for the Study of the Multi-Ethnic Literature of the United States,* 8:2 (Summer 1981): 22–34.

Anaya, Rudolfo A. *Bless Me, Ultima.* Berkeley, Cal.: Quinto Sol Publications, 1972.

———, and Simon Ortiz, eds. *Ceremony of Brotherhood, 1680–1980.* Albuquerque: Academia Publications, 1981.

———. *Silence of Llano, Short Stories.* Berkeley: Tonatiuh-Quinto Sol International Publishers, 1982.

———. *The Adventures of Juan Chicaspatas.* Houston: Arte Publico Press, 1984.

———, and Antonio Marques, eds. *Cuentos Chicanos.* Albuquerque: University of New Mexico, 1980. Revised edition, Albuquerque: University of New Mexico Press, 1984.

———. *The Legend of La Llorona: A Short Novel.* Berkeley: Tonatiuh-Quinto Sol International Publishers, 1984.

———. "Iliana of the Pleasure Dreams," *ZYZZYVA,* 1:4 (Winter 1985): 50–61.

———. *A Chicano in China.* Albuquerque: University of New Mexico Press, 1986.

———. "An American Chicano in King Arthur's Court," in *Old Southwest, New Southwest: Essays on a Region and Its Literature.* Ed. Judy Nolte Lensink. Tucson, Ariz.: The Tucson Public Library, 1987.

———. *Lord of the Dawn, the Legend of Quetzalcoatl.* Albuquerque: University of New Mexico Press, 1987.

———. *Heart of Aztlán.* Albuquerque: University of New Mexico Press, 1988.

———. "In Search of Epifano," in *Voces/Voices,* edited by Rudolfo A. Anaya. Albuquerque: University of New Mexico Press, 1988.

———. *Tortuga.* Albuquerque: University of New Mexico Press, 1988.

———, ed. *Voces/Voices. An Anthology of Nuevo Mexicano Writers.* Albuquerque: University of New Mexico Press, 1988.

———, and Edward Gonzales. *Farolitos for Abuelo.* New York: Hyperion Books for Children, 1998.

———. *Isis in the Heart.* Albuquerque: Valley of the Kings Press, 1998.

———, ed. *Chicanos/a Studies: Writing into the Future.* Norman: University of Oklahoma, 1999.

———, and Amy Córdova. *My Land Sings: Stories from the Rio Grande.* New York: Marrow Junior Books, 1999.

———. *Shaman Winter.* New York: Warner, 1999.

———. *Elegy on the Death of César Chávez.* El Paso, Tex.: Cinco Puntos Press, 2000.

———, and David Diaz. *Roadrunner's Dance.* New York: Hyperion Books for Children, 2000.

———, and Gus Arriola. *El Gato.* Salt Lake City: Green Cat Press, 2004.

———, Amy Córdova, and Enrique E. Lamadrid. *The Santero's Miracle.* Albuquerque: University of New Mexico Press, 2004.

———. *Serafina's Stories.* Albuquerque: University of New Mexico Press, 2004.

———. *Jemez Spring.* Albuquerque: University of New Mexico Press, 2005.

———. *Curse of the ChupaCabra.* Albuquerque: University of New Mexico Press, 2006.

———. *The Man Who Could Fly and Other Stories.* Norman: University of Oklahoma Press, 2006.

———, Amy Córdova, and Enrique E. Lamadrid. *The First Tortilla.* Albuquerque: University of New Mexico Press, 2007.

Anzaldúa, Gloria. *Borderlands/La Frontera: The New Mestiza.* San Francisco: Aunt Lute Books, 1987.

———, ed. *Making Face, Making Soul/Haciendo Carus: Creative and Critical Perspectives by Women of Color.* San Francisco: Aunt Lute Books, 1990.

————. *Prietita Has a Friend/Prietita tiene un Amigo.* N.p.: Children's Book Press, 1991.

————. *Friends from the Other Side/Amigos del otro Lado.* N.p.: Children's Book Press, 1998.

Arias, Ron. *The Road to Tamazunchale.* Reno, Nev.: West Coast Poetry Review, 1975.

————. *The Castle.* Jamaica, N.Y.: Bilingual Press, 1976.

————. *Five Against the Sea: A True Story of Courage and Survival.* N.Y.: New American Library, 1989.

————. *Moving Target: A Memoir of Pursuit.* Tempe, Ariz.: Bilingual Press Editorial/Editorial Bilingüe, 2003.

Avalos, Hector. *Strangers in Our Own Land: Religion in Contemporary U.S. Latina/o Literature.* Nashville, Tenn.: Abingdon, 2005.

Barrio, Raymond. *The Plum Plum Pickers.* Guerneville, Cal.: Ventura Press, 1969.

Bauder, Thomas A. "The Triumph of White Magic in Rudolfo, Anaya's *Bless Me, Ultima,*" *Mester,* 14:1 (Spring 1985): 41–54.

Bernal, Vicente. *Las Primicias.* Dubuque, Iowa: Telegraph-Herald, 1916.

Brito, Aristeo. *Diablo en Texas / The Devil in Texas.* Tempe, Ariz.: Bilingual Press Editorial/Editorial Bilingüe, 1990.

Bruce-Novoa, Juan. *Chicano Authors: Inquiry by Interview.* Austin: University of Texas Press, 1980.

————. *RetroSpace: Collected Essays on Chicano Literature, Theory and History.* Houston: Arte Público Press, 1990.

Calderón, Hector. "To Read Chicano Narrative: Commentary and Metacommentary," *Mester* 1 1:2 (1983): 3–14.

————. "At the Crossroads of History, on the Borders of Change: Chicano Literary Studies Past, Present, and Future," *Left Politics and the Literary Profession,* edited by Lennard J. Davis and M. Bella Mirabelli. New York: Columbia University Press, 1990. 211–235.

————, and Jose David Saldivar, eds. *Criticism in the Borderlands: Studies in Chicano Literature, Culture and Ideology.* Durham, N.C.: Duke University Press, 1991.

————. *Narratives of Greater Mexico: Essays on Chicano Literary History, Genre, and Borders.* Austin: University of Texas Press, 2004.

Candelaria, Cordelia. *Chicano Poetry: A Critical Introduction.* Westport, Conn.: Greenwood Press, 1986.

Candelaria, Nash. *Inheritance of Strangers.* Ypsilanti: Bilingual Press Editorial/ Editorial Bilingüe, 1977.

————. *Memories of the Alhambra.* Ypsilanti, Mich.: Bilingual Press Editorial/ Editorial Bilingüe, 1977.

———. *Not By the Sword*. Ypsilanti, Mich.: Bilingual Press Editorial/Editorial Bilingüe, 1982.

———. *The Day the Cisco Kid Shot John Wayne*. Tempe, Ariz.: Bilingual Press Editorial/Editorial Bilingüe, 1988.

———. *Leonor Park*. Tempe, Ariz.: Bilingual Press, 1991.

———. *Uncivil Rights, and Other Stories*. Tempe, Ariz.: Bilingual Press Editorial/ Editorial Bilingüe, 1998.

———. *A Daughter's a Daughter*. Tempe, Ariz.: Bilingual Press Editorial/Editorial Bilingüe, 2007.

Castillo, Ana. *The Invitation*. U.S.A.: A. Castillo, 1979.

———. *Sapagonia: An Anti-Romance in 3/8 Meter*. New York: Anchor Books, 1990.

———. *So Far From God*. New York: Plume, 1994.

———. *Massacre of the Dreamers: Essays on Xicanisma*. New York: Plume, 1995.

———. *My Father Was a Toltec and Selected Poems*. New York: W.W. Norton, 1995.

———. *Loverboys: Stories*. New York: Norton, 1996.

———. *Peel My Love Like an Onion: A Novel*. New York: Doubleday, 1999.

———, and Dolores Prida. *Carmen la Coja*. New York: Vintage Español, 2000.

———, and Susan Guevara. *My Daughter, My Son, The Eagle, The Dove: An Aztec Chant*. New York: Dutton Books, 2000.

———. *I Ask the Impossible: Poems*. New York: Anchor Books, 2001.

———. *Psst. . .: I Have Something to Tell You, Mi Amor: Two Plays*. San Antonio, Tex.: Wings Press, 2005.

———. *Watercolor Women, Opaque Men: A Novel in Verse*. Willimantic, Conn.: Curbstone Press, 2005.

———. *The Guardians: A Novel*. New York: Random House, 2007.

Chabran, Angie and Rosalinda Fregoso, eds. *Chicana/o Cultural Representations: Reframing Critical Discourses*. Special issue of *Critical Studies*, 4:3 (1990).

Chacón, Felipe Maximiliano. *Obras de Felipe Maximiliano Chacón. "El Cantor Neomexicano," Poesia y prosa*. Albuquerque: Chacón, 1924.

Chavez, Fray Angelico. *Clothed with the Sun*. Santa Fe, N.M.: Writer's Editions, 1939.

———. *New Mexico Triptych*. Paterson, N.J.: St. Anthony Guild, 1940.

———. *Eleven Lady Lyrics and Other Poems*. Paterson, N.J.: St. Anthony Guild, 1945.

———. *From an Altar Screen: Tales from New Mexico*. New York: Farrar, Straus & Cudahy, 1957.

———. *The Virgin of Port Lligat*. Fresno, Cal.: Academy Literary Guild, 1959.

———. *The Lady from Toledo*. Fresno, Cal.: Academy Guild Press, 1960.

————. *Selected Poems with an Apologia.* Santa Fe, N.M.: Press of the Territorian, 1969.

Chavez, John R. *The Lost Land: The Chicano Image of the Southwest.* Albuquerque: University of New Mexico Press, 1984.

Christian, B. Marie. *Belief in Dialogue: U.S. Latina Writers Confront Their Religious Heritage.* New York: Other, 2005.

Cisneros, Sandra. "Cactus Flowers: In Search of Tejana Feminist Poetry," *Third Woman* 3:1–2 (1986): 73–80.

Cordova, Teresa, Norma Cantu, Gilberto Cardenas, Juan Garcia, and Christine M. Sierra, eds. *Chicana Voices: Intersections of Class, Race, and Gender.* Austin, Tex.: Center for Mexican American Studies, 1986. (Proceedings of the National Association of Chicano Studies Annual Meeting, Austin, Tex., 1984)

Cota-Cardenas, Margarita. "The Chicana in the City as Seen in Her Literature," *Frontiers: A Journal of Woman Studies* 6:1–2 (Spring–Summer 1981): 13–18.

Dalleo, Raphael, and Elena Machado Sáez. *The Latino/a Canon and the Emergence of Post-Sixties Literature.* New York: Palgrave Macmillan, 2007.

Dick, Bruce Allen. *A Poet's Truth: Conversations with Latino/Latina Poets.* Tucson: University of Arizona Press, 2003.

Ellizondo, Sergio D. "A Question of Origins and Presence in Chicano Literature," *Latin American Literary Review* 11:21 (Fall–Winter 1982): 39–43.

Fahey, Felicia Lynne. *The Will to Heal: Psychological Recovery in the Novels of Latina Writers.* Albuquerque: University of New Mexico Press, 2007.

Flores, Lauro. *The Floating Borderlands: Twenty-Five Years of U.S. Hispanic Literature.* Seattle: University of Washington Press, 1998.

Grajeda, Rafael. "The Pachuco in Chicano Poetry: The Process of Legend-Creation," *Revista-Chicano-Riquena* 8:4 (1988): 45–59.

Gruesz, Kirsten Silva. *Ambassadors of Culture: The Transamerican Origins of Latino Writing.* Princeton, N.J.: Princeton University Press, 2002.

Habell-Pallán, Michelle. *Loca Motion: The Travels of Chicana and Latina Popular Culture.* New York: New York University Press, 2005.

Herrera-Sobek, Maria, ed. *Beyond Stereotypes: The Critical Analysis of Chicana Literature.* Binghamton, N.Y.: Bilingual Press, 1985.

————, and Helena Maria Viramontes. *Chicana Creativity and Criticism: Charting New Frontiers in American Literature.* Houston: Arte Público Press, 1988.

Hinojosa, Rolando. *Generaciones, Notas, y Brechas = Generations, Notes, and Trails.* San Francisco: Casa Editorial, 1978.

————. *Estampas del Valle y Otras Obras = Sketches of the Valley and Other Works.* Berkeley: Quinto Sol, 1973; Editorial Justa, 1977, 1980.

———. *Crossing the Line: The Construction of a Poem.* Milwaukee: University of Wisconsin-Milwaukee, College of Letters and Science, Spanish Speaking Outreach Institute, 1981.

———. *Rites and Witnesses: A Comedy.* Houston: Arte Público Press, 1982.

———. *Dear Rafe.* Houston: Arte Público Press, 1985.

———. *Partners in Crime: A Rafe Buenrostro Mystery.* Houston: Arte Público Press, 1985.

———. *Claros Varones de Belken / Fair Gentlemen of Belken County.* Tempe, Ariz.: Bilingual Press Editorial/Editorial Bilingüe, 1986.

———. *Klail City: A Novel.* Houston: Arte Público Press, 1987.

———, Vernon E. Lattin, and Gary D. Keller, eds. *Tomas Rivera, 1935–1984: The Man and His Work.* Tempe, Ariz.: Bilingual Press Editorial/Editorial Bilingüe, 1988.

———. *The Useless Servants.* Houston: Arte Público Press, 1993.

———. *El Condado de Belken—Klail City.* Tempe, Ariz.: Bilingual Press Editorial/Editorial Bilingüe, 1994.

———. *Estampas del Valle.* Tempe, Ariz.: Bilingual Press Editorial/Editorial Bilingüe, 1994.

———. *We Happy Few.* Houston: Arte Público Press, 2006.

Horno-Delgado, Asuncion, Eliana Ortega, Nina M. Scott, and Nancy Saporta-Sternbach, eds. *Breaking Boundaries. Latina Writings and Critical Readings.* Amherst: University of Massachusetts Press, 1989.

Jimenez, Francisco, ed. *The Identification and Analysis of Chicano Literature.* New York: Bilingual Review Press, 1979.

Kanellos, Nicolás. *Hispanic Literature in the United States: A Comprehensive Reference.* Westport, Conn.: Greenwood Press, 2003.

Kevane, Bridget. *Latino Literature in America.* Westport, Conn.: Greenwood Press, 2003.

Márquez, Antonio C. "Richard Rodriguez' *Hunger of Memory* and the Poetics of Experience," *Arizona Quarterly* 40:2 (Summer 1984): 130–141.

Miller, Beth, ed. *Women in Hispanic Literature: Icons and Fallen Idols.* Berkeley: University of California Press, 1983.

Moraga, Cherrie, and Gloria Anzaldúa, eds. *This Bridge Called My Back: Writings by Radical Women of Color.* New York: Kitchen Table / Women of Color Press, 1983.

Morales, Alejandro. *The Brick People.* Houston: Arte Público Press, 1988.

———. *The Death of an Anglo.* Tempe, Ariz.: Bilingual Press Editorial/Editorial Bilingüe, 1988.

———. *The Rag Doll Plagues: A Novel.* Houston: Arte Público Press, 1991.

Mujcinovic, Fatima. *Postmodern Cross-Culturalism and Politicization in U. S. Latina Literature: From Ana Castillo to Julia Alvarez*. New York: Peter Lang, 2004

Olivares, Julian, ed. *International Studies in Honor of Tomás Rivera*. Houston: Arte Público Press, 1985.

Ordóniez, Elizabeth. "The Concept of Cultural Identity in Chicana Poetry," *Third Women* 2:1 (1984): 75–82.

Padilla, Genaro M. "The Recovery of Nineteenth-Century Chicano Autobiography: 'tis not vengeance, 'tis regaining a loss,'" *American Quarterly* 40:3 (1988): 286–307.

Poey, Delia. *Latino American Literature in the Classroom: The Politics of Transformation*. Gainesville: University Press of Florida, 2002.

Rivera, Tomás. ". . . *y no se lo tragó la tierra*." Berkeley: Quinto Sol Publications, 1971.

———. *Always and Other Poems*. Sisterdale, Tex.: Sisterdale Press, 1973.

———. *The Migrant Earth*. Houston: Arte Público Press, 1985.

———. *The Harvest: Short Stories*. Houston: Arte Público Press, 1988.

———. *The Searchers: Collected Poetry*. Houston: Arte Público Press, 1990.

Romero, Orlando. *Nambé—Year One*. Berkeley: Tonatiuh International, 1976.

Romo, Ricardo, ed. *Chicana Voices: Intersections of Class, Race and Gender*. Austin: Center for Mexican American Studies Publications, 1986.

Saldivar, Jose David, ed. *The Rolando Hinojosa Reader. Essays Historical and Critical*. Houston: Arte Público Press, 1985.

———. "The Ideological and the Utopian in Tomás Rivera's . . . *y no se lo tragó la tierra* and Ron Arias' *The Road to Tamazunchale*," in *Missions in Conflict: Essays on U.S.-Mexican Relations and Chicano Culture*. Renate von Bardeleben et al., eds. Tubingen: Narr, 1986. 203–214.

———. "Towards a Chicano Poetics: The Making of the Chicano-Chicana Subject, 1969–1982," *Confluencia: Revista Hispanics de Culture y Literature* 1:2 (Spring 1986): 10–17.

Saldivar, Ramón. *Chicano Narrative: The Dialectics of Difference*. Madison: University of Wisconsin Press, 1990.

Sánchez, Marta Sánchez. *Contemporary Chicana Poetry: A Critical Approach to An Emerging Literature*. Berkeley: University of California Press, 1985.

Sanchez, Rosaura. *Chicano Discourse: Socio-Historic Perspectives*. Rowley, Mass.: Newbury House, 1983.

———. "Postmodernism and Chicano Literature," *Aztlán* 18:2 (Fall 1987): 1–14.

Sandín, Lyn Di Iorio. *Killing Spanish: Literary Essays on Ambivalent U. S. Latino/a Identity*. New York: Palgrave Macmillan, 2004.

Sommers, Joseph, and Tomas Ybarra-Frausto, eds. *Modern Chicano Writers: A Collection of Critical Essays*. Englewood Cliffs, N.J.: Prentice-Hall, 1979.

Soto, Pedro Juan. *Spike, Short Stories.* Mexico: Los Presentes, 1956.

———. *Usmail.* Puerto Rico: Club del Libro, 1959.

———. *Hot Land / Cold Season.* New York: Dell, 1973.

———. *Memoria de mi Amnesia.* Puerto Rico: Editorial Cultural, 1981.

———. *Palabras ad Vuelo.* Havana: Casa de las Americas, 1990.

———. *La Sombra Lejana.* Puerto Rico: Editorial Plaza Mayor, 1999.

Stavans, Ilan. *The Riddle of Cantinflas: Essays on Hispanic Popular Culture.* Albuquerque: University of New Mexico Press, 1998.

Vásquez, Richard. *Chicano.* New York: Avon, 1970.

Villarreal, Jose Antonio. *Pocho.* Garden City, N.Y.: Doubleday, 1959.

Zamora, Bernice. *Restless Serpents.* Menlo Park: Disenos Literarios, 1976.

———. *Releasing Serpents.* Tempe, Arizona: Bilingual Press Editorial/Editorial Bilingüe, 1994.

Acknowledgments

Juan Bruce-Novoa. "Chicano Theater: Editing the Origin Myth." Originally published in *GESTOS, Teoria y Practica del Teator Hispanico,* Volume 7, Number 14 (November 1992): pp. 105–116. Copyright © 1992 GESTOS. Reprinted by permission of the publisher.

Jeffrey Cass. "A White Man's Fantasies: Orientalism in Rudolfo Anaya's *A Chicano in China.*" Originally published in *Critica: A Journal of Critical Essays* (Spring 1998): pp. 43–51. Copyright © 1998 Jeffrey Cass.

Juliana de Zavalia. "The Impact of Spanish-American Literature in Translation on U.S. Latino Literature." Originally published in *Changing the Terms: Translating in the Postcolonial Era,* edited and introduced by Sherry Simon and edited by Paul St. Pierre. Perspectives on Translation Series (Ottawa, O.N.: University of Ottawa Press, 2000): pp. 187–206. Copyright © 2000 University of Ottawa Press. Reprinted by permission of the publisher.

Silvia Spitta. "Of Brown Buffaloes, Cockroaches and Others: *Mestizaje* North and South of the Rio Bravo." Originally published in *Revista de Estudios Hispánicos,* Volume 35, Number 2 (May 2001): pp. 333–346. Copyright © 2001 Silvia Spitta. Reprinted by permission of the author.

Anne Connor. "Desenmascarando a Ysrael: The Disfigured Face as Symbol of Identity in Three Latino Texts." Originally published in *Cincinnati Romance Review,* Volume 21 (2002): pp. 148–162. Copyright © 2002 Cincinnati Romance Review. Reprinted by permission of the publisher.

Miriam DeCosta-Willis. "Martha K. Cobb and the Shaping of Afro-Hispanic Literary Criticism." Originally published in *CLA Journal: Official Quarterly Publication of the College Language Assocition*, Volume 45, Number 4 (June 2002): pp. 523–541. Copyright © 2002 College Language Association. Reprinted by permission of the publisher.

Richard F. Patteson. "Oscar Hijuelos: 'Eternal Homesickness' and the Music of Memory." Originally published in *CRITIQUE: Studies in Contemporary Fiction*, Volume 44, Number 1 (Fall 2002): pp. 38–48. Copyright © 2002. Published by Heldref Publications and reprinted with permission of the Helen Dwight Reid Educational Foundation.

B. Marie Christian. "Many Ways to Remember: Layered Time in Mora's *House of Houses*." Originally published in *MELUS: The Journal of the Society for the Study of the MultiEthnic Literature of the United States*, Volume 30, Number 1 (Spring 2005): pp. 135–148. Copyright © 2005 MELUS. Reprinted by permission of the publisher.

Fiona Mills. "Living 'In Between': The Identification of Afro-Latino/a Literature." Originally published in *Anglistik und Englischunterrict*, Volume 66 (2005): pp. 33–55. Copyright © 2005 Universitätsverlag WINTER GmbH. Reprinted by permission of the publisher.

Jason Frydman. "Violence, Masculinity, and Upward Mobility in the Dominican Diaspora: Junot Díaz, the Media, and *Drown*." Originally published in *Columbia Journal of American Studies*, Volume 8 (Spring 2007): pp. 270–281. Copyright © 2007 Columbia Journal of American Studies. Reprinted by permission of the publisher.

Nicolás Kanellos. "Recovering and Re-constructing Early Twentieth-Century Hispanic Immigrant Print Culture in the U.S." Originally published in *American Literary History*, Volume 19, Number 2 (Summer 2007): pp. 438–455. Copyright © 2007 American Literary History.

Index